John Hughes FAQ

John Hughes FAQ

All That's Left to Know About the Man Behind the Movies

Thomas A. Christie

APPLAUSE
THEATRE & CINEMA BOOKS
An Imprint of Hal Leonard LLC

Published in 2019 by Applause Theatre & Cinema Books
An Imprint of Hal Leonard LLC
7777 West Bluemound Road
Milwaukee, WI 53213

Trade Book Division Editorial Offices
33 Plymouth St., Montclair, NJ 07042

The FAQ series was conceived by Robert Rodriguez and developed with Stuart Shea. Photos are from the personal collection of the author except where otherwise noted. Printed in the United States of America

Book design by Snow Creative

Library of Congress Cataloging-in-Publication Data is available upon request.

ISBN 978-1-4950-7466-0

www.applausebooks.com

This book is dedicated to everyone who is fortunate enough
to call themselves a child of the eighties

Contents

Acknowledgments

I would like to thank Professor Robert Lecker of the Robert Lecker Agency and Marybeth Keating of Applause Books for their much-appreciated advice and support during all stages of the research and writing of this book. I am also grateful to my family, Julie Christie and Mary Melville, and to my friends Professor Roderick Watson, Amy Leitch, Alex Tucker, and Dr. Elspeth King for their fellowship and encouragement throughout the project.

.

Introduction

John Hughes was one of the most popular figures in 1980s and 1990s filmmaking. But to an entire generation, he was something much more than that.

For many people growing up in the eighties, Hughes was a *bona fide* legend of cinema: the man who single-handedly reinvented the teen movie, making the genre both accessible and relevant to mainstream audiences of all ages around the world. Even for those viewers whose teenage years were far behind them, Hughes became a household name thanks to his crowd-pleasing comedies that examined the pleasures and the pitfalls of modern American life. And throughout the nineties Hughes would enrapture an entirely new generation with his range of screenplays for family movies; features which proved to be as popular with the public as they were profitable at the box office.

But what exactly were the reasons behind the success of Hughes's creative approach? Why did so many people, both in the United States and across the world, find themselves attracted to the engaging yet often thought-provoking scenarios he produced during a career spanning three decades? And why have his films retained such enduring appeal since their first appearance in theaters, to the point that their fan base even continues to grow?

John Hughes: Eighties Icon, Nineties Mogul, Modern Legend

This book has been written with the intention of providing an entertaining yet comprehensive account of John Hughes's contribution to modern cinema, explaining his considerable influence both as a director and screenwriter. It aims to explore many aspects of Hughes's filmmaking, ranging from the numerous themes he presented to the lasting artistic inspiration he evoked among other industry figures and the general public alike. This text will focus not only on the profound impact of his work on 1980s popular culture, but also on the legacy of his ongoing output throughout the nineties—a period that would also bear witness to his growing eminence as a highly successful producer.

Hughes's films have delighted audiences and captured the imagination of other filmmakers since their 1980s glory days, while the universality of the issues he presented has meant that many of the movies he created have long outlived the period of their initial release. Much more than simply evocative time capsules of American life, Hughes's eighties output in particular has continued to reach out to viewers ever since their first screenings in theaters; though firmly rooted in the music, styles, and fashions of a particular decade, the relatable and captivating subject matter of his films remains appealing to viewers of all ages.

While Hughes has become especially well known for the eight films he directed between 1984 and 1991—including *Sixteen Candles* (1984), *The Breakfast Club* (1985), and *Ferris Bueller's Day Off* (1986)—he arguably made a far greater contribution to cinema as a result of the dozens of high-profile screenplays he developed for production throughout the eighties and nineties. A prolific and famously exacting writer, his sensitive characterizations, clever dialogue, and the meaningful dramatic situations he brought about would eventually earn him a solid reputation as one of the American film industry's most sought-after screenwriters.

Though an issue often less explored, Hughes was also a highly successful movie producer whose company, Hughes Entertainment, would be the power behind numerous cinematic releases during his lifetime. With an inspired and often eclectic catalogue of films to his name, Hughes's work in a production capacity can sometimes be overshadowed by his stature as a leading director, and yet it was in this role that he would administer the creation of some of his most noted titles. As a producer, Hughes would remain active throughout the 1990s, continuing to ensure the financing of features even after he had retired from his directorial endeavors.

John Hughes: A Man of Many Talents

John Hughes seems forever destined to be regarded as one of the most iconic figures in 1980s American filmmaking, having written, directed,

John Hughes (1950–2009): film director, producer, screenwriter, and one of the most immediately recognizable figures in American cinema during the 1980s and early 1990s.
© *Paul Natkin*

and produced movies which continue to prove instantly recognizable to audiences worldwide. Though his films would help to launch the career of many actors who would go on to even greater success in the world of show business—not least the famous "Brat Pack" of young performers, who continually made headlines in the industry press during the eighties—he would also work with a wide range of established acting talent, with highly memorable results. From the adroit characterization and droll interactions presented in his screenplays to his directorial ability to encourage affecting, meaningful, and sometimes sidesplitting performances from his cast, Hughes left no stone unturned in his determination to present his observations about modern life in a manner that was as relevant as it was absorbing.

Demonstrating a razor-sharp eye for the cultural zeitgeist of the time, his youth cinema—which dealt with many different aspects of teenage life—was considered iconoclastic and genre-defying when first released, and these films have since become the yardstick by which all later teen movies are judged. The value of Hughes's contribution to this genre cannot be overstated, whether depicting technological fantasy in *Weird Science* (1985), or exploring class consciousness in *Pretty in Pink* (Howard Deutch, 1986), or *Some Kind of Wonderful* (Howard Deutch, 1987).

Beyond the monumental impression made by his teen movies, Hughes was also a hugely accomplished writer and producer of mainstream comedies and family features, with films such as *Planes, Trains and Automobiles* (1987) and *Home Alone* (Chris Columbus, 1990) achieving significant critical and commercial success at the time of their initial release. Yet the continuing ability of his films to entertain and amuse cannot simply be explained by their nostalgia value; though many John Hughes movies are packed with cultural references which place them indelibly within an America of a very particular period, several of his features have demonstrated the ability to reach out to new viewers who had not been born when Hughes's popularity was at its height.

John Hughes: Knowing Laughs with Hidden Depths

John Hughes FAQ will explore many facets of Hughes's prolific and critically acclaimed career in film, discussing his flair for creating amusing and engaging characters, his enthusiasm for new technology and eventful road trips, and his insightful social commentary on class and culture. While much attention has been focused over the years on the lasting cultural relevance of his canon of teen movies, his more outrageous comedies also include subtly underplayed themes which belied their seemingly innocuous exterior.

This book will cover the entire sweep of Hughes's work in the film industry both as a director and screenwriter. A detailed picture will be constructed of a career which was complex and often unpredictable in nature. A creative, perfectionistic force who regularly challenged audience and industry anticipation, Hughes toyed proficiently with genre boundaries, exploring the lines of demarcation between categories of film to highly inventive effect.

John Hughes FAQ will also consider aspects of his movies that have often been overlooked, including the director's patriotic love for his country, his fervor for vacations and the holiday season, his lasting affection for the state of Illinois, and the premises for films that he would contribute under the pseudonym Edmond Dantès.

Each of the chapters will focus on a particular theme arising from Hughes's work, relating it to his wider catalogue of movies as well as, where relevant, other films of the time. While many people will remember Hughes's films for their profound truths about human nature, their lasting success has been due in no small part to their infectious sense of fun and energy—the eccentricity and liveliness that so regularly typified his movies throughout a long career. The hidden depths of his writing often managed to convey complex emotional themes through seemingly lighthearted means.

John Hughes: King of Contemporary Popular Culture

How many people today can look at a 1961 Ferrari 250 GT California without immediately thinking of *Ferris Bueller's Day Off*, or listen to the Simple Minds song "Don't You Forget About Me" without finding themselves recalling the events of *The Breakfast Club*? Whether in distinctive concepts, including a 1980s home computer that proved capable (with a little supernatural assistance) of producing a human being from thin air in *Weird Science*, comic highlights such as Clark Griswold's hopelessly unreliable Wagon Queen Family Truckster in *National Lampoon's Vacation* (Harold Ramis, 1983), or unforgettable sights like Macaulay Culkin as *Home Alone*'s Kevin McCallister aping Edvard Munch's 1893 painting *The Scream*, the imagery of John Hughes's cinema has never slackened its grip on the cultural consciousness. Even on occasions where Hughes was not the director of a particular movie, his creative imprimatur is nonetheless unmistakable in films where he was overseeing production responsibilities or contributing the screenplay.

There was never a lack of variety in Hughes's choice of subject matter. Alongside the towering reputation of his cycle of teen movies, Hughes was equally comfortable handling chaotic suburban comedies, such as *Mr. Mom* (Stan Dragoti, 1983) and *Uncle Buck* (1989), providing a witty commentary on the great American getaway in *National Lampoon's Vacation* and *The Great Outdoors* (Howard Deutch, 1988), following the trials of exasperated travelers in *Planes, Trains and Automobiles* (1987) and *Dutch* (Peter Faiman, 1991), and even exploring the duties and anxieties of parenthood in *She's Having a Baby* (1988) and *Curly Sue* (1991). Throughout his career, he took care to painstakingly construct a comprehensive montage of themes and subjects which reflected many different aspects of the American character, utilizing comedy both bawdy and urbane to create a stimulating and persuasively well-disposed impression of life in the United States, always providing a warm but ultimately sincere interpretation of his country's idealism and quirks. Hughes's films create a contemporary cultural patchwork which has proven to be as ingenious it is remarkable.

By evaluating a wide range of traits of Hughes's creative output and discussing his films' significance in the wider context of their era of production, his soaring reputation as a writer and filmmaker will be contemplated in depth, and his involvement in American popular cinema evaluated with regard not only to his significance at the time but also his lasting effect on the field. Hughes's abundant work had a matchless effect on the American film industry of the 1980s and 1990s, and—often popular with critics as well as proving financially lucrative at the box-office—it is difficult to overemphasize the import of his movies' consequence on commercial filmmaking during an exhilarating and often tempestuous period in the history of United States cinema.

After Hughes's input into the teen movie, the subgenre would no longer inevitably encounter languid critical classification as unrefined campus-based farces and portentous melodramas. His trailblazing involvement with this category of film led to sophisticated and skillfully rendered features, blending the astute portrayal of diverse individuals with sharp and incisive wordplay to challenge widespread convictions. Hughes's deliberate selection of idiosyncratic, but nonetheless likable, characters became a fundamental quality of a majority of his movies. The results were an unconventional prism through which he could present a curiously charming, and always unique, worldview.

By employing subtle nonconformity and the offbeat in order to shine a light on various traits of mainstream assumptions about society, and thus surveying the outer margins of orthodoxy and conventionality in the rapidly shifting American culture of the eighties and nineties, Hughes presented his audience with a complex fusion of comedic mayhem and insightful, often sensitive, social observation. His groundbreaking involvement with the teen movie genre has, in the eyes of some critics, eclipsed his numerous accomplishments in other areas of screenwriting. Perhaps the most noteworthy achievement of his career was the way in which he underscored the vital worth of societal harmony and the central role of the family unit within a harshly avaricious and materialistic period of recent history. He consistently fostered cooperation, resisted oppression (in many forms), and celebrated the family as a core factor of social stability, even if the unit did not follow conventional structural expectations. Considering the fact that many of his films were produced at a time when the shadow of the Cold War and an age of elevated material acquisitiveness had combined to proliferate a substantial degree of conceptual and social cynicism, the steadfast advocacy of meaningful, personal, and professional relationships championed by Hughes seemed invigoratingly optimistic in an otherwise hostile and aloof modern world.

Hughes typically featured sympathetic characters, applying an acerbic comicality and skillful discourse to popular genres in ways that elicited appreciation from both critics and cineastes. Even now, Hughes's cinema succeeds in transcending clichéd genre tropes and the historical context of the movies' production in order to focus on issues of a more universal nature. While fully in synch with the social and cultural apprehensions of their initial times of release, the overarching relevance of these films' representations of suburbia, social mores and teenage anxieties were to establish a unique quality which has allowed his range of movies to endure the passing of time and survive shifting generational attitudes in ways that few other features of the time could. The nostalgic appeal of Hughes's work has been further enhanced by the fact that his agreeable panoply of larger-than-life characters, many of which were brought into being by some of the most famous actors of the 1980s and '90s, continue to loom large within the wider confines of American pop culture. Irrespective of whether we are to distinguish his artistic aims through the dreams and trepidations of adolescents and teenagers advancing towards the deep-seated ambiguities of adult life, or in adults dealing with disenchantment and silently pining for the bygone days, Hughes's films were to present the public with a credible, coherent, and unquestionably compelling interpretation of American lives in a volatile and erratic age.

In the light of cinema history, John Hughes's work has become a celebrated contribution to American film. Many of the movies he either directed or wrote—during the eighties in particular—are now considered a benchmark among other motion pictures of the period. Despite achieving a significant amount of commercial success thanks to the family movies produced later in his career, most especially the first three titles in the *Home Alone* cycle, it seems highly likely that his groundbreaking films produced throughout the 1980s will remain his central creative accomplishment. Movies such as *The Breakfast Club* and *Ferris Bueller's Day Off* have become virtually synonymous with the period in which they were made, comfortably seated alongside other icons of the decade, such as the Blues Brothers, John Rambo, the Ghostbusters, and Marty McFly. While other cultural phenomena from the eighties have declined into obscurity, Hughes's stirringly affirmative, confident, and authentic judgments of ordinary day-to-day existence are still being appreciated by enthusiastic audiences.

Today, a decade since John Hughes's untimely passing, the genres and subjects of his many features construct a tapestry of this incomparable figure of American cinema. *John Hughes FAQ* evaluates the wide-ranging impetus of his creative output. It will offer the fullest possible picture of a career behind the camera that managed to spark international acclaim, helping to define the hopes and dreams of a generation. And, finally, it will reveal a true representation of a well-loved but complicated figure; a character whose creative legacy still casts a very long shadow.

John Hughes

The Man Behind the Movies

While John Hughes may well be remembered as one of the most respected figures in filmmaking during the 1980s and '90s, even in his heyday he preferred to let his work speak for itself. During his lifetime, Hughes was considered to be a deeply private individual who—in general—favored the notion that his public profile would be defined by the quality of his cinematic output. However, behind this professional persona lay a dedicated family man whose personal and ideological beliefs are regularly reflected in the content of his work. From his early days as a screenwriter to the later years of his career as director and producer, Hughes was a prolific talent who retained the same core values at the heart of his work even when the tone and concerns of his writing gradually evolved to adapt to a rapidly evolving cultural environment. His withdrawal from the public spotlight during the 1990s earned him a reputation for reclusiveness, a factor which further enhanced his status as a cult director. Indeed, his solitary nature became the basis for Matt Austin's acclaimed documentary film *Don't You Forget About Me* (2009), wherein Hughes's lofty professional standing was contrasted with his later self-imposed departure from Hollywood. But who was John Hughes, and how did he come to secure such a lasting legacy of goodwill among the moviegoing public?

The Write Stuff: How John Hughes Got Ahead in Advertising (and Publishing)

John Wilden Hughes Junior (1950–2009) was born in Michigan's capital city of Lansing on February 18, 1950. Raised by a father whose professional background was in sales, and a mother who was a charitable sector volunteer, Hughes spent his formative years in the Detroit town of Grosse Point before moving to the Chicago suburb of Northbrook in 1963. The town had been established in 1901 under the name of Shermerville—in tribute to influential local resident Frederick Schermer (1817–1901), upon whose land the town's first train station was built—before being given its current name in 1923. The town's original designation would later become familiar to Hughes's fans as the name given to his fictional Chicago suburb of Shermer, which regularly featured in many of his films. He attended the local Glenbrook North High School, where his youthful experiences would inform several of his most persistently popular movies in the same way his suburban upbringing influenced the central venues of many filmic narratives he was later to pen.

Following his graduation from high school in 1968, Hughes relocated to the city of Tucson, where he attended the University of Arizona. However, he left his undergraduate studies before completing his degree, instead embarking upon a career as a professional joke writer for stand-up comedians. His talents soon won him employment with advertising agencies, where he became a copywriter for companies such as Needham, Harper and Steers, and, later, a creative director at Leo Burnett Worldwide. In 1970 he married Nancy Ludwig, with whom he would have two children: John Hughes III and James Hughes.

By the mid-seventies, the Chicago-based Hughes was regularly visiting New York City as a result of his work, and his imaginative writing style eventually brought him to the attention of *National Lampoon* magazine. A humorous periodical which had been established a few years earlier, in 1970 (an offshoot of the much older *Harvard Lampoon* satirical magazine, which had been founded almost a century beforehand, in 1876), *National Lampoon* was considered pioneering in its day and achieved major popularity. With his nostalgic short story "Vacation '58," a humorous retrospective published in the magazine's September 1979 issue, Hughes suitably impressed the editorial team, earning himself a place on the writing staff.

At the time, *National Lampoon* magazine was expanding beyond the realm of print, eventually encompassing a multimedia empire that branched out into radio, theater, television, commercials, books, anthologies, and—perhaps most notably—cinema. The first movie to bear the magazine's famous name, *National Lampoon's Animal House* (1978), was directed by John Landis and featured a screenplay penned by *National Lampoon* writing alumni Chris Miller and Harold Ramis as well as the magazine's co-founder, Douglas Kenney. Set at the fictional Faber

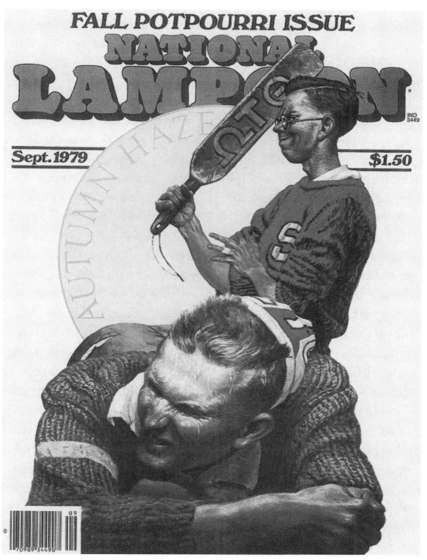

The September 1979 "Fall Pot Pourri" issue of *National Lampoon* magazine, which was to feature the first appearance of John Hughes's "Vacation '58" short story.

College, the film was a wildly successful campus comedy which sparked a boom in the genre, giving way to numerous imitations for several years afterwards. Produced on a small budget, *Animal House* was to amass an immense amount of profit at the box office at the time of its release, guaranteeing that further cinematic outings bearing the *National Lampoon* brand name would follow.

Building upon the monumental success of *Animal House* proved to be a challenging proposition, however. The company's first attempt to follow its commercial triumph, Joshua White's *Disco Beaver from Outer Space* (1978), was not to bear fruit. A surreal but frustratingly uneven parody of cable television of the time, White's feature was broadcast on HBO but achieved popularity with neither the critics nor the public. Another film, this time for the cinema, *National Lampoon Goes to the Movies* (1981), is a comedic anthology directed by Henry Jaglom and Bob Giraldi. The movie satirizes popular genres, but lacks coherence. It was eventually re-edited and received a delayed release in 1983 under the new title *National Lampoon's Movie Madness*, though reviewers were left largely unimpressed.

Now determined to recapture some aspect of the earlier success of *Animal House*, *National Lampoon* moved ahead with a production that eschewed the anthology format in favor of a single narrative more in keeping with the trailblazing original movie. Directed by Michael Miller, *National Lampoon's Class Reunion* marked John Hughes's first screenwriting credit. (While Hughes had earlier been contracted to complete a screenplay for "Jaws 3, People 0"—a spoof of the well-known shark-attack franchise—in collaboration with fellow writer Tod Carroll in 1979, that script was ultimately to remain unproduced.) A fusion of a high school reunion comedy and a sendup of the slasher horror subgenre that was gaining popularity in the early eighties, the film was an obvious attempt to evoke the chaotic entertainment of *Animal House* while introducing enough originality to attract new audiences. In spite of considerable public expectation, the film was not a commercial success, and performed poorly with critics. Though he would later voice dissatisfaction with the way his screenplay had been presented, noting that the content of his work bore little resemblance to what had eventually been shown

National Lampoon's Animal House. Director: John Landis. Release date: July 28, 1978.

in theaters, *Class Reunion* was nonetheless to signal Hughes's transition from prose into the realm of writing for the big screen.

Onward and Upward: From Screenwriting to the Director's Chair

Hughes would write for a handful of TV series early in his career, such as episodes of *Delta House* (1979)—a short-lived ABC comedy based on characters from *Animal House*—and *At Ease* (1983), a military-themed sitcom which aired on CBS for one season. However, he would continue to work on scripts for cinematic features, including Stan Dragoti's domestic comedy *Mr. Mom* (1983) and Ferdinand Fairfax's high-seas adventure film *Nate and Hayes* (1983), the latter—co-written by David Odell from his original story—forming what would be a rare big-screen writing collaboration for Hughes. The big break for his screenwriting career came in the form of his script for *National Lampoon's Vacation* (1983), a movie which was directed by one-time *National Lampoon* staff writer Harold Ramis (who had earlier helmed 1980's *Caddyshack* to a warm critical reception) and was to be based on "Vacation '58," the same short story that had gained Hughes the approval of the magazine's top brass several years earlier. *National Lampoon's Vacation* would prove to be a huge success, achieving considerable profitability in theaters and also winning the approval of many reviewers. Now considered one of the most popular and satisfying of all films to carry the *National Lampoon* name, *Vacation* has firmly embedded itself in the public consciousness—its endlessly quotable dialogue and peculiar mode of transport have ensured that it is still referenced in pop culture decades after its first release.

Given the lucrative performance of *Vacation*, Hughes's profile within the industry was on the rise, and as a result he was signed by Universal Studios to direct three movies. His directorial debut, *Sixteen Candles*, appeared in 1984 and was to be the first of his now-legendary cycle of teen movies. The film's inventive approach sent a shockwave through the industry; in a market which had been saturated by portentous coming-of-age dramas and ribald teen comedies, suddenly audiences were confronted by teenaged characters who used credible patterns of speech and faced believable problems within realistically portrayed situations. *Sixteen Candles* was to make a major star of Molly Ringwald, who would collaborate with Hughes again over the following two years, and the film's understated wit and relatable supporting cast would lay the foundation for many of his later teen comedies.

Hughes was highly prolific throughout the mid-eighties, writing and directing additional teen movies, such as the widely admired ensemble drama *The Breakfast Club* (1985), the sci-fi fantasy *Weird Science* (1985), and the offbeat comedy *Ferris Bueller's Day Off* (1986). He was simultaneously the writer-producer of two other films, the social class–focused *Pretty in Pink* (1986) and *Some Kind of Wonderful* (1987), both of which were directed by Howard Deutch. This cycle of teen features, from 1984 to 1987, came to be popular with audiences and critics alike, and their cultural prominence has been regularly cited (to a greater or lesser degree) as being among the most significant American movies of the eighties. Hughes was to single-handedly redefine all expectations of the teen movie's capability to connect with audiences and reflect a kind of cultural authenticity which had been theretofore lacking. A generation came to feel that their voice had been articulated more accurately by Hughes, and that he had truly understood their hopes and anxieties.

Hughes's six features in this category would have cemented his legacy on their own merits alone, but given their monumental success he was determined not to be pigeonholed within the confines of one particular genre. Alongside his teen cycle, he co-wrote (with Robert Klane) the screenplay for *National Lampoon's European Vacation* (Amy Heckerling, 1985), based on Hughes's original story. While accounts have varied over the years with regard to the extent of Hughes's actual involvement in the development of the final script (though he was given sole story credit), there was no doubting the debt owed to his original *Vacation* characters and his trademark dialogue. A return to the disaster-prone Griswold family featured in the original *Vacation* movie, the sequel was considered patchily amusing by most reviewers. However, from 1987 onward, he was to write and direct a number of mainstream comedies which—with their emphasis on family, suburbia, and domestic life—would hark back to his earlier feature *Mr. Mom*. At this point, he founded his production company—Hughes Entertainment—which would continue as a commercial entity until the late nineties. His keen interest in music was reflected by the formation of his independent record label, Hughes Music, also in 1987.

With *Planes, Trains and Automobiles* (1987), one of the best-received of all Hughes's directorial offerings, a mismatched pair of impromptu traveling companions forge a difficult and sometimes fraught friendship as they make their way from New York to Chicago during the Thanksgiving holiday. The film's subtle commentary on family and companionship, alongside its many adept cultural observations, mark it as perhaps the quintessentially Hughesian comedy of the eighties. The following year's *She's Having a Baby* (1988) was an uncharacteristically subdued affair by contrast, following the joys and tribulations of a newly married couple as they plan to have their first child. The noticeably heightened degree of dramatic content divided critics, and today the film is arguably among the most obscure of all Hughes's directorial efforts. A return to form was demonstrated by the success of *Uncle Buck* (1989), which shared the suburban setting of *She's Having a Baby* but reshaped its central subtexts of personal responsibility and family duty by instead conveying them through a clash of personalities between the titular, garrulous man of leisure and his reluctant wards.

Alongside his directorial output in the late eighties, Hughes was also to take up the duties of executive producer and screenwriter for *The Great Outdoors* (Howard Deutch, 1988), a vacation comedy set in scenic rural Wisconsin. The film made little impact on the reviewers of the time. He would take up production and screenwriting responsibilities for *National Lampoon's Christmas Vacation* (Jeremiah S. Chechik, 1989) the following year, and would meet with greater success. His final engagement with the Griswold family (who would later be revisited by other writers), the film was based on the events of Hughes's short story "Christmas '59," which had originally been published in the December 1980 issue of *National Lampoon* magazine. Though he was to end the decade with an immeasurably greater professional stature than when he had begun it, it seemed ironic that he would leave the eighties by reflecting the source of his earliest screenwriting contributions.

Voice of the Family: The Versatility of Hughes, the Producer

Hughes was to begin the 1990s in high style. *Home Alone* (Chris Columbus, 1990), which he was to both produce and write, would quickly establish itself as one of the most commercially profitable comedy films of all time. *Home Alone* tells the tale of a resourceful young boy who is accidentally left behind when his family flies off to Paris on vacation. The Christmas-set narrative and the now-famous scenes of the boy's ingenious methods of defending his family's home against burglars combine to make *Home Alone* a lasting favorite. With the youthful Macaulay Culkin as its lead, the movie would mark the beginning of a sea change in Hughes's cinematic output, one that would continue as the nineties progressed.

The following year, Hughes acted as screenwriter and producer for *Career Opportunities* (Bryan Gordon, 1991), a romantic comedy which mirrored some aspect of his eighties work in its personality conflicts and exploration of individual insecurities. A less successful film, *Dutch* (Peter Faiman, 1991), is a Thanksgiving-situated road-trip movie which paled in comparison to the similarly themed *Planes, Trains and Automobiles*. The same year, he also produced (but, unusually, neither wrote nor directed) the touching *Only the Lonely* (Chris Columbus, 1991), a comedy-drama centering around the attempts of a middle-aged police officer to find a balance between his love life and the care of an elderly parent. None of these films came close to matching Hughes's high-profile eighties output, much less the meteoric box-office success of *Home Alone*. In fact, these early nineties features are now largely forgotten by all but the most devoted aficionado of his work.

Hughes released his final film as director, *Curly Sue*, in 1991. Making plain his shift in gear from mainstream comedy to family movies, this offered an increase in slapstick as well as a lively, charming child star in the form of Alisan Porter. A studied mix of romance, comic situations, and social commentary, *Curly Sue* would share Hughes's preoccupation with the family unit which had characterized many of his earlier works. Nevertheless, it was criticized in some quarters for being emotionally manipulative in comparison to his other films.

Only the Lonely. Director: Chris Columbus. Release date: May 24, 1991.

Renewed commercial prosperity was to accompany the release of *Home Alone 2: Lost in New York* (Chris Columbus, 1992), where Hughes again took up production and screenwriting duties. Though the film was to reunite almost the entire cast from the first film and would perform strongly at the box office, it was unable to match the exceptional profitability of the original and faced skepticism from some reviewers who noted a large number of similarities between the plotline and several of the film's scenarios. The same year saw Hughes—in the guise of his writing pseudonym Edmond Dantès—collaborating on the screenplay for *Beethoven* (Brian Levant, 1992) with Amy Holden Jones. An unabashedly family-centric film which placed its focus on its lovable canine star, the ever-capable St. Bernard of the title, the movie was successful enough that it would spawn many sequels, though none of them would feature any participation from Hughes.

From the mid-nineties onwards, Hughes's involvement with the film industry gradually began to lessen. Though he had generally never been one to court public awareness, his withdrawal from the attention of the mainstream media would commence when he departed from the entertainment industry epicenter of California in favor of Lake Forest, Illinois. The number of interviews he granted diminished, and his public profile declined over the coming years. However, his solid reputation never waned, and he remained prolific both as a producer and screenwriter until the end of the decade. Hughes acted as writer-producer on a range of family-oriented films from the mid-1990s, including *Dennis the Menace* (Nick Castle, 1993), *Baby's Day Out* (Patrick Read Johnson, 1994), *Miracle on 34th Street* (Les Mayfield, 1994), *101 Dalmatians* (Stephen Herek, 1996), and *Flubber* (Les Mayfield, 1997), as well as a belated return to an earlier franchise with *Home Alone 3* (Raja Gosnell, 1997).

A surprising sidestep into character-based drama was made by Hughes near the end of the decade when he wrote and produced the claustrophobic *Reach the Rock* (William Ryan, 1998). Exploring the interconnected lives of a lawman and a troubled young man in a small Illinois community, the film signified a return to the refined characterization and adroit dialogue of Hughes's earlier output. However, this re-visitation of past glories would be short-lived. *Reach the Rock* received a limited

Market Square in Lake Forest, Illinois. Based along the shore of Lake Michigan, the city was home to John Hughes in his later years.

release, and marked the last time Hughes would engage in widespread media coverage to coincide with a movie's release.

Gone but Never Forgotten: Hughes in Retirement

Moving into the 21st century, Hughes's involvement with the entertainment industry continued to ebb. He composed the screenplay for the time-travel fantasy *Just Visiting* (Jean-Marie Poiré, 2001), better known as *Les Visiteurs en Amérique* within the international market. He also acted as executive producer for *New Port South* (Kyle Cooper, 2001), a high school–based drama which demonstrated some faint resonance with the subject matter of his mid-eighties work. Hughes's script treatments were also used as the source material for film comedies in later years, under his Edmond Dantès pen-name. These included the stories for *Maid in*

Manhattan (Wayne Wang, 2002), which was developed into a screenplay by Kevin Wade, and *Drillbit Taylor* (Steven Brill, 2008), where the Hughes plot outline formed the basis of Kristofor Brown and Seth Rogen's script.

Even after his retirement from the film industry, Hughes could not resist continuing his lifelong passion for writing. Though he was no longer penning screenplays for movie studios, he developed a talent for flash fiction—very short stories which were published under another pseudonym, "J. L. Hudson" (an obscure nom de plume which had been drawn from the name of a department store in Detroit that Hughes had frequented in his youth). But while his abandonment of the movie world meant he was no longer active within the industry, his films—especially his teen movie cycle from the mid-eighties—had not only retained their popularity, but were attracting new fans with every passing year. His legacy, and that of his creative output, continued to grow unabated. There was even widespread speculation within the trade press that Hughes could be persuaded out of retirement to make a return to the director's chair, and numerous articles emerged concerning the likely trajectory of sequels to his most famous films, such as *The Breakfast Club*, *Ferris Bueller's Day Off*, and *Sixteen Candles*. Ultimately, however, Hughes was to resist any suggestion of a comeback.

On August 6, 2009, while visiting Manhattan, Hughes suffered a fatal heart attack at the age of fifty-nine. The untimeliness of his passing rocked the entertainment world; a testament to his longevity as a filmmaker, given the number of years that had passed since his retirement. Tributes poured in from performers and directors who had worked with him, including many filmmakers who cited the profound influence his work had on them. Stories circulated of his numerous unproduced story treatments and screenplays, further accentuating his productivity and imaginative drive as a writer beyond even the abundance of his established output. A celebration of his body of work took place at the 82nd Academy Awards in 2010, and the surge in public interest regarding his career led to the reissue of many of his films (including some of the more obscure entries in his canon) on DVD.

Today, the life and professional reputation of John Hughes continues to inspire writers and directors. Whether drawing from the inventiveness of his groundbreaking teen movies, the accomplished wit of his comedies,

New Port South. Director: Kyle Cooper. Release date: September 7, 2001.

or the hyperkinetic quality of his family adventures, his work has continued to be referenced, parodied, and applauded. Hughes left behind a unique legacy which touched lives, stimulated minds, and moved hearts. His movies continue to endure to the present day, and beyond.

When You Grow Up, Your Heart Dies

John Hughes and the Teen Movie

The contribution made by John Hughes to the teen movie genre is incalculable. Between 1984 and 1987, he redefined the genre with confidence and stylistic assurance, sweeping away audience preconceptions about the ways in which teenagers were depicted in motion pictures. Hughes's teen protagonists were intelligently written, layered with substantial emotional depth, and exhibited characterization that was never allowed to lapse into the realm of tired cliché.

Primarily intended for consumption by young adults, the teen movie had been a staple of Hollywood for decades before Hughes made his directorial debut in 1984. Such films focused on issues that were of particular relevance to a teenage audience: early romance, peer pressure, anxiety about entering adulthood, divergence from parental authority, rebellion against the establishment, among other themes. This genre had achieved commercial profitability but the films themselves were also regularly derided for their stilted dialogue, formulaic storylines, and highly predictable structures. Frequently relying on stereotypical archetypes and faddish teenage argot relating to their time of production, teen movies can undoubtedly be seen as interesting snapshots of modern history, but they regularly relied on glossy presentation over thematic substance, which led to accusations of perceived triviality or superficiality from critics.

Although the American teen movie had manifested itself as early as the 1950s, with renowned films such as *The Wild One* (Laslo Benedek, 1953) and *Rebel Without a Cause* (Nicholas Ray, 1955) emphasizing the allure of the genre's "coolness," the briskly evolving fashions and cultural practices over the coming decades would require creative teams to rapidly adapt features in this category to meet constantly shifting social considerations. While certain conventions remained prevalent, such as a high school setting or engagement with perennial issues surrounding the process of growing up, as the years passed a growing reliance on sexual themes and bawdy humor were also increasingly observable. Ranging from early contributions to the genre such as *High School Confidential* (Jack Arnold, 1958) and *The Party Crashers* (Bernard Girard, 1958) to the innumerable beach movies of the sixties, subtle refinements to the genre could be detected by the arrival of the 1970s. With Robert Mulligan's *Bildungsroman*-style *Summer of '42* (1971), George Lucas's nostalgic but sophisticated *American Graffiti* (1973), and Jonathan Kaplan's darkly urbane *Over the Edge* (1979), the teen movie was beginning to come of age. Relying on an audience's familiarity with the stock characters and established precepts of the genre, filmmakers were starting to artfully reconfigure conventions and subtly undermine expectations to frequently notable effect.

With the dawn of the eighties, America's teenagers had become ever more stylish and astute, highly attuned to the increasingly consumer-driven society which formed the backdrop to their young adulthood. Many prominent teen movies of the early eighties—including *Times Square* (Allan Moyle, 1980), *Porky's* (Bob Clark, 1981), *Flashdance* (Adrian Lyne, 1983), and *The Outsiders* (Francis Ford Coppola, 1983)—highlighted different facets of the teen culture of this new decade, building upon the generic reinvention throughout the seventies while also continuing to diversify. Hughes's own engagement with the teen movie was to come at a point when films such as *Class* (Lewis John Carlino, 1983) and *St Elmo's Fire* (Joel Schumacher, 1985) were beginning to defy long-standing critical suppositions about the teen movie's aptitude for articulating contemporaneous cultural commentary and meaningful philosophical content.

Emerging at an opportune time in the genre's history, Hughes was to profoundly reinvigorate the teen movie with the production of six landmark features: *Sixteen Candles* (1984), *The Breakfast Club* (1985), *Weird Science* (1985), *Ferris Bueller's Day Off* (1986), and—directed by Howard Deutch—*Pretty in Pink* (1986) and *Some Kind of Wonderful* (1987).

Occasionally working in collaboration with young actors from the famous "Brat Pack" group of performers, such as Molly Ringwald, Anthony Michael Hall, Andrew McCarthy, Ally Sheedy, and Judd Nelson, Hughes was to demonstrate considerable determination in meticulously applying faithful, contemporary dialogue, up-to-the-minute fashions and music styles into each of his teen films. Yet beyond the assertive modernity of his scrupulous attention to detail, Hughes's mid-eighties output always utilized humor and a range of engaging situations which very often concealed profound universal messages about the difficulties of growing up in an uncertain and turbulent world. For all the prolificacy of his output, it is for his teen movies that Hughes is likely to be most closely associated, and his exacting yet thoughtful approach has come to inspire directors as varied as Whit Stillman, Kevin Smith, and Cameron Crowe.

Looks Like Teen Spirit: Youth Culture in *Sixteen Candles* and *The Breakfast Club*

When John Hughes's *Sixteen Candles* was first released, the effect on critics and the general public was immediate. Though his later films were arguably to become more iconic within eighties popular culture, with his debut directorial feature Hughes proved that he had the ability to convey the authentic voice of teen culture with both understanding and accuracy. He demonstrated that his characters were the product of a different kind of age than the stock figures so often employed in the earlier years of youth cinema. Confident and hopeful in many respects, they were nonetheless also emotionally vulnerable and quietly apprehensive about an uncertain future. Their apparent social assurance was inevitably filtered through a lens of peer pressure and, while perennial anxieties of seeking parental acceptance were holdovers from the established conventions of the teen movie, audiences were also left in no doubt that these characters were indicative of a new and fresh approach to the genre; affecting, without ever straying into mawkishness. *Sixteen Candles* marked the point where youth cinema evolved beyond the need for crude stereotypes and formulaic conventions, striving instead for a heightened degree of realism and relatability.

Sixteen Candles recounts the trials of a teenaged girl named Samantha Baker (Molly Ringwald), who must balance the anxieties of having a seemingly doomed crush on one of the most unattainable boys in her high school, with the hurt and frustration of her parents forgetting her landmark sixteenth birthday—the "sixteen candles" of the title—due to the upheaval caused by her older sister's fast-approaching wedding. While the movie established that Hughes's thoughtful style of direction corresponded to the elegance and sensitivity of his screenwriting—maintaining brisk momentum without treating its situations in an ephemeral or shallow manner—it was for his appreciation of effective characterization that *Sixteen Candles* has become best-known. Exemplifying his well-honed knack for reproducing the era's teenage vernacular while avoiding eighties-specific buzzwords or idiomatic lingo, the film highlights many central themes of Hughes's later teen movies while remaining a highly entertaining experience.

Among the most notable features of *Sixteen Candles* was its early manifestation of Hughes's deft ability to subvert the recognized character archetypes of the teen movie in ways which were diverting, amusing, and usually unanticipated. This slyly creative *legerdemain* is at the heart of the film's main premise; for much of the narrative, Samantha remains convinced that the object of her affections—Jake Ryan, played by Michael Schoeffling—is unreachable simply because of his elevated status within the school's complex social order. The logic governing high school factions may determine that a romantic relationship between the two will be impossible, meaning that it never occurs to Samantha to accommodate the possibility that Jake's own emotional attraction to her may override the lines of demarcation laid down by the inflexible hierarchy of their peers. Similarly, Gedde Watanabe's amorous exchange student Long Duk Dong bucks all cultural assumptions, transcending his setting in humorous and sometimes surreal ways. Anthony Michael Hall's nerdish Farmer Ted is never allowed to stray into the realm of generic truism, always being drawn in a manner which emphasizes his individuality and astuteness rather than leaning on the lazy clichés of geekdom. Hughes even turns the most unimaginative of teen movie staples on their head, challenging expectations of the burly, idolized high school senior and the self-obsessed, one-dimensional prom queen. Developing these well-worn

Sixteen Candles. Director: John Hughes. Release date: May 4, 1984.

stereotypes into fully fleshed-out characters, Hughes presented figures who were more reflective and convincing than audiences of the time would generally have anticipated. With his insight into the distinctive personalities of his teen protagonists, he exercised a lively and erudite discourse between these individuals which expounded upon their social trepidation just as much as it highlighted their interpersonal appeal.

The convincingly rendered environment Hughes created became successful with audiences precisely because of its accessibility; the central characters of *Sixteen Candles* would be immediately recognizable to anyone who had ever attended high school. A world of bickering relatives, sibling rivalry, and awkward encounters, the film's comedic elements were just as effective as its dramatic aspects. Hughes's subtly underplayed study of the clumsiness and shy discomfiture of young love seemed a world away from boisterously ribald contemporaries within the teen movie genre, such as *Meatballs* (Ivan Reitman, 1979), *Fast Times at Ridgemont High* (Amy Heckerling, 1982), and *Screwballs* (Rafal Zielinski, 1983), and his perceptive and socially aware departure from convention would come to be regarded as a major reason for the lasting success of *Sixteen Candles*.

Though Hughes had laid the groundwork for an examination of the multifarious social dynamics which operate within high schools, he was to consider the theme with considerably greater focus in *The Breakfast Club* the following year. A judicious and cerebral study of peer expectations and communal undercurrents within mainstream youth culture, Hughes was to populate the film with examples of the very kinds of genre archetype that audiences would have assumed to be present within a teen movie of the time, only to then gradually and meticulously dismantle these notions. Gathering together a cross-section of long-standing high school figures, including a rebel, a cheerleader, a jock, a geek, and an oddball individualist, Hughes took great care to play directly against expectation by assiduously setting up these established stereotypes only to then dispute and reconfigure assumptions regarding their attitudes, relationships, and respective mindsets.

Signaling an even more premeditated divergence from contemporary teen movie tropes, *The Breakfast Club* has become arguably the most renowned among all of Hughes's entries in the genre. Beyond his realignment of generic lodestones previously considered sacrosanct within the category of the teen movie, actively redefining its boundaries as a result, *The Breakfast Club* was also celebrated at the time for its introduction of the talented young performers who made up the "Brat Pack." Along with Joel Schumacher's *St. Elmo's Fire*, which was released in the same year, this loosely defined group rose to prominence throughout the eighties and was comprised of such actors as Molly Ringwald and Anthony Michael Hall (who featured in *The Breakfast Club*); Andrew McCarthy, Demi Moore, and Rob Lowe (who appeared in *St. Elmo's Fire*), and Ally Sheedy, Emilio Estevez, and Judd Nelson (who performed in both of these films). A play on the "Rat Pack" of the 1950s and 1960s—a high-profile group of actors led by Humphrey Bogart and Frank Sinatra respectively—the term "Brat Pack" is thought to have been coined in an article by David Blum, published in the June 10, 1985, issue of *New York* magazine, entitled "Hollywood's Brat Pack." The Brat Pack collective was considered flexible enough to accommodate other performers under the same umbrella, but the aforementioned actors are commonly deemed to be the principal figures associated with the term.

Building skillfully on the central scenario of five very different students being sent to a Saturday detention session in their high school's library—the unruly John Bender (Judd Nelson), popular Claire Standish (Molly Ringwald), athletic Andrew Clark (Emilio Estevez), nonconformist Allison Reynolds (Ally Sheedy), and bookish Brian Johnson (Anthony Michael Hall)—Hughes establishes a claustrophobic setting that forces interaction between a group of people who would generally never have chosen to fraternize. Conflict immediately erupts between them, but they find a common antagonist in Paul Gleason's tyrannical Assistant Principal Richard Vernon: an overbearing and dictatorial authority figure whose contempt for his unwilling charges is palpable. As had been the case with its predecessor *Sixteen Candles*, various established themes of the teen movie—such as the challenging of conventional authority structures and the suffocating weight of peer pressure—were only to denote the starting point for Hughes's subsequent, exacting process of cultural inquiry that would unfold within the confines of *The Breakfast Club*'s narrative.

Ringing the changes between digital-age teen angst that was specific to the eighties, and apprehensions which were universal enough to have traversed generations, Hughes considered, with much panache, the veritable chasm that lay between the disenchanted, hyper-competitive adult world and the increasingly urbane viewpoints and feelings of the independently minded group of youths who are on the cusp of colliding with it. Central to *The Breakfast Club* was Hughes's sly deliberation of the cliques which constitute the structure of the unyielding social system that operates within high school culture, but he additionally grapples with a recurrent motif in teen movies: that of the drive towards individuality being at variance with the importance of belonging to a larger group. This topic is expertly contemplated in the very brief essay which Brian composes as the voice of the entire group, with his reading of the work both opening and closing the movie. This short treatise was to become one of *The Breakfast Club*'s most fascinating highlights, and is so representative of Hughes's quirky but discerning creative approach that it has been continuously imitated (and lampooned) in popular culture from the eighties onward.

That Hughes had been able to successfully sustain a full-length feature based solely on the conversations and dealings which take place between five teenagers in a single room is remarkable in itself; that he was able to do so while demonstrating such charm, wit, and sheer entertainment value was nothing less than astonishing. Just as the subtle social observations and poignant romance of *Sixteen Candles* had felt like an opportune withdrawal from the hedonistic chaos of so many teen movies emerging throughout the early eighties, *The Breakfast Club* would prove to be a momentous departure from the established conventions of the campus comedy subgenre. The spiky interchange, serrated wit, and eventual bonding which takes place between Hughes's band of appealingly offbeat characters abundantly exhibits the reason *The Breakfast Club* was to become, in the views of the critical community as well as the viewing public, one of the most extraordinary entries in 1980s American film, with the movie's principal themes of teenage iconoclasm, the determination to establish personal independence, and the elusiveness of true belonging still resonating with audiences even today.

Such Stuff as Dreams Are Made: The Comedy Fantasy of *Weird Science* and *Ferris Bueller's Day Off*

If Hughes had re-energized the teen movie with the release of *Sixteen Candles* and *The Breakfast Club*, his engagement with the genre would not always be quite so intensely focused on the social dynamics of young adult life. Indeed, some of his films were to shun a high school setting altogether in favor of rather more fantastical or audacious situations. With *Weird Science*, for instance, he brings about an inventive cross-generic fusion between the teen movie and a rather tongue-in-cheek brand of science fiction. The effect is arresting, not just in terms of its retreat from the down-to-earth realism of Hughes's other youth cinema but also in its groundbreaking creative resolve to present audiences with a novel viewing experience. The end result is a bracing and lively caper, which blends vigorous generic reinvention with identifiable precepts originating from the respective annals of both constituent categories of film.

Weird Science was a rare foray into sci-fi territory for Hughes, though he would return to the realms of fantasy and magical realism during his screenplays of the nineties in films, such as Les Mayfield's *Miracle on 34th Street* (1994) and *Flubber* (1997), as well as the later *Just Visiting* (Jean-Marie Poiré, 2001). In the spirit of the EC Comics title *Weird Science*, a bi-monthly anthology series created by William Gaines and Al Feldstein which ran from 1950 to 1953, Hughes's movie combines the allegorical potential of the sci-fi genre with its capacity for communicating a strong moral message. The film's plot revolves around the efforts of gifted teen outsiders Wyatt Donnelly (Ilan Mitchell-Smith) and Gary Wallace (Anthony Michael Hall) to overcome their social outcast status by crafting a beautiful woman (Kelly LeBrock), using technological means. However, their creation—named Lisa—proves to be significantly shrewder and more worldly-wise than her designers, leading to some timely life lessons for the mystified young boffins. Given the movie's far-fetched storyline, however, it is perhaps more accurate to consider *Weird Science* under the generic umbrella of "science fantasy," not least when pondering its high concentration of deliberately humorous scenarios. Hughes's narrative implements cheerfully implausible technology

Weird Science. Director: John Hughes. Release date: August 2, 1985.

alongside an insightful exploration of teenage desire—not least in its manifold fantasies and uncertainties—which lend the feature a sense of jovial offhandedness and knowing whimsy. There is no small amount of amusement to be found in watching Wyatt's early home-computer system, connected via jury-rigged means to a top-secret government facility full of backing storage units (sporting frantically spinning tape reels in tribute to innumerable seventies sci-fi movies) miraculously succeeding in creating from nothingness the perfect specimen of female wisdom and beauty.

It is fair to say that by today's standards, the gender politics of *Weird Science* are highly problematic. While the notion of a pair of single, lonely teenage boys creating a stunning woman is a scenario fraught with potential accusations of sexism and chauvinistic caprice, Hughes briskly evades any such pitfalls by immediately emphasizing Lisa's independence, intellect, and confidence; he is always at pains to highlight her role as counselor and life coach to her naïve inventors rather than being merely the living personification of male desire that Wyatt and Gary may have initially anticipated. Kelly LeBrock, still fresh in the public memory from her role as the eponymous *femme fatale* in the previous year's *The Woman in Red* (Gene Wilder, 1984), plainly exults in the flamboyant character's sharp wit and fierce individuality. Always holding authority over her own destiny, Lisa drives the film's plot with unwavering conviction, even choosing to voluntarily remove herself from the lives of her clueless architects at the film's conclusion once she is satisfied that her guidance has been followed.

Hughes's examination of the nature of heterosexual male desire is only sporadically hinted at throughout *Weird Science*, alternating between Wyatt and Gary's foiled desire for Lisa (whom they soon discover to be vastly more mature and free-spirited than they had ever begun to predict) and their creation's rapid development of proxy parental attributes, such as empathy and compassion towards her two guileless "designers"—not least as she aims to resolve their insecurities regarding a lack of experience with the opposite sex. Via some transformative hijinks, including a memorably wild house party (another staple of the teen movie turned on its head by Hughes), these lessons in love eventually lead to the realization that their futures lie with fellow students Hilly (Judie Aronson) and

Deb (Suzanne Snyder), who forge a genuine and shared attraction with Wyatt and Gary in ways that outclass the relative inauthenticity of Lisa and her inexplicable powers of manipulation and invention. Thus, the teenagers discover that a more consequential and profound romantic relationship is possible with their contemporaries than had ever been the case with their impulsive creation, causing them to realize that while science can achieve noteworthy results, true love is likely to remain a mystery beyond human understanding.

Though Hughes had taken a markedly different creative approach to *Weird Science* than had been the case with his earlier *The Breakfast Club*, he was to use the movie to pick up on a number of the same themes that had been explored in his earlier work—most notably, the daunting burden and far-reaching effects of parental expectation on teenagers, and the inherent conflict between the allure of peer approval and the essential need to establish qualities of personal individuality. With significant artistic grace, Hughes had playfully disrupted the methodology of his earlier, thoughtful studies of teenage life in America by releasing the unpredictable and fantastic into the unwary suburbs of the United States. For his next film, however, he was to combine the whimsicality of attention-grabbing situations with the perceptive characterization and social commentary of his earlier works, all to extraordinary effect. The result would be one of the most critically acclaimed movies of his entire career.

Ferris Bueller's Day Off is a film that exhibits many dexterously exercised paradoxes. A movie which focuses on a group of high school students and a deeply misguided senior educator, but which features high school only on a handful of occasions, it would become one of John Hughes's most unconventional entries in the teen movie genre. Though one of the most explicitly comical of his youth cinema features, and demonstrating a multi-layered narrative that observes the benefits of a compassionate family unit and supportive community while highlighting the damage that can be caused (personally and collectively) by conflict within the domestic environment, the film was an entertaining travelogue through Chicago and its suburbs, filled with droll insights and startling character moments.

The film centers around the independently minded high school senior Ferris Bueller (Matthew Broderick), who decides to feign illness in order to skip his classes in favor of an incredible day in the city with his girlfriend, Sloane Peterson (Mia Sara), and best friend, Cameron Frye (Alan Ruck). However, his breezy attitude towards his studies is treated with deep suspicion by the school's autocratic dean of students, Ed Rooney (Jeffrey Jones), leading to a game of cat and mouse around Chicago as the streetwise teenager outsmarts both the authorities and his well-meaning parents. Filled with many inimitable sights, such as the ultra-rare 1963 Ferrari owned by Cameron's father (commandeered by Ferris for the day), a wearisome class with Ben Stein's droning economics teacher, and eye-catching trips to such varied venues as the top of the Sears Tower (subsequently rechristened as the Willis Tower in 2009), the home of the Chicago Cubs at Wrigley Field, and the visual riches of the Art Institute of Chicago, *Ferris Bueller's Day Off* has subsequently become a who's-who of 1980s pop culture iconography.

Although the film may not have been quite as overt a fantasy as its predecessor *Weird Science*—more of a wish-fulfillment scenario that makes manifest every teen's dream of running rings around the adult establishment—it nonetheless teases ingeniously with audience anticipation both as a highly effective comedy and a thought-provoking drama. Beyond its relentless good humor, the film soon moves clear of the realms of quirky eccentricity to consider deeper issues than may at first seem apparent. Hughes exercises considerable self-discipline in his exploration of Ferris's obvious disquiet towards the predicament of his close friend Cameron, whose life has been blighted by a domineering father and disaffected mother. Given Cameron's dysfunctional upbringing, Ferris is eager to avoid any possibility that his old confidante will unwittingly stumble into a similarly despondent adult life, and his efforts throughout the day—along with Cameron's own painful, dawning realization of his psychological and emotional shortcomings—lead to a moment of truly affecting epiphany at the film's conclusion. Similarly, Hughes's restraint is also tangible in his examination of the surprisingly deep emotional bond which exists between Ferris and Sloane. Though their mutual affection is always well-realized, Ferris is clearly troubled by the prospect that his impending admission to college and the pressures of adulthood will inevitably put an all-but-terminal strain on their flourishing relationship.

While other characters in Hughes's teen movies were heavily influenced by the demands of peer expectation, Ferris instead was to lead the pack rather than follow it. His effortless outmaneuvering of his parents and the school system has elevated him to a mythical status among his fellow students, while word of his *faux* ailments was so compellingly proliferated around his suburban community—and even the city of Chicago itself—that everyone from his classmates to the school faculty are cheering on his recuperation. But though he may have a wisecrack for every occasion, for all his trickery and gleeful duplicity Ferris is, at heart, a character who cares deeply for those around him. In his efforts to improve the lifestyles and broaden the mindset of friends and acquaintances, he is a truly life-enhancing individual in a world of increasingly gray uniformity.

Ranging from eye-catching views of the Windy City's famous skyscrapers to a whirlwind race around the landmarks and unique cultural identity of Chicago, Hughes makes clear his love of this area of Illinois; switching with ease from verdant, well-maintained suburbs to the drearily impersonal corridors of Ocean Park High School, the movie offers an abundance of visual variety. It was also to denote an intriguing variation in style for Hughes in his agreeable conceit of having Ferris candidly address the audience. As he breaks the confines of the fourth wall, this most alternative of characters forthrightly airs his thoughts throughout the movie, discussing not only the action but also his life philosophies and sharing numerous lighthearted asides as the narrative unfolds.

Ferris Bueller's Day Off was not only one of Hughes's most successful teen movies; with enough artistic verve to win over audiences from teenagers to adults, the film is so steeped in mid-eighties urbanity that it is one of the most fondly remembered comedies of the decade, both among critics and the public. While its sustained popularity has proven that the themes of personal freedom and autonomy championed by Hughes have remained as relatable and universally relevant in the 21st century as they did in the eighties, the film's continued reputation has also underlined the fact that Hughes's more fanciful entries in his cycle of teen movies have demonstrated just as much longevity as his more pragmatic, issue-based features.

A Touch of Class: Social Issues in *Pretty in Pink* and *Some Kind of Wonderful*

With *Pretty in Pink* and *Some Kind of Wonderful*, Hughes produced what would become arguably the most socially analytical entries in his teen movie canon. The films also saw the beginning of his professional relationship with director Howard Deutch, who was to develop a number of Hughes's screenplays into movies throughout the course of the late eighties. Although this loose duology would be the only two teen movies in Hughes's youth cinema cycle that he did not personally direct, the screenplays he wrote were manifestly redolent of the deep-seated problems that so often reveal themselves throughout teenage life. His return to the issues relating to the intricate social order of high school was so evocative that, in the view of many, the two films would together come to form an exemplary consideration of the class politics that affected American youth in the eighties.

With *Pretty in Pink*, Hughes took a conscious step away from the fantastical trimmings of *Weird Science* and the freewheeling whimsy of *Ferris Bueller's Day Off*, instead resuming his preoccupation with the carefully delineated characterization and discerningly depicted interpersonal relationships of his earlier teen movies. The film also allowed him to further hone a central issue that had been presented in both *Sixteen Candles* and *The Breakfast Club*: that of the convoluted, rigid, and often tacitly enforced structure which administered interaction between high school students, both individually and in groups, as well as the acute manner in which these unspoken social rules were to impact their lives and expectations.

Perhaps the most noticeable aspect of *Pretty in Pink* to occur to audiences and critics was that it seemed considerably more sober in its tenor than any of Hughes's preceding teen movies. Although the film was hardly without humorous content—indeed, the comic timing and witty dialogue of its supporting cast have since come to be regarded among its most memorable features—such was the profundity of the narrative that

Hughes was to prudently make the creative choice to diminish the more explicitly comedic situations which had so typified his previous films, instead placing greater focus upon relational dynamics and addressing emotional needs. The narrative centers on Andie Walsh (Molly Ringwald), a sensitive and caring but somewhat ostracized—if not entirely unpopular—teenager whose straitened economic circumstances isolate her from many of her well-to-do peers. Though usually inseparable from her zany childhood friend Phil "Duckie" Dale (Jon Cryer), who has unrequited feelings for her, Andie is taken aback when she develops a shared attraction with Blane McDonnagh (Andrew McCarthy)—an affluent and widely admired fellow student. Though Blane is unconcerned by Andie's comparatively humble background, their romance faces many obstacles: not least the disapproval of Blane's snooty acquaintances who will stop at nothing to ensure that the young couple's relationship never has the chance to take shape.

Though the pain of unreciprocated attraction plays a fairly major role in *Pretty in Pink* (Andie's rejection of the loyal, devoted Duckie in favor of sympathetic teen playboy Blane was to split the opinion of critics and audiences alike), the dominant issue to be expounded by Hughes is that of the tense interactions which take place between representatives of different social strata. It is testament to Hughes's skill as a screenwriter that he demonstrates the ability to avoid slipping into the realms of truism in his assessment of inter-class subtleties, just as he evades maudlin sentimentality when dealing with the subject of unrequited romance. While it cannot be denied that the general tendency of the screenplay is more disparaging of the attitudes demonstrated by the movie's more prosperous characters—especially the nominal antagonist, James Spader's spitefully Machiavellian Steff McKee—Hughes does take pains to circumvent any allegation of "inverse snobbery." Himself no stranger to the conflict between social classes during his own adolescence and teenage years, Hughes continually accentuates the key argument that any individual's personal qualities and moral character must be of primary importance; ready access to disposable income, their dynastic breeding, and other such considerations are irrelevant by comparison.

Pretty in Pink is a signpost of an intriguing change in pace for Hughes's engagement with the teen movie. Conspicuously light in terms of the off-the-cuff humor of his earlier work, it present a moodier, more reflective approach to the genre. Hughes had decided on a different creative approach with the film, choosing to explore the divisions and challenges surrounding issues of class while also shining a light on the ways in which these social disharmonies can have a deleterious effect on individuals as well as wider communities. Never preachy or emotionally manipulative in pursuing its aims, *Pretty in Pink* restated Hughes's enthusiasm for surveying the confines of the teen movie, pushing the genre's perceived margins in order to explore issues of emotional and cultural import with growing self-assurance and insight.

Some Kind of Wonderful was to mark the final entry in Hughes's cycle of teen movies, and—as had been the case with *Pretty in Pink*—it was to signify a greater maturity of approach which distinguished it from the cultural satire and sophisticated humor of his earlier features. Again directed by Howard Deutch, with Hughes taking up screenwriting and production responsibilities, *Some Kind of Wonderful* presents a series of issues which make it the perfect film to conclude this mid-eighties engagement with the genre. Dealing with young adults approaching the end of their teenage years, the challenges of maturity and personal responsibility were brought to the forefront in a film which pulled no punches when it came to the subject of life development and its many challenges.

An understated sense of contemplation and even mild dejection is apparent within the events of *Some Kind of Wonderful*, differentiating it from the lightheartedness of Hughes's earlier teen movies and indicating a correspondence with the thoughtful commentary of the preceding *Pretty in Pink*. The narrative concerns college-bound teenager Keith Nelson (Eric Stoltz), an artistically gifted loner in the dog days of high school, who unexpectedly lands a date with the beautiful and popular Amanda Jones (Lea Thompson). This enrages Amanda's former boyfriend Hardy Jenns (Craig Sheffer), a prosperous contemporary who is incensed by the notion of his erstwhile partner entering a relationship with someone he considers socially subordinate. As Hardy plots malign reprisals against the unsuspecting Keith, there is a further complication when Watts (Mary Stuart Masterson)—a tomboyish mechanic who has been

02-03 *Some Kind of Wonderful*. Director: Howard Deutch. Release date: February 27, 1987.

Keith's closest confidante since childhood—discovers that she too has feelings for her considerate but emotionally intense friend.

As the above summation may suggest, at the film's time of release more than a few reviewers noted the inescapable similarities between *Some Kind of Wonderful* and its predecessor *Pretty in Pink*. Some even went so far as to venture that the later film was a gender-swapped version of its precursor, with the Amanda-Keith-Watts love triangle being a deliberate reflection of the Duckie-Andie-Blane romantic entanglement—only with more of a crowd-pleasing conclusion, which saw the more prosperous prospective partner being passed over in favor of the long-standing platonic friend who finds that their close bond of companionship has developed into something more significant. Thus, while both films share other areas of thematic overlap, not least in the exploration of parental wealth and its effect on determining the class structure of high school as much as it did in society at large, *Some Kind of Wonderful* most obviously mirrored *Pretty in Pink* through its reflections on unanswered romantic longing. While Watts's affections are eventually responded to in ways that would forever evade the star-crossed Duckie Dale, Hughes's twist on this particular plot development shaped the film in profoundly different ways than had been the case with its forerunner.

While Hughes preserves the same type of understated humor that had worked so effectively in his later teen movies (most noticeable in the off-the-wall behavior of Elias Koteas's quirky Duncan), the muted comedy of the film was never allowed to overshadow the earnestness of Hughes's handling of the predominant issues at hand. Beyond the analysis of social divisions, *Some Kind of Wonderful* had much to say about the importance of friendship, the value of the family unit, and the intrinsic longing to address the needs of the self in the face of a group mentality. Like *Pretty in Pink*, there is an exploration of factionalism between (and within) social classes, and yet Hughes's focus always tends to accentuate the importance of fine details as they relate to individual people rather than the groups to which they belong. Thus, we see Keith's anxieties over his future from his own perspective, that of his concerned but well-meaning parents, and from the viewpoint of Watts (who has always believed in him, even when he has doubted himself). Keith's love for his family is always made apparent, not least when he is at variance with his father's wishes relating to his admission to college, and this is juxtaposed with Watts's covert desire for a secure and supportive family unit to which she may herself belong—a fact which only occurs to her when the depth of her feelings for Keith begin to become apparent, leading her to realize the true significance of the connection they share. Even Amanda, with her comparatively privileged background, is forced to appreciate the extent to which she is a prisoner of peer expectation; with everything from her fashion style to her personal comportment being shaped by the collective standpoint of her contemporaries, it is only when she is ultimately cut loose from this overpowering state of attitudinal pressure that she discovers she is finally at liberty to find her true self.

Some Kind of Wonderful may not have been the last time Hughes would deal with teenaged characters in his cinematic work, but it did mark the end of his mid-eighties teen cycle with substantial assurance. While all six films have remained hugely popular in the years since their first appearance, their appeal has extended far beyond the nostalgic allure of Hughes's famous ability to capture the atmosphere of a particular time and place. By always treating his characters and their situations with respect, rendering their thoughts in convincingly realized dialogue and delineating their motivations in ways that are both persuasive and absorbing, Hughes elevated the teen movie far beyond the territory it had once occupied. With his idiosyncratic but believable range of characters, his observance of family life, and his commemoration of the elation and fretfulness of being young and in love, Hughes had encapsulated the essence of being a teenager not only in the mid-1980s, but for many years to come. While his filmography ultimately encompassed numerous other styles and subjects, it seems certain that in the annals of popular culture he will always be remembered most fondly as the king of the teen movie.

Life Moves Pretty Fast

John Hughes, Travel, and Transport

The movies of John Hughes regularly featured vehicles which were almost as distinctive as the characters themselves. A filmmaker who always exhibited a keen eye for technology and machinery, Hughes often presented unexpected and unusual modes of travel in his cinema—and as his films were so often acutely concerned with liberty, few things spoke so readily of freedom as the ownership of a car. The automobiles presented in Hughes movies range from the stylish to the arcane, but they are always presented with entertainment in mind. Some of the vehicles were the very height of prestige at the time of production, whereas others are deliberately played for laughs. Occasionally, Hughes even rewarded his audience with some transport-related in-jokes—many of them quite surprising in nature, and all the more amusing for it.

Car-nage: *Ferris Bueller's Day Off* and the 1961 Ferrari 250 GT California

Perhaps the most famous of all automobiles to appear in a John Hughes film is the iconic 1961 Ferrari 250 GT Spyder California, which was "borrowed" by Matthew Broderick's Ferris Bueller as an integral part of his day out in Chicago. The perfect fusion of affluence and stature, this esteemed sports car perfectly typified Ferris's free-wheeling but aspirational attitude to life, and it has become one of the most recognizable of all vehicles to appear in eighties cinema. After convincing his edgy best friend, Cameron Frye (Alan Ruck), to let him take the inestimably costly vintage car for a spin (risking the ire of Cameron's intimidating but never-seen father in the process), the audience is treated not only to its presence on a travelogue of the city but also some less-than-expected depictions of its capabilities as this stylish automobile leaves the road in more ways than one.

The Ferrari 250 series was produced by Ferrari between 1953 to 1964; a successful line of highly prestigious sports cars, the company manufactured a number of variants during its lifetime—many of which have come to be sought-after collector's items. The 1961 250 GT Spyder California featured in *Ferris Bueller's Day Off* (1986) was a particularly exclusive specimen, with fewer than a hundred having been produced by Ferrari. But much to the relief of vintage car enthusiasts the world over, all was not quite as it seemed when this rare vehicle eventually met its demise—in one of the most striking scenes of the movie, we see the automobile crashing through the glass wall of the Fryes' elevated garage and landing several feet below, a shattered travesty of its former self. With so few specimens of the 250 GT California Spyder in circulation, the genuine article was used very sparingly by Hughes on occasions where close-up shots were required.

A fiberglass-bodied replica of the 1961 Ferrari 250 GT Spyder California.

For all other sequences, including those of Ferris and his friends driving around Chicago, replicas were used to safeguard the ultra-rare automobile's well-being. After much consideration, Hughes settled on the Modena Spyder California, an extremely faithful replica produced by Modena Design, which used fiberglass bodywork to imitate the original Ferrari's appearance. This allowed the production team the use of an aesthetically similar vehicle for shots where filming the hugely expensive Ferrari was considered to be unnecessarily risky in commercial terms.

A small number of these fiberglass-bodied replicas, actually based around an MG sports car, were constructed for the film. The use of the Modena reproduction of the genuine article permitted Hughes to attempt adventurous sequences that would never have been possible using the real Ferrari 250 GT, due to the astronomical costs that would have been involved in the event of even minor damage. These included the notorious scene where two garage attendants take the automobile on a joyride, speeding through the air to the sound of John Williams's renowned main theme from *Star Wars* (George Lucas, 1977), to say nothing of the car's eye-watering fate at the film's climax. Nonetheless, there has been some discord among automobile experts regarding the replica's odometer, which some have claimed is more suited to a British-based MG vehicle than the Italian-style gauge which would have been installed in a genuine Ferrari 250 GT of this type. Others have claimed that if an authentic Italian odometer had been used, Ferris's scheme to run back the accrued miles by putting the car in perpetual reverse may actually have worked, defusing Cameron's later fit of rage and robbing the film of its reflective climax.

The wreckage of the mock-Ferrari provoked angry reactions among vintage car aficionados at the time, given that they were unaware of its replica nature. However, as the more eagle-eyed viewer would no doubt have taken note, the impact as the facsimile "Ferrari" smashes into the foliage behind the Frye family garage actually causes visible damage to the fiberglass outer shell of the mockup car—external breakage which is clearly discernible to the trained eye when the vehicle comes to rest. Thus, the outward appearance of the crash affects the vehicle in a manner that is quite different in comparison to the effects of a catastrophic collision on a real Ferrari of this vintage. While the car's onscreen ruination may well have brought a tear to the eye of many an automobile devotee on viewing the film, they would no doubt have been relieved to know that the true Ferrari was not alone in emerging undamaged by the filming—all three of the Modena Design reproductions are said to have survived in private hands.

You Auto Know: Cars and Characterization in John Hughes Movies

John Hughes's use of vehicles often revealed a great deal about the characters who drive them. For instance, Cameron Frye's father owns a custom-built garage which contains not only the aforementioned Ferrari but also a number of other highly collectible classic cars, such as a Mercedes 300 convertible and a vintage MG J2, and yet Cameron himself is left to drive a comparatively run-down 1982 Alfa Romeo Alfetta. Though Cameron is less than impressed by the condition of his vehicle, it is the focus of much envy from Ferris himself—in spite of being desperate for a car of his own, he was gifted an expensive computer system for his birthday while his sister Jeanie received a sporty white 1985 Pontiac Fiero (much to his continual irritation). Sophisticated automobiles are also used heavily by Hughes throughout his teen movies to denote social status or prosperity; Kelly LeBrock's Lisa gifts teenagers Gary (Anthony Michael Hall) and Wyatt (Ilan Mitchell-Smith) with an impossibly classy black 1984 Porsche 928 in *Weird Science* (1985), the affluent but self-important Steff McKee (James Spader) drives a chic red Porsche 911 in *Pretty in Pink* (Howard Deutch, 1986), and Ferris Bueller's upwardly-mobile father Tom (Lyman Ward) makes his way around Chicago and its suburbs in a stylish 1985 Audi 5000.

However, not all of the cars that appeared in Hughes's movies were to be quite as lavish in their style. Often, the automobiles were chosen for their comic potential, and none more so than the Wagon Queen Family Truckster, which featured in *National Lampoon's Vacation* (Harold Ramis, 1983). Arguably one of the most humorous vehicles to be showcased in all of 1980s cinema, the visual style of the Truckster was actually based around the real-life 1979 Ford LTD Country Squire station wagon—albeit with some major modifications. The memorably shoddy fictional car was designed by George Barris, an automobile customization expert whose name will forever be synonymous with famous vehicles, such as the Batmobile driven by Adam West in the 1966–1968 ABC *Batman* television series, and the Munster "Koach," used by the endearingly macabre family in CBS's 1964–1966 TV series *The Munsters*. Intended to parody large American station wagons of the late 1970s and early '80s, the Truckster was deliberately planned to be as visually unappealing as possible. It featured a gaudy paint scheme in a metallic shade of avocado, and imitation wood-paneling (achieved by using decals) liberally applied around the car's bodywork. The Truckster had a number of other design oddities designed for the audience's amusement, including eight separate headlights and a gas cap which was purposely awkward to operate, leading to considerable inelegance whenever refueling was required.

Though not the car that was originally ordered by Clark Griswold (Chevy Chase) when he had sought a reliable vehicle to take his family on the long drive from Illinois to California, the Truckster has become closely correlated with the *Vacation* series and, over the years, has become

The Wagon Queen Family Truckster station wagon, designed by George Barris.

the very epitome of the unreliable and nauseatingly styled family car in modern popular culture. Though Jonathan Goldstein and John Francis Daley's 2015 sequel—entitled simply *Vacation*—was to replace the fabled automobile with an updated, similarly bizarre family vehicle named the Tartan Prancer, the Wagon Queen Family Truckster did make a cameo near the end of the film when it can be seen at the bed-and-breakfast operated by a now-retired Clark and Ellen Griswold. This was not, in fact, the original Truckster, but a painstakingly realized recreation, which had been crafted by Steve and Lisa Griswold of Atlanta, Georgia, who had given their consent to have their custom-built car included in the scene. This real-life Griswold family had built their own exacting replica of the Truckster in order to go on vacation with their daughters, and made the news in 2014 when they embarked on a cross-country road trip across America together, visiting many of the locations depicted in the original Harold Ramis film.

The Truckster was also to receive a spiritual successor of sorts in the form of the garish hired car which appears in *Planes, Trains and Automobiles* (1987). While again not the ideal choice of weary travelers Neal Page (Steve Martin) and Del Griffith (John Candy), the two luckless passengers only make use of the vehicle due to their shared desperation to return to Chicago—and in a film which centers on the use of transportation in all of its many forms, a supremely ugly car was required for maximum comic impact. To this end, Hughes introduced us to the 1987 Gran Detroit Farm and Country Turbo—a completely fictitious vehicle which was never likely to win awards for either its performance or general appearance. Like the Truckster before it, the car was actually a camouflaged version of a genuine automobile—in this case, the Chrysler LeBaron Town and Country convertible—with a conspicuous line in wood-effect decal panels and a tasteless shade of green that is eerily similar to the paint job adorning Clark Griswold's infamous earlier vehicle. In a regrettable development for the ill-fated pair, the Farm and Country Turbo winds up being even less fortunate than the Truckster, with mechanical failure, a catastrophic fire, and the results of dangerous driving—all plaguing the insipid-looking car as the film unfolds.

Perhaps the most decrepit of all automobiles to grace a John Hughes film was the run-down 1977 Mercury Marquis Brougham driven by Buck

The 1986 Chrysler LeBaron Town and Country station wagon.

Russell (John Candy) in *Uncle Buck* (1989). Affectionately known as "The Beast" by its owner, this rickety vehicle seemed to be held together almost entirely by rust and goodwill. Designed to be as disheveled and character-ful as its slovenly but lovable owner, Buck's Marquis Brougham is fondly remembered for its propensity to backfire deafeningly—a fearsome noise that was achieved by audio engineers combining the sound of an explod-ing firecracker and a gunshot. Grimy, badly maintained and carrying a worn sticker which indicates that the car had once been mistaken for an abandoned vehicle, Buck's beleaguered automobile seems only barely capable of motion; some careful engineering on the part of the produc-tion team ensures that the car's tailpipe emits enough greasy smoke to leave no one in any doubt of the engine's state of health. Chock-full of the clutter and ephemera that would be expected of the film's amiably slobby protagonist, Buck's gas-guzzling Marquis Brougham was not exactly the powerful, high-end vehicle that it would likely have seemed in its late seventies heyday. Covered with dents, its fender badly corroded and with some of its original fittings missing, the car is in a sorry state—a testament to Buck's constant neglect of its upkeep. Yet like its owner, while this forlorn automobile may have appeared ramshackle and on the verge of falling apart, it was not to be underestimated: the capacious vehicle was the perfect match for such a larger-than-life individual, and, by some miracle, it always seemed to come through in the end.

Creative License: The Vehicular In-Jokes of John Hughes

One of John Hughes's most notorious directorial trademarks came in the form of subtle in-jokes he placed within the license plates of his characters' cars. These appeared in many of the films he directed in the eighties, and, in several cases, they referred to other movies he produced. In *Sixteen Candles* (1984), the car used by Samantha Baker's grandparents bears a license plate reading "V58," referring to Hughes's short fiction work "Vacation '58," published in the *National Lampoon* magazine and later the basis of *National Lampoon's Vacation*. Also, the car driven by Jake Ryan (Michael Schoeffling) is licensed with the number "21850"—a subtle reference to Hughes's date of birth (Saturday February 18, 1950). In *The Breakfast Club* (1985), the vehicle carrying the scholarly Brian Johnson (Anthony Michael Hall) has a license plate reading "EMC2," calling to mind Albert Einstein's famous law of mass-energy equivalence, whereas the automobile belonging to Jefferson "Jake" Briggs (Kevin Bacon) in *She's Having a Baby* (1988) has the titular acronym "SHAB" as its license code.

The most famous of all Hughes films to feature license plate in-jokes was *Ferris Bueller's Day Off*, which contains several incidents of this running sight gag. The formidable Ed Rooney ironically drives a car with a license plate reading "4FBDO" is not just an acronym of the movie's title; it is also paradoxical in the sense that he constantly expends every effort in trying to thwart Ferris's famous day of leisure. Ferris's mother, Katie, has a vehicle license of "VCTN," referring to *National Lampoon's Vacation*, while his father Tom's car is registered with the license "MMOM"—an allusion to *Mr. Mom* (Stan Dragoti, 1983). Jeanie's Pontiac bears the license plate "TBC" after *The Breakfast Club*, but—perhaps most appropriately of all—the famous 1961 Ferrari 250 GT California has a license registration of "NRVOUS," perfectly summing up Cameron's mindset for most of the film's running time.

For John Hughes, cars were more than a way of getting his characters from one point to another. The style and condition of a character's vehicle would often say a great deal about them. For Ferris Bueller, the prospect of owning his own vehicle was symbolic of the social liberty and individual freedom he always sought from life; that he is unwilling to settle for any car from Mr. Frye's garage other than the irreplaceable Ferrari speaks volumes about his aspirations. By contrast, for characters such as Clark Griswold or the unlucky traveling companions Neal Page and Del Griffith, their vehicles are characterful but essentially hopeless—the very embodiment of trying to make the most of a bad situation. Juxtaposing Clark's perennially unsound Truckster with the pristine red Ferrari 308 GTS driven by Christie Brinkley's unnamed woman of mystery in the same film was to draw inevitable comparisons between the purposeful functionality of family life and the excitement of new romance. (As was the recurrent Hughes theme, Clark soon learns that his depth of affection for his loved ones transcends the temptation of any potential fleeting affair; the Truckster may be a banal and unreliable automobile, but it nonetheless proves capable of getting him to his destination long after the flamboyant Ferrari and its sophisticated, independent owner have gone by the wayside.) In the case of Buck Russell, the automobile acts as a mirror of his character; disheveled and largely given up for junk, it somehow manages to remain steadfast enough to be relied upon when needed—just like its ebullient owner.

Hughes's films often feature cars that had been meticulously chosen to achieve maximum impact upon the audience—either because of their opulence or their comic value. But as was so often the case in a Hughes movie, outward appearances sometimes proved to be deceptive; the Ferrari so coveted by Ferris Bueller may have signified prosperity and ambition to him, but to Cameron Frye it was a symbol of his distant father's elevation of material possessions over the love of his own family. Likewise, the inspired comical appearance of the cars in *National Lampoon's Vacation*, *Planes, Trains and Automobiles*, and *Uncle Buck* may have lacked glamor and consistent dependability, but they nonetheless reflected their drivers' good intentions in their sense of utilitarian but unconventional practicality. Hughes's characteristically sharp eye for comedic possibilities certainly never let him down when it came to the choice of cars he made for his films, and some of his unrivaled selections have remained mainstays of popular culture ever since.

How Can You Give Kris Kringle a Parking Ticket on Christmas Eve?

John Hughes and the Christmas Movie

While he has been widely lauded for his pioneering teen movies and eighties comedies, John Hughes also had a significant impact upon Christmas cinema. The festively themed features produced by Hughes Entertainment may not have reached quite the same level of lasting admiration that has accompanied many of his other movies, but they have nonetheless earned their place within a well-populated and commercially popular genre, ensuring that they are still regularly screened and appreciated.

Jingle Hell: *National Lampoon's Christmas Vacation*

Although films such as *Planes, Trains and Automobiles* (1987) and *Uncle Buck* (1989) had featured the unmistakable visual tones of late autumn, Hughes's involvement with the Christmas movie would not truly begin until 1989 and the arrival of *National Lampoon's Christmas Vacation*. Directed by Jeremiah S. Chechik, who would later helm such whimsical films as *Benny and Joon* (1993) and *Tall Tale* (1995) alongside numerous television features, Hughes's screenplay for the film would establish several areas of shared ground which existed between his established narrative themes and those of Christmas cinema in general. Eschewing the road-trip motif of the first two films in the *National Lampoon's Vacation*

National Lampoon's Christmas Vacation. Director: Jeremiah Chechik. Release date: December 1, 1989.

cycle, this festive outing for Clark W. Griswold and his star-crossed clan was a significantly less ribald offering; emphasis was placed more firmly on family-oriented entertainment, while the film's core theme centered on the role of domestic goodwill and the importance of familial bonds—subjects of crucial significance in many Christmas movies. Yet, in the true Hughes spirit, a careful balance is struck to ensure that the deceptively cozy Yuletide atmosphere does not compromise laughs for the sake of emotional sentiment.

Once again featuring Chevy Chase as the well-meaning but hugely accident-prone Clark Griswold, and Beverly D'Angelo as his long-suffering wife, Ellen, *National Lampoon's Christmas Vacation* presents a temporary break in the family's chaotic travels by bringing the holiday season into their well-appointed suburban home as they enjoyed festive celebrations with their many peculiar relations. Much to the chagrin of the Griswolds' fraught children, Rusty (Johnny Galecki) and Audrey (Juliette Lewis), this involved the wholesale invasion of their house over the Christmas period by Clark's well-meaning parents, his significantly less accommodating in-laws, and the strange pairing of Aunt Bethany and Uncle Lewis (played to addled perfection by Mae Questel, one-time voice of Betty Boop, alongside William Hickey, forever remembered for his turn as the affable barfly in Mel Brooks's Academy Award-winning 1968 comedy *The Producers*). The disarray is further intensified by the unexpected—and distinctly unwelcome—arrival of Ellen's down-on-his-luck cousin, Eddie Johnson, and his family, who have traveled from the state of Kansas to spend the holidays with the Griswolds. Reprising and expanding on his role as Cousin Eddie from the original *National Lampoon's Vacation* (Harold Ramis, 1983), Randy Quaid somehow managed to re-enact the impossibly deft juggling act which made this disheveled character simultaneously repellent and oddly endearing. Quite brazenly present at Clark's home with the sole intent of scrounging his way through the festive period—sponging gifts for his children and even himself—it is difficult to entirely dislike Eddie, considering his mix of general cluelessness and boundless geniality. Sadly for Clark, this overbearing relative is only one part of a growing festive nightmare.

Although the film takes place almost entirely in one snowy suburban locale, director Chechik skillfully made full use of every situation for well-timed comedy effect, reflecting Hughes's witty and well-paced script. This is true of everything from Clark's high-wire stunts as he staples Christmas lights to the roof of his house (a scenario which predictably does not go according to plan) all the way through to the slow-motion, if unintentional, demolition of his yuppie neighbors' pretentiously decorated home. The screenplay makes good use of the intermittent interludes away from the Griswold family home, be they at Clark's swanky inner-city office or the pleasant woodland regions surrounding his neighborhood (captured beautifully by cinematographer Thomas E. Ackerman). Hughes employs these vignettes both sparingly and efficiently in a way that enhances the film's festive flavor rather than eroding it. Angelo Badalamenti, who would achieve huge success with his haunting music for David Lynch's *Twin Peaks* television series (1990–1991) soon afterwards, provided a dynamic score which neatly accompanies *Christmas Vacation*'s sense of manic action, as well as delivering the obligatory holiday atmosphere whenever required. (Given the static nature of the family Christmas celebrations, Lindsay Buckingham's "Holiday Road"—a song which had accompanied the earlier Griswold outings—was this time replaced by the energetic title song, "Christmas Vacation," performed by Mavis Staples.)

Though few could have suspected it at the time, *National Lampoon's Christmas Vacation* performed an important transitionary function for the Christmas film during the point of its release. While Hughes's screenplay had engaged with arguably the most prominent theme to emerge in the genre throughout the eighties—that is, depicting the conflict between the philanthropic nature of the festive spirit and commercial self-interest. This topic had predominated in other Christmas movies of the decade, such as Jeannot Szwarc's *Santa Claus: The Movie* (1985) and Richard Donner's *Scrooged* (1988). But Hughes was also to lay the foundations for what would become the predominant concern of Christmas features throughout the 1990s: the unchanging value of the family unit. With *Christmas Vacation*, he brought the two subjects into collision by introducing, at the film's climax, a showdown between the Griswold family and Clark's irascible boss, Frank Shirley (a memorably cantankerous performance by Brian Doyle-Murray). Having covertly canceled the annual Christmas bonus in a blatant attempt to save money, Mr.

Shirley is forced to re-examine his actions when he witnesses first-hand the effect that his miserliness has had at the grass roots level. (The extent to which anyone could consider the Griswolds an "ordinary family" is another issue entirely, but the impact of the abolished bonus is made plain enough.) Whether Frank's change of heart can be explained by the transformative power of Christmas or the prospect of the lumbering Cousin Eddie glowering over him with pugilistic intent, the fact that his *volte-face* has been brought about at all is clearly depicted by Hughes as a triumph of the family unit over faceless corporate avarice.

Christmas Vacation was followed by a belated made-for-television spin-off, Nick Marck's *National Lampoon's Christmas Vacation 2: Cousin Eddie's Island Adventure* (2003), written by Matty Simmons. Although Chase and D'Angelo did not feature this time around, and the TV movie would have no involvement from John Hughes in any capacity, it did star Randy Quaid and Miriam Flynn—once again reprising their roles as Eddie and Catherine Johnson—as well as Dana Barron as Audrey Griswold (who had previously assumed the role in 1983's original *Vacation* movie). The sequel made only a minimal impression on the public, however, and has never seriously competed with the original in either critical response or in the memory of audiences.

Home for the Holidays: *Home Alone*

By the early 1990s, the world was changing, and so too were the expectations surrounding the Christmas movie. Cultural attitudes were beginning to shift, with the "greed is good" ethos of the eighties (popularized by films such as Oliver Stone's 1987 finance industry drama *Wall Street*) giving way to concerns that lay beyond the economic factors dominating much of the social commentary throughout the earlier decade. Just as these sweeping changes would affect the world of cinema in general, so too would the Christmas film need to adapt in order to reflect the newly developing domestic and international outlook. Hughes was at the forefront of redefining the genre with these emerging issues in mind. The energetic defense of the Christmas spirit in the face of corporate excess was to steadily fade, being gradually usurped by a move towards

Home Alone. Director: Chris Columbus. Release date: November 16, 1990.

a greater celebration of the family, friendship, and the community as well as the re-emergence of a another traditional theme—the need for a sense of belonging in a world that seemed to be more profoundly in flux than ever before.

Home Alone (Chris Columbus, 1990) would further develop the theme of familial affection and its importance to the festive season. Although the film would share some common factors with *National Lampoon's Christmas Vacation*—an inviting home in the Chicago suburbs, eccentric characters, and Christmas plans that go drastically awry—the approach that Hughes would adopt for his screenplay on this occasion would prove to be drastically different. *Home Alone* was also to feature popular child actor Macaulay Culkin, a performer with whom Hughes had worked during his earlier family comedy *Uncle Buck*, back in 1989. Culkin's wryly mature performance in that film had been favorably received by the critics of the time, but few could possibly have predicted the meteoric box-office success that would arrive following his next collaboration with Hughes.

Home Alone came relatively early in the filmography of director Chris Columbus, who at the time was arguably best known for helming the cult comedy *Adventures in Babysitting* (1987) and Elvis Presley–themed fantasy *Heartbreak Hotel* (1988). Later a producer of note, he was also a well-regarded screenwriter by the early nineties, having written scripts for films such as *Gremlins* (Joe Dante, 1984), *Reckless* (James Foley, 1984), and *Young Sherlock Holmes* (Barry Levinson, 1985). Working with Hughes, who would again fulfill a dual role as producer and screenwriter, Columbus's professional profile was to be greatly enhanced by the huge commercial impact achieved by *Home Alone*.

Home Alone is a heartfelt tribute to the nuclear family by Hughes, and one which appears unerringly traditional in comparison to later nineties films with similar themes of domestic relationships and reconciliation at Christmas. In the same manner is such movies as Robert Lieberman's *All I Want for Christmas* (1991), *Home Alone* promotes the traditional benefits of marriage and the stable family unit, whereas the decade's later offerings became significantly more inclusive, emphasizing that the term "family" can encompass a very diverse range of relationships which transcend mere blood relations. But as was the case with his other Christmas features, Hughes seemed much more intent upon ensuring that his audience was being entertained than attempting to overtly influence their worldview with excessively profound socio-political points, meaning that he and Columbus would work in tandem to maintain a warm-hearted, festive atmosphere throughout the film.

Following the tribulations of young Kevin McCallister, who is accidentally left at home by himself when his parents and siblings fly off on holiday to Paris, the film takes place during the build-up to Christmas—a confluence of events which leaves Kevin with mixed emotions, as he revels in his newfound freedom while simultaneously regretting his family's absence during the festive season. Although the film has, of course, become most affectionately regarded for its climactic sequence where Kevin repels a pair of incompetent burglars ("The Wet Bandits") from his home, it is also notable for the poignancy of the sensitive emotion at its heart, which accentuates the need to belong and feel wanted—especially at Christmas—without ever drifting into treacly sentimentality. Certainly Hughes is always careful to take a decidedly lighthearted approach to the film's events as they unfold, providing a sort of ironclad internal logic which belies the relative implausibility of much of the plot. The McCallisters' luxurious home in an affluent suburb offers Kevin the widest possible range of opportunities to defend his property against the Wet Bandits (a sublime pairing of Joe Pesci and Daniel Stern), and indeed his inspired range of improvised security countermeasures are never less than a joy to behold.

Columbus's direction is always capably efficient, neatly contrasting the frantic, accelerated mayhem of the bustling McCallister house in the early scenes with Kevin's later escapades while alone in his deserted home. There are also many pleasing sight gags, such as the McCallisters' constantly capsized garden statue, which always appears to be directly in the line of every car or van that approaches it. There is also wry humor, such as the street corner Santa's gift of lime-favored Tic-Tacs (being the night of Christmas Eve, he had given all of the remaining candy canes to his assistant before closing up for the evening). The film features a number of nicely understated supporting performances, such as Gerry Bamman's sneeringly crass Uncle Frank, moaning snidely one minute and then shamelessly loading up on complimentary airline giveaways the next, and John Candy's cameo appearance as kindhearted bandleader Gus Polinski (a character who is heavily influenced by Candy's earlier role as the cheerful traveling salesman Del Griffith in Hughes's *Planes, Trains and Automobiles*). Additionally, *Home Alone* profits immensely from an excellent score by legendary film composer John Williams. Moving effortlessly between tender contemplation and frenetic action, the soundtrack is uniformly impressive, though the atmospheric title theme and up-tempo "Holiday Flight" are standout pieces.

While Hughes's stellar reputation as a producer and filmmaker had been well established throughout the eighties, no one beyond the most optimistic of pundits could have predicted just how well *Home Alone* would perform at the box-office when it was released in November 1990. According to BoxOfficeMojo figures, with an estimated budget of $15 million, the film would eventually accrue a combined worldwide gross of $476,684,675, meaning that *Home Alone* would not only become the top-grossing film to be released in 1990, but that it would be one of the twenty most profitable movies in film history.

Given the film's massive box-office success, a sequel seemed inevitable, and, sure enough, the main cast and production team soon reunited for *Home Alone 2: Lost in New York* (1992). Once again directed by Chris Columbus and featuring a John Hughes screenplay, the similarly Christmas-situated *Home Alone 2* focuses upon a strangely familiar mishap, which sees Kevin separated from his family on the way to a vacation in Miami and eventually winding up (as the title suggests) in New York City instead. Once there, he manages to trick his way into renting a well-appointed room at a high-class hotel, and is soon faced with the twin difficulties of reuniting with his family while simultaneously thwarting an attempt by the recently escaped Wet Bandits (now rechristened the "Sticky Bandits") to burgle an enormous toy store in the city over the holidays. As well as the returning main cast, the sequel also featured excellent supporting performances by the ever-charismatic Tim Curry as a snooty hotel concierge, and Irish actress Brenda Fricker, who portrays a character with a very similar function to Roberts Blossom's surprisingly cordial loner Mr. Marley in the original film. Although the film was a huge financial success, it was unable to replicate the monumental box-office achievement of the first *Home Alone*, and the implausible number of similarities which lay between the sequel's narrative and incidents which had taken place in the original were not lost on the critics who gave *Lost in New York* a deeply mixed response at the time of its launch. Neither of the later sequels, Raja Gosnell's *Home Alone 3* (1997) or made-for-TV movies *Home Alone 4: Taking Back the House* (Rod Daniel, 2002) and *Home Alone: The Holiday Heist* (Peter Hewitt, 2012), were to engage quite so closely with the conventions of festive cinema.

The commercial triumph of *Home Alone* heralded a new boom-time for Christmas-themed films. Although it has been noted that the film contained a faint whiff of criticism towards upper-middle-class lifestyles, calling attention to the fact that the value placed on materialistic pursuits and striving for a comfortable quality of life was undermining the value of family interaction and highlighting the need for parents to ensure that they adequately prioritized their offspring, *Home Alone* nonetheless signified a move away from the discernible (and often heavy-handed) cultural commentary that had been so conspicuous in Christmas movies of the eighties. By emphasizing traditional values in a manner that was relevant to—and popular with—contemporary audiences, the influence of *Home Alone* was far-reaching enough that it would set the pace for many later family-oriented features in the Christmas film genre throughout the coming decade.

The New Old-Fashioned Way: *Miracle on 34th Street*

Hughes was to continue his engagement with festive filmmaking in the form of what would debatably be the most challenging entry in his loose sequence of Christmas movies, namely a popular remake of George Seaton's iconic silver screen classic *Miracle on 34th Street* (1947). With its genesis in a formative period in the history of Christmas cinema, when the tropes defining the genre were being laid down throughout the 1940s and '50s, the original *Miracle on 34th Street* had long been established as a *bona fide* landmark in the development of the festive film, with none of the subsequent TV updates coming close to supplanting its towering status. Even today, Seaton's film remains one of the best-loved of all Christmas movies. There are very few motion pictures in any genre which

Miracle on 34th Street. Director: Les Mayfield. Release date: November 18, 1994.

encapsulate so vividly the excitement of childhood expectation towards the festive season, or which underscore with such panache a willingness to retain a healthy faith in that which remains indefinable—irrespective of anyone's ideological, philosophical, or religious background.

Directed by Les Mayfield, who would collaborate with Hughes again a few years later on the whimsical comedy remake *Flubber* (1997), this new cinematic revision of *Miracle on 34th Street* opened in 1994. Hughes's screenplay was forced to perform a difficult balancing act in the sense that his audience would expect a degree of fidelity to the original film while also anticipating heightened relevance to modern-day sensibilities. Reworking Seaton's earlier screenplay (which itself had been based on a story by Valentine Davies), Hughes was at pains to take into account the social and cultural changes that had occurred in the intervening decades. As in the original film, a kindly old gentleman named Kriss Kringle ("Kris" in the Seaton movie) finds himself persuaded to become a department store's Santa Claus over the holiday period, but winds up a victim of his own success—when Kris's (Richard Attenborough) kindly nature brings about enthusiastic publicity and new customers in their droves, a vindictive rival seeks to call his mental stability into question, leading to his incarceration. (The antagonist in the original film is a crank psychologist named Granville Sawyer; a rival department store takes up a similar adversarial role in the remake.) This causes particular distress to one of the store's executives, Dorey Walker (Elizabeth Perkins), and her daughter Susan (Mara Wilson)—a skeptical child whose friendship with Kris slowly makes her question her incredulity towards Santa Claus and his mythical powers. Dylan McDermott's compassionate city lawyer Bryan Bedford (named Fred Gailey in Seaton's original) takes up the subsequent court case resulting from Kris's evaluation, leading to a lengthy legal battle which ultimately proves not only that Santa Claus exists, but that he does so in the form of the humble Mr. Kringle.

Mayfield and Hughes's remake offers a number of key narrative changes from Seaton's movie; much of the explicit psychological content is eliminated from the plot, including the character of Sawyer himself, meaning that the guileless Kris's downfall is engineered in a more premeditated way. Just as prominently, the Macy's and Gimbels department stores of the 1947 film are now replaced by the fictional companies

"Cole's" and "Shopper's Express." However, at its core the film retains the same message of remembering the vital importance of belief in the individual, substituting the earlier film's conclusion (where mailbags full of letters to Santa are decanted into a New York courtroom) for a rather more low-key climax which contains an understated subtext focusing on the very concept of faith, drawing subtle parallels between belief in the spirit of Christmas and the simple act of trust.

The remake of *Miracle on 34th Street* benefits greatly from Richard Attenborough's performance as the avuncular Kris Kringle; the veteran actor throws everything into the creation of a thoroughly appealing character who embodies the very essence of the festive season. Wisely, he chooses not to emulate Edmund Gwenn's original portrayal of Kringle, instead carving out a very different individual who retains his intended connection to the traditions of Christmas while remaining engaging and relevant to modern audiences. Elizabeth Perkins and Dylan McDermott made for appealing leads, while Mara Wilson's youthful Susan appears suitably star-struck by old Mr. Kringle's effortless invocation of the wonder of the holiday season as she makes the transition from jaded cynic to a true believer in Santa Claus.

Perhaps the most noteworthy aspect of Hughes's screenplay is its ability to update Seaton's original concerns for the fast-paced world of the 1990s. With the 1947 film first appearing in an America that was only just beginning to emerge from the austerity of the war years, the note of caution it sounded regarding the commercialization of Christmas would doubtless have seemed timely. Mr. Kringle states quite emphatically his concern that the festive season is ceasing to focus on the importance of giving, and is now in danger of becoming more concerned with materialism and self-interest. Hughes preserves Kris's altruistic scheme of conveying parents to stores other than Cole's in order to track down hard-to-find gifts or better quality presents—a strategy which baffles the corporate top-brass with its simplicity and ability to generate public support for the company (even though they risk losing some Christmas revenue, many customers pledge to become loyal shoppers there throughout the year). *Miracle on 34th Street* is one of the earliest and best-known exponents of the need to recognize the importance of unselfishness and philanthropy at Christmas, and yet rather than appearing preachy the film quite profoundly blurs the boundaries between commercial trade and individual generosity. In Hughes's film, as in the original, Kris seems perfectly happy to enter the employ of Cole's, and though he is an unconventional staff member (to say the least), he has few qualms about jumping through any and all corporate hoops that are presented to him. While he is eager to encourage parents to seek out the best bargains when purchasing gifts for their children so that their money can go further, he has no difficulty in accepting the fact that mass-production is the most expedient way of ensuring that as many toys as possible are available at affordable prices to satisfy the present-buying public.

While Bryan and Dorey's blossoming romance answers Susan's secret Christmas wish for the security of a nuclear family with two loving parents (a classic Hughesian motif if ever there was one), by approaching Kris in the belief that he can make this desire come true, Susan mirrors Kevin McCallister's late-in-the-day visit to the street corner Santa in *Home Alone* as he tries to find new, untried options in his quest to be reunited with his family. Yet Hughes spends more time on preserving the dual purpose evident in Seaton's original screenplay, celebrating the commoditization of Christmas—the energetic cultural spread of festive customs made possible through the mass-market—at the same time as it presents anxieties about the aggressive encroachment of commercialism into the season of giving, which saw the inclusiveness of the traditional Christmas challenged with the demands of unchecked materialism. Yet, at its heart, *Miracle on 34th Street* is a film about faith—a simple yet robust belief in the Christmas spirit and the positive effects which can derive from it. Kris repeatedly makes the point that it is a matter of human nature to sometimes put our faith in things which may appear indefinable or intangible, such as love itself, and that we should never give up hope even when the odds are stacked against us. But Hughes also emphasizes that it is important to choose carefully what it is that we put our faith in, because those beliefs will ultimately shape and define us. We see this optimistic outlook at work not just in Susan, whose natural youthful exuberance has been stymied by hard-hearted pragmatism, but also in the staid matter-of-factness evident in her mother Dorey's melancholic worldview, her glacial temperament eventually thawing as a result of Kris's wistful encouragement and the idealistic Bryan's romantic advances. No one, it seems, can stand in the way of Mr. Kringle's irrepressible festive spirit; he has no interest in gaining the upper hand over those who oppose his message of goodwill, for his only goal appears to be propagating a universal message of benevolence to all, typified by Christmas but relevant the whole year through.

John Hughes's Christmas movies may not have reached the level of instant recognition that has been achieved by many of his other films, but their annual appearances on TV and via home entertainment platforms have ensured that they are certainly not forgotten. Carrying forward several of the central themes established in his earlier work, not least the importance of the traditional family unit, the need for social responsibility, and the significance of the individual, the festive cinema that he produced has not only retained an audience over the years but has also assumed a prominent position within the broader canon of Christmas filmmaking.

I Predict Me and Her Will Interface

Technology in John Hughes Films

Once the exclusive bastion of large businesses and science labs, the digital electronics boom of the late seventies and early eighties had started to bring computers into the lives of the public at an unprecedented rate. This period of rapid technological change met with a variety of responses within the creative industry at the time, with numerous films—such as Ridley Scott's *Blade Runner* (1982), Steve Barron's *Electric Dreams* (1983), and most especially James Cameron's *The Terminator* (1984)—trading upon audience anxieties surrounding the swift development of new digital equipment as it became an increasingly ubiquitous part of peoples' lives. This cautionary approach was, however, never one followed by John Hughes.

In Hughes's cinema, the availability and development of digital devices was not cause for apprehension, but celebration. Fully aware of the many potential ways in which lives could be enhanced by the convenience of accessible computer systems and other high-tech solutions, Hughes knew that the rise of the microcomputer was heralding a new age of affordable technological access which was being made available to the mainstream public, and many of his movies offer an appealing glimpse at the early popular computer systems of this period.

An Electric Atmosphere: Personal Computing in Hughes Movies

Hughes demonstrated a keen awareness of the need to underscore the growing part that new technology was playing in the lives of teenagers and adults alike, and in reflecting the near-inescapabilty of new digital devices in the 1980s, he was also to foreshadow the era of widespread Internet access that would follow in the next decade. In *Pretty in Pink* (Howard Deutch, 1986), we see teenagers Andie and Blane (Molly

The IBM PCjr, an early home computer system released by IBM in 1984.

WarGames. Director: John Badham. Release date: June 3, 1983.

Ringwald and Andrew McCarthy) working on networked terminals in their high school's library during an early scene. Much to Andie's surprise, her fact-finding session is interrupted by Blane, who engages her in conversation from elsewhere in the room via a text prompt (a sight familiar to users of the time, most of whom would likely have an acquaintance with disk-operating systems such as MS-DOS). Blane is able not only to communicate through a textual interface, but also transmits an image of his face over the network to introduce himself to Andie. It may have been decades before the advent of Facebook Messenger and other chat applications, but Hughes had already determined the capacity of digital technology to bring people together—a stark departure from other contemporary filmmakers who were warning of the same systems' ability to alienate and divide. (Hughes also foreshadows the widespread use of information technology in modern education: the library at Shermer High School appears unusually well-stocked with computer terminals for 1986, with more than a dozen in the scene.)

Another evocation of mid-eighties computer technology appears in *Ferris Bueller's Day Off* (1986), where Matthew Broderick's eponymous character can be seen making creative use of his home computer—the disk-based IBM PCjr. A somewhat controversial system at the time due to its limited compatibility with the more widely available IBM PC and its expensive price tag (the machine had actually been discontinued in 1985, a year before the film's release), the PCjr was a sophisticated personal computer which fitted perfectly with Ferris's ostentatious personality. Manufactured by Teledyne, the system boasted 256-color VGA graphics and a 5.25-inch disk drive, along with less common features for the period, such as a wireless keyboard.

Though Ferris can be seen making use of the system's color monitor to compose images in a graphic design package, the main use of the PCjr in the film is made evident when he hacks into his high school's file system and deliberately reduces the number of recorded absences on his record—much to the bafflement of the Dean of Students, Ed Rooney, who watches Ferris's online handiwork in real time. The character's use of a dial-up modem to achieve his aims is a playful tip of the hat to John Badham's *WarGames* (1983), a Cold War thriller also starring Broderick. Portraying teenage hacker David Lightman, Broderick's earlier character had illicitly

The E-mu Systems' Emulator II digital sampling keyboard, released in 1984.

broken into his high school's network and inflated his grades to impress his new girlfriend, Jennifer, played by Ally Sheedy. (This turns out to be far from Lightman's worst offense, given that he later comes close to triggering global thermonuclear war after hacking into a U.S. Defense Department mainframe.) Interestingly, there is another reminder of the breakneck pace of technological development to be found in the fact that the computer system used in *WarGames*—the IMSAI 8080, developed by IMS Associates—would have been obsolete at the time of the film's production. With an archaic 8-inch floppy drive and 1200-baud modem, the IMSAI 8080 had been discontinued by its manufacturer in 1978—some five years before Badham's movie would appear in theaters.

Ferris's involvement with technology did not stop with computer systems, however. He can also be seen using an E-mu Emulator II (produced by E-mu Systems)—a state-of-the-art digital synthesizer—to hoodwink his friends into thinking he is ill by producing a variety of increasingly disgusting sound samples, which range from coughs and sneezes to belches and a thunderous vomiting noise. While Ferris regularly bemoans his luck in being given a computer as a gift when his sister, Jeanie, received a car, he would presumably have had little reason to feel short-changed with the ownership of an Emulator II, which retailed between $7,995 and $9,995 when first released in 1984. An 8-bit digital sampling keyboard that used floppy disks for data storage (though hard drives were available as an optional upgrade), the E-mu Emulator II was regularly used by high-profile musicians and bands, including Ultravox, Jean-Michel Jarre, Genesis, Vangelis, Tangerine Dream, and many others. Although Ferris's unorthodox use of the synthesizer may have been something of a rarity, the Emulator II was widely used in soundtrack composition throughout the 1980s, with composers such as John Carpenter and Michael Kamen making regular use of the machine for original scores written during the period. While the Emulator II would be superseded by its more powerful successor, the Emulator III, which was released in 1987, this popular system has become so immutably associated with the decade that it has experienced something of a revival among nostalgic musicians in recent years. Anyone seeking Ferris's customized disk of illness-related sound samples may be fated to scour online auction sites for a very long time, however.

The Game's the Thing: Computer Gaming and Video Arcades in Hughes's Cinema

While home-computing applications played a big part in the 1980s electronics boom, the period is also famed for the rise of video gaming as a popular pastime—especially among America's youth. While some seminal console-based games had been available during the previous decade, the eighties would see the video game explode in popularity as electrical devices became more readily available. We see the two faces of home computing in collision during *National Lampoon's Vacation* (Harold Ramis, 1983), where the hapless Clark Griswold (Chevy Chase) tries, with somewhat limited success, to interrupt the gaming session of his son Rusty (Anthony Michael Hall) by using an early home computer to plot the route of their forthcoming road journey from Illinois to California. In 1983, many years before GPS satellite navigation and online tools such as Google Maps, this was something of an innovation, and again Hughes's screenplay was somewhat prophetic in its presentation of technological applications with positive lifestyle uses. In true *Vacation* style, however, Clark's good intentions do not go according to plan, and the onscreen sprite representing his Family Truckster is soon pursued with injurious intent by a character from one of Rusty's games. Accompanying this action is a range of authentic sound effects from the Mattel Intellivision, an early cartridge-based games console, initially released in 1979 as a challenge to the market dominance of the bestselling Atari 2600 system. The sounds that can be heard are sampled from games, including Mattel's *NFL Football* (1979) and *NBA Basketball* (1980), APh Technology Consultants' *Las Vegas Poker and Blackjack* (1979), and CBS Electronics' *Donkey Kong* (1982), which was a conversion of the famous 1981 Nintendo arcade platform game of the same name.

Video games were not confined to the home during the 1980s, however, as the decade was also host to the glory days of the coin-operated arcade machine. "Coin-ops," as they were affectionately known in the electronics industry, were most usually found in specialized video arcades, where players could deposit their hard-earned dimes and quarters into game cabinets in order to play titles from many different genres. Important for its social function as a hang-out spot as much as for its entertainment value, the video arcade was a mainstay of eighties popular culture, and the phenomena was immortalized in films such as Michael Nankin and David Wechter's *Midnight Madness* (1980), Steven Lisberger's *Tron* (1982), and Nick Castle's *The Last Starfighter* (1984). Hughes's involvement with arcade games is presented in *Ferris Bueller's Day Off*, when high school dean Ed Rooney (Jeffrey Jones) heads off in pursuit of his crafty nemesis Ferris and wrongly assumes that the absconding teenager is to be found in a downtown bar. Approaching a figure at an arcade machine, Rooney incorrectly tries to apprehend his prey only to discover—too late—that he is mistaken. A deeply unimpressed woman spits a mouthful of soda over him before calmly returning her attention to the game.

The amusements shown in the arcade are two popular titles from the 1980s, namely Nintendo's *Donkey Kong* (1981) and Data East's scrolling martial arts game *Karate Champ* (1984). Judging by the cabinet artwork, Rooney's adversary is watching the action of the latter title, but the sound effects that are heard throughout the exchange are actually samples from Namco's famous maze-based game *Pac-Man* (1980). This was presumably an artistic decision, as the sample that plays when

The short-lived Memotech MTX500 home computer, sister model of the MTX512 and RS128. The range was manufactured between 1983 and 1984.

Rooney is soaked by the young woman is the same sound that is heard when a player is caught by a ghost and loses one of their lives in *Pac-Man*. It is ironic that Matthew Broderick was not involved in the video arcade scene, as he had practiced gaming extensively during rehearsals for John Badham's *WarGames*; training intensely for a sequence involving arcade titles to demonstrate believable prowess, he had reputedly become very proficient with games such as Namco/Midway's *Galaxian* (1979) and *Galaga* (1981).

Indistinguishable from Magic: The Technological Fantasy of *Weird Science*

Perhaps Hughes's most momentous implementation of computer technology was the use of an eighties home microcomputer to create life in *Weird Science* (1985). This modern-day take on the parthenogenetic themes of Mary Shelley's *Frankenstein* (1818) was given a playful twist by Hughes, where teenagers Wyatt (Ilan Mitchell-Smith) and Gary (Anthony Michael Hall) make inventive use of an early personal computer to hack into a mainframe at the Pentagon and, later, bring about the existence of a brand new entity. Though the government facility they hijack is filled to capacity with the kind of tape-based data access machines so beloved of old sci-fi movies, the computer used by the protagonists is actually a humble Memotech MTX512—a home system which boasted 64Kb of memory, roughly the size of a reasonably lengthy e-mail message by today's standards. The Memotech machines were based around the Zilog Z80 microprocessor, commonly used throughout the 1980s in popular home computers such as the Microsoft MSX, Commodore 128, and Sinclair ZX Spectrum, and thus Hughes uses a recognizable and widely available system for the duo's anarchic experiments to make the characters' efforts seem more relatable to viewers. Here, the film's foray into outright fantasy begins in earnest, however, as the Memotech needed a substantial upgrade just to operate a floppy disk drive, much less create human beings from thin air. While there is no end of enjoyment to be had in watching a rather convenient lightning storm flaring up (in the tradition of many old Universal horror movies) and a major government mainframe going temporarily haywire as the teenagers put their scientifically creative plans into action, Hughes knows that his audience is unlikely to waste much time in gauging the plausibility of the action; *Weird Science* is unabashed technological fantasy from start to finish.

The events of the movie are the closest that Hughes ever came to sounding a note of caution over the precipitous pace of technological advancement in contemporary society, though his lightness of touch is commendable. Sidestepping entirely the Mary Shelley motif of a besieged creator being tormented by the actions of his reanimated creature, Hughes instead focuses upon the moral hubris of bringing about life by scientific means. Socially inept and shunned by their fellow students, Wyatt and Gary struggle to gain peer approval, and thus the creation of Lisa (Kelly LeBrock)—the beautiful woman who is the outcome of their computer-driven experiments—comes as a result of a desire to generate, by technological methods, what they are unable to achieve naturally: finding the perfect partner. But from the moment of her first appearance, Lisa proves that she will not be objectified by her teenaged progenitors: intelligent, witty, and worldly-wise, she immediately runs rings around her two maladroit creators. The students repeatedly fall short of her expectations, unable to act meaningfully on her personal advice and regularly disappointing her by allowing their desperation to please their classmates to prevail over their own self-respect. Though their creation is an independent being who is never compliant or subservient, she does directly influence events to ensure that Gary and Wyatt change their outlook on what is truly important in life; though they may have technological knowledge in abundance, they slowly come to realize that their intellectual prowess is nothing without emotional heart—an appeal by Hughes not to neglect compassion and empathy in an age that was in danger of being characterized by increasing reliance on specialized scientific skill over concern for the well-being of society (a not uncommon topic during the Cold War and its ever-present shadow of nuclear annihilation). Such ethical concerns, though often subtly drawn, are at the core of Hughes's work, and here we see a timely entreaty for an increasingly technophile culture to ensure that emergent digital systems were used for the benefit of the majority—rather than the elite or the individual—in order to uphold a persisting concern for one's fellow human being. Many years prior to the emergence of social networking as a major mode of online behavior, Hughes's concerns seemed prescient; given the apprehensions reflected in many computing-themed films of the 1980s, it is heartening to know that computer technology has exhibited a positive ability to bring people and communities together, establishing a kind of digital egalitarianism across the world in a way that was difficult to conceive when the technology was still in its infancy.

Weird Science was also adapted into a spin-off television series some years later. Airing from 1994, the show—which was produced by St. Clare Entertainment in association with Universal Television—ran for a total of five seasons, and saw Gary and Wyatt's computer equipment suitably updated to meet the changing technological environment of the nineties. Though the series retained the catchy Oingo Boingo theme song from the original film, the characters were all recast—most notably with Vanessa Angel succeeding Kelly LeBrock in the role of Lisa. While Hughes had no involvement in the television series (the creators of the TV adaptation being Alan Cross and Tom Spezialy), the origins of the characters are irreverently acknowledged in the pilot episode when John Mallory Asher's Gary points out that he believes the creation of life by technological means is eminently achievable due to having seen the process happen in an old John Hughes film.

Though our modern age of mobile devices and wireless Internet access is infinitely more technologically sophisticated than any of Hughes's characters could ever have imagined back in the eighties, he showed commendable foresight in acknowledging the growing role that computer systems would play in the lives of teenagers—and, by extension, society at large. Just as Andie and Blane's flirting over a school library's local area network presaged the omnipresence of Facebook, WhatsApp, and Snapchat decades later, and Clark Griswold's primitive route-planning program foreshadowed satellite navigation in the same way that his son Rusty's gaming habits portended many subsequent generations of video game consoles in the years to come, Hughes's films not only reflected growing audience fascination with technological developments but actually prefigured the increasing dependence of society upon instant access to up-to-date information, the social aspects of communication systems, and the convenience and cultural benefits of having useful applications available to the widest possible number of people. Hughes was often applauded by critics for the way in which he guaranteed the relevance of his cinematic output by so vibrantly echoing the styles, fashions, and pop culture phenomena of the time in which his movies were produced. When it came to technology, however, he proved beyond doubt that he was not only capable of faithfully representing the shifting attitudes towards computing in the eighties but—in his determination to stress the advantages of that era-defining digital boom—he was also well ahead of his time in many ways.

6

What Aren't We Going to Do?

John Hughes and the Great American Vacation

John Hughes was a noted perfectionist, and his exacting standard of professionalism meant that he also knew the importance of recognizing when it was time to take things easy. Many of Hughes's films have featured vacationing as a prominent part of the storyline, and while relaxation may be the intention of his characters, the end result all too often verges on the surprising, the bewildering, and even the chaotic. The act of unwinding (or, at least, attempting to unwind) away from home formed the basis of several of his comedies, ranging from the most prominent to some of his lesser-known movies.

On each occasion that his screenplays were to engage with the act of vacationing, Hughes was to highlight a different aspect of this traditional family activity. While a trip away from home may have seemed like an ostensibly harmless endeavor, in Hughes's cinema it is an invitation to expect the unexpected. In this chapter, Hughes's exploration of holidaying (both within the United States and further afield) is described in relation to the individual journeys experienced by his characters, explaining the way in which the American vacation has come to take a place among his most persistently popular plot scenarios.

By Road and By Air: At Home and Abroad in *National Lampoon's Vacation* and *European Vacation*

Almost certainly Hughes's most famous creative involvement with the topic of getting away from it all, the first two entries in the *National Lampoon's Vacation* cycle have been acclaimed precisely because of the universality of their audience appeal. Not only was the desire to enjoy a family holiday with loved ones (however reluctant they may be) the kind of goal that most people could relate to, but the journey of Clark Griswold and his largely unenthusiastic family as they cross America in *National Lampoon's Vacation* (Harold Ramis, 1983) was to be a comic triumph full of social satire and eyebrow-raising predicaments. Following a roughly Route 66–style excursion from Chicago to Los Angeles, the Griswolds'

The Great Sand Dunes National Park near Alamosa, Colorado; a United States National Park and Preserve located in the San Luis Valley.

trip alternates between fleeting but rich cultural experiences and occasionally insipid amusements along the way. Clark's stated intention is to ensure that his family is treated to a vacation that is a little out of the ordinary, and in this aim he succeeds in ways that he presumably could never have begun to anticipate.

The wide geographical area involved in the movie's location filming presented a logistical challenge for director Harold Ramis, and numerous states were visited as the now-famous Griswold vacation was plotted out. However, not all was necessarily as it appeared on-screen. For instance, the (fictional) Walley World theme park that was the intended endpoint of Clark's journey was really Six Flags Magic Mountain in Valencia, California, whereas other substitutions included the Griswolds' house in the Chicago suburbs actually being located in Los Angeles, and Cousin Eddie Johnson's rural Kansas home which, in reality, was located in Boone, Colorado. (Both were private residences which still exist in their respective locations.) Humorously, famous sights such as the breathtaking Grand Canyon National Park in Arizona are visited only very briefly, whereas scenes in dingy motels and holiday camps are given significantly greater screen time—testament to the somewhat awry nature of the vacation as it inevitably deviates from Clark's best attempts to remain on schedule. Extensive filming took place in Colorado, Utah, and Arizona (in particular, the wilderness scenes—where the family's Wagon Queen Family Truckster breaks down in a remote desert area—were shot in the Great Sand Dunes National Park near Alamosa, Colorado), while Californian studio backlot locations in Burbank were used to double for numerous destinations from other parts of the United States, such as inner-city St. Louis, Missouri, and the historical site of Dodge City, Kansas.

Hughes both salutes and satirizes the American vacation, underscoring its potential for family bonding (even Clark's kids, Rusty and Audrey, get into the right spirit eventually) while also sounding a note of caution regarding the idealization of the experience. Just as erratic characters such as Cousin Eddie and Aunt Edna have the capacity to effortlessly derail Clark's carefully planned agenda, his objective of appreciating as many national landmarks and places of interest as possible during the journey is inevitably thwarted by circumstances and outcomes which never quite meet his expectations. This culminates in the family's arrival at Walley World at the film's conclusion, where Clark discovers to his apoplectic fury that—in spite of all the difficulties and indignities which have taken place in order to get them there—the amusement park is temporarily closed for renovations. Spiraling into a state of mania, he then takes a security guard hostage (a superbly understated turn from John Candy) and insists that he and his family enjoy all that the park has to offer—at any cost. Though wary of Clark's increasing unpredictability, the family finds themselves forced into a travesty of the theme park experience, compelled to appear as though they are enjoying the rides while actually merely enduring them for the sake of defusing the situation. The film's climax thus reveals the reality of the vacation in microcosm: Clark's good intentions and subsequent determination to overcome disappointment, and his family's attempts to support his efforts no matter how unhinged he eventually becomes.

Though generally less popular with the critics, *National Lampoon's European Vacation* (Amy Heckerling, 1985) picked up the story of the Griswold clan (here spelled the "Griswalds" for the only time in the Vacation series) after they win a trip around Europe as the top prize in a TV game show. Trading in the Family Truckster for an international flight to London's Heathrow Airport, director Amy Heckerling was to make the most of the European location filming to include a mind-boggling array of famous landmarks from Britain, France, and Italy. These include the Tower Bridge, the Palace of Westminster, Buckingham Palace and Notting Hill in London; Paris's Eiffel Tower, the Notre Dame Cathedral and Louvre Museum; and the Colosseum, *Scalinata di Trinita dei Monti* (Spanish Steps), and Piazza Navona in Rome. Though some critics protested that the film's endless procession of renowned visitor attractions effectively made the film's locations seem like a rather predictable string of regularly visited European tourist destinations, in actuality the screenplay uses the highly recognizable nature of these places as a means to highlight the Griswolds' fish-out-of-water ingenuousness while vacationing outside the comfort zone of their home continent.

As always, Clark builds the experience up to such an elevated point that the reality can never come close to matching his aspirations. Thus, he envisions the prospect of rubbing shoulders with British royalty only to wind up in a rundown London hotel with a grandiloquent name (the closest he comes to encountering nobility during his stay), and tracks down some distantly related German kinfolk who turn out to be polite strangers who have no way of rebuffing his emotional family get-together as they don't speak a word of English. While Clark fantasizes in a dream sequence about visiting Austria, he appears in an Alpine-themed tribute to *The Sound of Music* (Robert Wise, 1965), which was filmed in roughly the same location as the original. However, other scenes shot in Europe proved rather less straightforward. Filming at the ancient location of Stonehenge in Wiltshire—a protected heritage site—was not possible, which necessitated the construction of a replica stone circle elsewhere in England. This had the benefit of making Clark's subsequent demolition of the Neolithic monument much easier; the reproduction was specially designed to topple in the manner of a row of dominoes when struck.

Hughes (whose screenplay was later co-written by Robert Klane) ensures that Clark retained his characteristic enthusiasm for vacationing, and the foreign settings created the potential for some choice cultural reflections. These included the Griswold kids' incredulity that British television consists of only four channels (the film being produced before the advent of satellite, cable and digital TV in the UK), an encounter with a breathtakingly rude French waiter which leads (unbeknown to the family) to microwaveable meals in place of the country's world-famous cuisine, and some Germanic folk dancing which abruptly turns violent due to an unfortunate *faux pas* on Clark's behalf. Once again, Hughes makes the point that while maintaining unreasonably high hopes of a vacation's venues will inevitably end in disappointment, the real enjoyment is likely to come in the less expected encounters which may present themselves. The family actually proves to be admirable ambassadors for their country, with Clark's wide-eyed zeal for transcontinental adventure, his cheerful comportment, and his unswerving resolve to make the most of his cross-cultural escapade. This demonstrates, beyond doubt, that while the Griswolds could be taken out of America, it was impossible to take America out of the Griswolds.

American Dream: Getting Back to Nature in *The Great Outdoors*

While the Griswold family became notorious for their cross-continental adventures, not all vacations in the movies of John Hughes take place over such a wide area. The action of *The Great Outdoors* (Howard Deutch, 1988) was situated entirely in one location of the United States, with the focus being much more on the aim of relaxing away from the urban rat race in wide-open spaces rather than seeking a whistle-stop tour of the country at large. Whereas the Vacation movies had been more directly concerned with cultural observation, however, *The Great Outdoors* would instead reserve the main thrust of its commentary for issues of social class—an ironic situation, as the film's director was Howard Deutch, who had previously helmed two of Hughes's most class-conscious teen movies, *Pretty in Pink* and *Some Kind of Wonderful*.

The Great Outdoors concerns Chicago-based family man Chet Ripley (John Candy), who takes his wife and kids to a remote lodge near a scenic lake in Wisconsin to spend some quality time together over the summer. His plans are soon thrown into disarray by the unwelcome arrival of his investment broker brother-in-law Roman Craig (Dan Aykroyd) and his upscale family, who constantly sneer at Chet's intended lineup of activities while belittling his efforts to recapture some aspect of the enjoyable vacations of the past in the same location—including his honeymoon with his wife, Connie (Stephanie Faracy). Thus the battle lines are drawn as Chet resolves to make the most of his time away from home while determining to deflate the pretensions of his yuppie nemesis in the process.

Though set in the rural town of Pechoggin, a lake resort in Wisconsin, *The Great Outdoors* was actually filmed around Bass Lake, California, which was located near Yosemite National Park. (The interior of Chet's "The Loon's Nest" vacation cabin was actually a set which had been constructed at Universal Studios in California.) In spite of the distance of more than 1,670 miles between the real Wisconsin and the Californian facsimile employed by Deutch for filming, Bass Lake is a more than creditable imitation of the genuine article; the lush forest greenery and pleasing lakeside views make for an appealing holiday destination. The

Wisconsin connection is further enhanced by small details, such as the presence of Point Beer, which is produced by Stevens Point Brewery and remains very popular throughout the state.

While *The Great Outdoors* has never achieved the level of popularity enjoyed by the *National Lampoon's Vacation* cycle, the film's shrewd meditations on class divisions and intergenerational bridge-building made it a very different viewing experience in comparison to its popular forerunners. The relentless clash between the good-natured Chet and the boorish Roman creates some entertaining moments of character conflict which remain in the memory far longer than the more overtly knockabout

Yosemite National Park in Northern California, which was declared a World Heritage Site in 1984.

situations such as the attack on the family's cabin by "the bald-headed bear"—an ursine opponent seeking revenge on Chet, who had outsmarted him at the resort many years beforehand. While the natural world plays

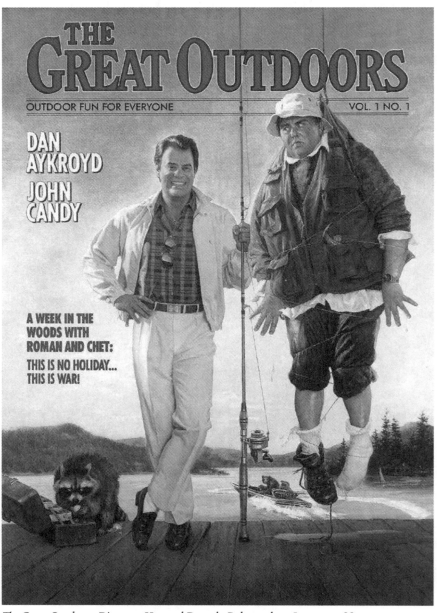

The Great Outdoors. Director: Howard Deutch. Release date: June 17, 1988.

a substantial part in augmenting the movie's rural charm—not least the subtitled raccoons which cause chaos by constantly plundering the contents of the Ripleys' trashcan—it also provides a useful counterpoint in the ongoing quarrel between the belligerent brothers-in-law. For Chet, the great outdoors of the title is a means of escaping from the stresses of mainstream society, growing closer to his family, and reconnecting with memories of a more innocent time. But Roman is unable to see things the same way, envisaging the expansive forest and abundant wildlife simply as natural resources to be exploited in the name of progress and monetary gain. This central argument is played out throughout the movie, with both men not only unable to reach common ground but—at a fundamental level—incapable of fully appreciating the view of the other due to their disparate worldviews and an irreconcilable philosophical gulf.

By the conclusion of *The Great Outdoors*, both the Craigs and the Ripleys have agreed to overcome their differences even if they can't necessarily find correspondence between their respective viewpoints, bonding over their experiences at the resort as events take an unforeseen turn. Roman's high-class affectations are punctured when it is revealed that he has lost his family's savings as the result of an inauspicious investment, and Chet's advocacy of a rustic vacation as a means of bringing people together eventually wins the day. While their stay in Wisconsin may not have caused the same level of widespread devastation as a Griswold vacation, it nonetheless has the same ultimate effect of encouraging harmony between family members, bridging different generations, and bringing the best out of people as they face the worst of situations—usually in the least expected of ways.

Bon Voyage: There and Back Again in *Home Alone* and *Home Alone 2*

While the first two movies in the *Home Alone* series are undoubtedly best remembered for the spirited home-defense sequences featuring its youthful protagonist Kevin McCallister (Macaulay Culkin), it is a fact often overlooked that the central premise of both films revolve around family vacations—to the French capital of Paris in the first feature, and Miami,

Home Alone 2: Lost in New York. Director: Chris Columbus. Release date: November 20, 1992.

Florida, in the sequel. While audiences follow the misadventures of adolescent Kevin as he revels in his newfound independence and then gradually begins to struggle as bungling adversaries close in on his home, it is
easy to forget the joyless experiences of his family as their long-distance
holidays are unexpectedly cut short.

Almost as a kind of karmic punishment for their inadvertent parental neglect in accidentally leaving Kevin at home in the first place, the
McCallister clan faces a rather grim experience on their intercontinental
excursion in the original *Home Alone* (Chris Columbus, 1990). Realizing
too late that their son is missing, parents Peter (John Heard) and Kate
(Catherine O'Hara) are forced to immediately spring into action as soon
as they arrive at Paris Orly Airport—actually filmed at Chicago's O'Hare
International Airport, the same location where the family depart at the
start of the movie. Crammed into a soulless Parisian hotel room, where a
traditional festive broadcast of Frank Capra's *It's a Wonderful Life* (1946)
can be seen on a television set (another reminder of annual Christmas
customs turned askew), Kate manages to head back to the United States
ahead of her family to reunite with Kevin. But unable to book a flight
to Chicago, she is forced to take a circuitous route (including accepting
a ride from a traveling polka band) before she eventually manages to
return home on Christmas Day.

A similar scenario unfolds in *Home Alone 2: Lost in New York* (Chris
Columbus, 1992), only with Kevin this time unintentionally embarking
on a flight to the Big Apple while the rest of the McCallisters head for
Miami. On this occasion, what should ideally have been an agreeable
family holiday in the Sunshine State is instead turned on its head as the
unfortunate tribe find themselves ensconced within a rain-soaked Miami
motel (in reality, the exterior shots were taken at a then-functioning motel
situated in Long Beach, California), formulating a plan to once again
return their wayward relative to the fold.

In both of the above cases it is made clear that for Hughes, vacationing
is a family endeavor which is at its best when the experience is uniting
people and allowing everyone to feel its benefits equally. Because the
McCallisters violate this premise, albeit accidentally, their time away
from home becomes a logistical and bureaucratic nightmare: all hope
of a restful break is abandoned as every effort is subsequently focused

on returning to Kevin as quickly as possible. Thus, while the unstinting efforts of well-intentioned paterfamiliases, such as Clark Griswold and Chet Ripley, eventually result in beneficial results by the time their respective vacations have reached a conclusion, the only way that the McCallisters (in both instances) can make things right is to effectively abort their holiday expeditions in favor of an attempt to reunify the family unit. This may not have been new ground for Hughes, whose championship of family stability is one of the key themes of his work, but in its incisiveness the motif of the vacation as a uniting and universal activity was to extend from his adult-oriented comedy to his more family-focused features.

7

A Letter Confirming Your Reservation at the Nuthouse

Comic Characterization and Eccentrics in John Hughes Films

If there is one feature which typifies a majority of John Hughes's movies, it is in his humorous and involving employment of eccentric, offbeat characters. Hughes's keen eye for characterization produced some truly striking oddballs, usually with a profoundly off-kilter look on life. Yet, far from simply fulfilling the role of comic relief, his less-than-conventional characters were fully fleshed out in their own right; they all had their own personal stories to tell, and they were to entertain audiences in the way that they were individually portrayed—often, but not always, through juxtaposition with the protagonists. Hughes's films have more than their share of colorful characters, and he often employed them not only to advance a movie's narrative but to reveal wide-ranging truths about the human condition and societal expectation.

Embracing Individuality: Self-Expression and Nonconformity in the Teen Movies of John Hughes

For many people, the teenage years are a period where different personas are experimented with, and a complex worldview begins to take shape, molded by environment, events, and personal experience. Because

Hughes knew all too well the various difficulties that are involved in growing up, his teen movies reflect the fact that character and personality are intricate factors to consider in any individual's life, especially when they are only on the cusp of adulthood. Thus, as far as Hughes was concerned, creating an eccentric character did not necessarily mean fabricating an outwardly flippant figure: many of his quirkier teenagers are imbued with intricate motivations and multi-layered dispositions.

Rarely did Hughes's teen characters come close to matching the degree of peculiarity exhibited by Gedde Watanabe's exchange student Long Duk Dong in *Sixteen Candles* (1984). A character so overwhelmingly incongruous that at times he almost seems to have wandered in from another movie entirely, Long Duk, the quintessential fish out of water, is able to fit into the challenging high school environment around him largely as a result of his charisma and inexhaustible geniality. Charming and amorous in roughly equal measure, Long Duk's behavior is occasionally unusual, but never to the point that he is in any danger of becoming alienated from the audience; indeed, quite the opposite is true, as his more bizarre idiosyncrasies actually become strangely compelling. Though nudging the age of thirty at the time of filming, Watanabe's youthful appearance and lively performance created a surprisingly credible teenager, and Long Duk became one of the highlights of a film which had no shortage of pleasing character moments. However, the way in which Hughes engenders humor from cultural differences has led to subsequent criticism from some quarters that the character was depicted in a racially insensitive manner. While it is true that more enlightened attitudes make such a character both inviable and unacceptable within a mainstream cinematic comedy today, it can also be argued that Hughes takes care to delineate Long Duk's clash with American mores in a manner which is drolly observed and cordial rather than intentionally offensive or given to the crudest forms of stereotyping.

While Phil "Duckie" Dale of *Pretty in Pink* (Howard Deutch, 1986) may have lacked Long Duk's stilted English and hard-earned reputation as a lady's man, actor Jon Cryer made the character both sympathetic and comical—a wise clown, undeniably, and one with both depth and sincerity. While Annie Potts may have lingered in the memory of audiences

Gedde Watanabe (1955–), stage and screen comedian and actor.

as the flamboyantly dressed Iona, the astute but exuberant manager of the town's record store, it was nonetheless Duckie who stands out as the wackier of the two: with the machine-gun delivery of his always-sharp dialogue, energetically rangy physicality, and an outlandish (but highly individual) fashion sense, Cryer forged his character into one of the standout figures of Hughes's entire sequence of teen movies. Widely remembered for his high-spirited dance routine, flailing his way around Iona's store as he lip-synchs unconvincingly to the dulcet tones of Otis

Redding's "Try a Little Tenderness," Duckie was a divisive character even at the time of the film's initial release; critics have disagreed for years over whether he is an endearing extrovert or an exasperatingly possessive neurotic. Yet, even considering his tendency to split critical opinion, Duckie nonetheless remains a unique character creation on Hughes's part, and Cryer never allows the madcap high schooler's alternative qualities to overshadow his kindhearted side. The pathos of his eventual realization that the only way to retain his bond with lifelong friend Andie (Molly Ringwald) is to accept that his ambitions of romance with her are doomed ultimately lends the character an implicitly benevolent aspect which belies his comic façade.

Similarly able to transcend the mantle of a figure of fun was Duncan, the intense skinhead played by Elias Koteas, who is encountered by protagonist Keith Nelson (Eric Stoltz) during detention in *Some Kind of Wonderful* (Howard Deutch, 1987). While Mary Stuart Masterson's no-nonsense tomboy Watts may have been an equally idiosyncratic and fiercely independent character, for out-and-out eccentricity Duncan manages to exceed her in nonconformity as the film progresses. Though Hughes's screenplay may trick the unsuspecting viewer into anticipating a straightforward comic character in Duncan, in actuality this rebel without a cause becomes increasingly likable and oddly entrancing over time, eventually developing into a kind of anti-heroic reflection of Keith. Koteas, in what was to be one of the earliest cinematic roles of his career, implements a highly energetic interpretation of the character's uncommon personality, adding unforeseen strata of dimension to an atypical figure who may otherwise have seemed like a collection of simple, humorous truisms. Whether he is developing new—and less-than-orthodox—creative skills, or concocting inventive ways to bamboozle the long-suffering staff of the high school he attends, Duncan invariably manages to step beyond the realm of cliché with much panache. Hughes was to make highly effective use of the character in order to alleviate the otherwise-contemplative disposition of one of his most powerfully meditative teen movie storylines

Mad, Bad, and Dangerous to Know: Humorous Characterization and Eccentrics in John Hughes Comedies

Hughes's comic characters were, of course, not confined to his teen movies. Many of his adult characters are similarly off-the-wall, and usually in ways that generate a degree of divergence from the qualities of a film's protagonist. Never is this more obvious than in the case of Randy Quaid's infamous "Cousin Eddie" Johnson, who was invariably the bane of Clark Griswold's existence during *National Lampoon's Vacation* (Harold Ramis, 1983) and, later, *National Lampoon's Christmas Vacation* (Jeremiah S. Chechik, 1989). Cousin Eddie is the very antithesis of Clark's middle-class cachet; crude and slobby yet still curiously captivating, this amiable loafer is a stalwart family man (perhaps a little too close to some of his family, as Cousin Vicky attests in *Vacation*) who is never quite as dim as he looks. Though going through a period of unemployment when he is first encountered at his Kansas farm in the original *National Lampoon's Vacation*, having been made redundant from his job at an asbestos factory, times become increasingly difficult for Eddie and his family over the years—to the point that he and his expansive progeny are living in a ramshackle RV during their appearance in *Christmas Vacation*. Thus, he is best remembered for his tendency to mooch (usually unsuccessfully) quantities of money from Clark in order to get by, even requesting tens of thousands of dollars from him during the first *Vacation* movie.

Though he would emerge again in later, non-Hughes-influenced entries in the *Vacation* series, it is in his first two appearances that Eddie's character is fleshed out to its full, humorous effect. While jokes at the expense of his monetary woes may seem rather ill-spirited in the present day (such as the barbecue he serves up in *Vacation*, which consists of tomato ketchup and a toasted bun as he is unable to afford any burger meat), humor is also generated from the antics and attitudes of Eddie's similarly eccentric family. This includes his easygoing wife, Catherine (played by Miriam Flynn in all of the character's appearances), an extensive array of offspring who tended to alternate from film to film, and, of course, his over-friendly Rottweiler named Snots, whom Eddie describes as being crossbred with a "Mississippi Leg Hound" due to his overly personable manner with strangers (to say nothing of his undisclosed sinus condition).

Whether complaining that the plastic plate in his head—the result of an unexplained accident—was not of adequate size to qualify for a United States Army pension, or dumping the contents of his RV's chemical toilet into the storm sewer of Clark's well-to-do suburban street, Cousin Eddie is an unforgettable character who remains lodged in the memory of the general public. Quaid succeeds brilliantly in balancing the contradictory traits of this extraordinary individual, crafting a figure that is both disconcertingly unhygienic and oddly engaging. Though it seems unlikely that anyone would willingly seek Eddie out as a companion on a vacation of their own, with his artless magnetism and scrounging craftiness he is never less than entertaining to watch.

Another character who proves to be an acquired taste is Del Griffith of *Planes, Trains and Automobiles* (1987), brought to life with great flair by John Candy. Del was one-half of a reluctant pairing with Neal Page, a prosperous Chicago businessman played by Steve Martin, and much of the film is concerned with the conflict between these two strong but clashing personalities as they make their way from New York to Chicago during Thanksgiving in spite of every possible delay, diversion, and catastrophe being strewn in their path. *Planes, Trains and Automobiles* was one of Hughes's most critically successful comedies, and its accomplishment is greatly aided by the exceptional performances of its two stars. While the movie balances the notions of incompatible dispositions and gradually developing friendship, it also addresses the concept of mutual understanding; while Neal is constantly aggravated by Del's annoying traits and questionably sanitary habits, his unexpected companion is so good-natured that he continues to provide unwavering support even when he is undergoing a barrage of verbal abuse from his prickly acquaintance.

With the unremittingly chatty Del, Candy created one of the most memorable characters of his entire cinematic career. Possibly the most ingenious shower curtain-ring salesman imaginable—at one point in the film, he sells the innocuous plastic hoops to the unsuspecting public via endlessly absurd pretexts, such as designer earrings—Del is a character who exhibits numerous poignant paradoxes. As the film continues, he evolves from an exasperating buffoon to a multifaceted and deeply empathetic individual: one whose motivations are much more complicated than the audience is initially led to believe. Though his more unusual inclinations drive his well-groomed, fastidious companion to distraction, including laundering his underwear in the sink of their shared hotel room or talking so incessantly during their ride in a rental car that Neal's ears seem to be at risk of bleeding, we eventually discover that Del is a widower who is so lonely that he will gladly elect to suffer a stranger's repeated, hurtful tirades about his behavior than risk being alone.

Whether leading a spontaneous sing-along on a bus full of otherwise cheerless travelers navigating the roads of Missouri, or attempting to trade a budget Casio watch in lieu of hard cash, Del is unfailingly quick-witted and practical and never once gives up in the face of adversity. While Neal is desperate to return to the comfort of his opulent home and loving family, Del's determination to assist him in his surprisingly tortuous trek becomes all the more touching when we realize that, at the end-point of his own journey, he has nowhere to go and not a soul waiting for him. In no way could this revelation have been nearly as heartrending if Del had been less affable, supportive, and endlessly thoughtful a traveling companion as he proved to be.

Candy's performance as Del would greatly influence his later cameo role as polka band leader Gus Polinski (the self-proclaimed "Polka King of the Midwest") in *Home Alone* (Chris Columbus, 1990), where, ironically, he and his group are forced to hire a truck to make a long road journey following the cancellation of his flight—a rather circuitous reference to the earlier film. Yet *Home Alone* also contains one of Hughes's most deftly developed nonconformist characters in the form of the elderly Mr. Marley: a formidable and shadowy figure forever known to the kids of Kevin McCallister's neighborhood as the sinister "Old Man Marley."

A well-observed performance played beautifully by Roberts Blossom, this sharp-featured, flinty-eyed gentleman is the stuff of legend in the Chicago suburb where he lived. With an ominous profile which would not have looked out of place in many eighties slasher movies, Marley is rarely seen without his snow shovel, with which he salts the sidewalks around his home and those of his neighbors. Yet it is not his threatening appearance (or so it may seem to youthful eyes) that is the cause of Kevin's panic whenever Marley is in his immediate vicinity. According to the tall tales of Kevin's older brother, the adversarial Buzz, Marley was better known as "The South Bend Shovel Slayer," explaining his solitary status being due to his having been a serial killer who had murdered his entire family—along with many of his neighbors—in the winter of 1958, using his inseparable shovel as a murder weapon. The unworldly Kevin takes his brother at his word, along with a subsequent warning that Marley had stashed away the corpses of his victims in a salt container, resulting in their being mummified. This leads to Kevin racing away in terror whenever he spots the oblivious senior citizen anywhere in the area.

In reality, however, Marley is a textbook example of the danger inherent in judging people by their appearance. Later encountering Kevin at a pre-Christmas church service, he soon neutralizes any anxiety by proving himself to be far from the homicidal maniac that the boy fears, but rather a friendly, lonely old man. The absence of his family, he reveals, is not the result of a massacre many years earlier, but rather the sad outcome of a still-ongoing feud. Kevin's realization of the depth of sadness experienced by Marley at his hermitlike status leads him to consider the antipathy he has felt towards his own family and the need to overcome any misunderstanding that may eventually develop into a more serious rift. Marley later turns his assumed role as nominal antagonist on its head by rescuing Kevin from the clutches of the two burglars who pursue the youngster following the abortive break-in of his home, using his snow shovel to knock them both unconscious. In true Hughes style, of course, the resilience of familial bonds and the redemptive power of Christmas (in keeping with the film's holiday season setting) combine by the time of the film's conclusion to ensure that Marley and his estranged son achieve rapprochement, thus bringing to an end his unwillingly reclusive existence.

The Freewheeling Life: John Hughes's Celebration of the Slacker

Not all of Hughes's more unconventional characters are out-and-out eccentrics; some are simply idlers who have rejected the daily grind in favor of a less-conformist lifestyle. In some cases, it is society which has somehow abandoned the characters, leading to a worldview tinged with resentment or disaffection towards a system which has excluded them for issues of circumstance usually beyond their control. Hughes often reveled in the individuality and unorthodox thinking of these resourceful slackers and quick-thinking wanderers, applauding their ability to survive and even thrive in a world that seems indifferent to both their successes and their difficulties.

Arguably the most prominent of Hughes's jovial shirkers is Buck Russell, the protagonist of *Uncle Buck* (1989). A gregarious and highly sociable character, Buck is content to coast through life; nearing middle age, he has only a disheveled bachelor apartment and an ancient, barely drivable car to his name. He is content to eke out an existence of suspect betting practices and any other insalubrious business opportunities that come his way. His insouciant attitude to life is resented by his hard-working, upwardly mobile brother Bob (Garrett M. Brown), who has little contact with his sibling until a family emergency forces him to request that the lovable rogue watch over his children while he is out of town.

In the capable hands of John Candy, Buck becomes much more than simply the indolent figure his brother and sister-in-law believe him to be. Taking care to explore the full range of humorous potential that the role offers him, Candy also does not neglect the significant dramatic capacity of the part, ultimately forging a charismatic and strangely appealing character who proves to be both comical and complicated. As his time with Bob's children continues, Buck slowly becomes aware of an underlying lack of purpose in his life, one that is unavoidably highlighted by his engagement with the many unforeseen duties and accountabilities of parenting by proxy. His fast-thinking nature comes in handy when he finds himself forced to develop unusual solutions to family problems as they occur, such as using a microwave to dry laundry when the tumble dryer breaks down, and putting together packed lunches for the kids which are far from orthodox in their ingredients.

Candy endeavors throughout *Uncle Buck* to imbue the title character with an affecting sense of credibility and a highly individualized sense of personal integrity, sketching out Buck's outsider status as a pariah in the eyes of his sibling's family before—little by little—overcoming his

Uncle Buck. Director: John Hughes. Release date: August 16, 1989.

perceived irresponsibility to gradually become assimilated into the lives of his relatives in a manner that would not previously have been possible. This theme of familial judgment and accountability was echoed by Hughes a few years later in the screenplay for *Career Opportunities* (1991), directed by Bryan Gordon, where the movie's protagonist Jim Dodge finds himself torn between a natural tendency towards free and easy living and a withering parental appraisal of his squandered vocational potential.

Portrayed by Frank Whaley, Jim is a silver-tongued operator who finds that his talent for fast talking and persuasiveness is not matched by an ability to retain gainful employment. His deep-seated insecurities have led to a predilection towards ever more implausible deceit, while his unreliability has led his parents to despair of the fact that he still hasn't flown the family nest in adulthood. Scarred by an alienating experience of high school, Jim's psychological behavior has been shaped in fascinating ways; jumping from one dead-end job to the next, he shows no degree of commitment or dedication to any aspect of his life, though his reliance on increasingly outrageous lies mark him as a social anomaly as much as a misfit in professional circles.

Hughes spends time carefully building up a picture of Jim as a listless and essentially lethargic individual before throwing him in at the deep end. Offered an ultimatum by his hard-working father—either find continuous work or be forced to leave home—he accepts a job as a night janitor in a well-frequented discount store situated in the small Illinois town where he lives. While there, he suddenly finds himself compelled to defend the store from burglars as well as protecting an unexpected guest: the wealthy daughter of a local land baron, who has been accidentally locked in overnight during a shoplifting spree. Together, the two discover a commonality over their shared experience of discord with parents, and Jim begins to realize—just as Buck Russell had—that true independence is a concept which is considerably more multifaceted than he had initially thought.

The free-thinking Jim would eventually decide to forge his own path voluntarily, but the responsibility for the strained relations with his father ultimately lies with the defiant son's dereliction of duty towards the family unit. Thus, it takes him to forge a relationship with his unanticipated visitor Josie McClellan (Jennifer Connelly) to see that building a more meaningful structure to his life has greater benefits than expecting support without reciprocation. In this sense, the convivial dissembler eventually becomes a compassionate and caring partner due to an eventual awareness that adulthood truly begins with an appreciation of the fact that each of us is responsible for the pattern of our own destiny; they cannot be shaped by the will or caprices of others, lest we lose ourselves in the process.

The issue of family is also crucial to Jim Belushi's character Bill Dancer in *Curly Sue* (1991). A homeless drifter who takes responsibility for his young friend—the Curly Sue (Alisan Porter) of the title—Bill has had no choice in life but to learn how to travel light and make the most of any opportunity which presents itself in order to survive another day. Faced with a society which proves largely unconcerned with his plight, he finds himself obliged to forge his own solutions to the problems he encounters. Hughes employs a muted line in social commentary by juxtaposing the impoverished but good-hearted Bill and Sue with Kelly Lynch's affluent lawyer Grey Ellison, whose life has become a succession of disinterested interactions as she finds herself slavishly and unthinkingly fulfilling the cultural expectations of her high-status occupation.

As Bill's charm slowly humanizes the hard-nosed, clinical Grey, he also realizes the extent to which Sue would benefit from living in a stationary family unit rather than continuing her itinerant existence. Because of Sue's emotional attachment to Bill and his nomadic but nonetheless authentic personal attitudes, she protests at his plans to transfer her guardianship, but in the end Grey's developing feelings lead to the three forming an unconventional nuclear family of their own, thus ensuring domestic security for Sue and a supportive partnership for both Bill and Grey. Although putting down roots is an essentially alien concept to Bill, he understands that the benefits of the collective family unit outweigh the appeal of the freedom of movement he has experienced while destitute. Thus, even the crucial security of having a fixed abode is subordinated to the emotional sustenance of good family relations, and he comes to view his life priorities anew.

Hughes created a plethora of out-of-the-ordinary characters throughout his screenwriting career, and many of these distinctive figures have

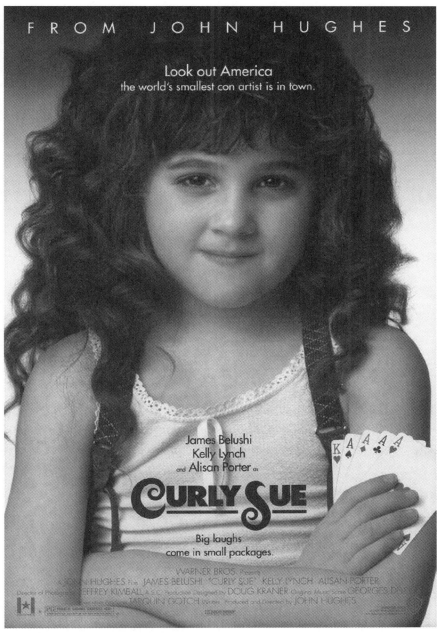

Curly Sue. Director: John Hughes. Release date: October 25, 1991.

retained a place in popular culture long after the initial release of the films. While some were inevitably more sympathetic than others, all had the capacity to grow and change as a result of the situations they encounter—sometimes in fulfilling and unpredictably extensive ways. Highly individual and usually demonstrating idiosyncratic attitudes of one kind or another, Hughes's eccentrics are another reason his films have continued to linger in the cultural consciousness.

8

If We Played by the Rules Right Now, We'd be in Gym

Sports and Games in John Hughes Films

John Hughes understood all too well the importance of sports and leisure in the lives of many Americans. Sports of different types are referenced throughout numerous Hughes movies, though the characters' interaction with these activities varies widely. Sometimes Hughes was to depict them engaging willingly with a sporting pastime, though occasionally physical exercise would be avoided because of its strenuous nature. In other instances, sports were subverted entirely for a variety of reasons, being presented in a manner quite different from that which might otherwise have been conventionally expected. Hughes's complex relationship with the world of sports, and games in general, shone an interesting light upon shifting cultural attitudes of his films' time of production, and the manner in which he situates leisure-time activities within the lives of his characters often reflects a great deal about their wider approach to life.

Competitive Spirit: Sporting Achievement and Personal Honor in *The Breakfast Club*

Perhaps the most prominent athletic character to appear in a John Hughes movie is Andrew Clark, portrayed by Emilio Estevez, in *The Breakfast Club* (1985). Andy, as he is known to his fellow students, is a high-achieving athlete who ostensibly has it all—the respect of his peers, a glowing record of sporting accomplishments, and a bright future. The reality of his life would soon be revealed as something quite different, however.

As is the case with all five students who make up the eponymous band of detention attendees, nothing is ever quite as it seems, and this popular competitor is no exception.

For Andy, success in sports appears to be everything. It informs his character, his relationships, and even his diet. The other students in the Breakfast Club immediately assume that this star of the school wrestling team fulfills a particular stereotype: namely, that he will use his elevated status to his own advantage, employ his superior physique to bully and intimidate others, and that his general comportment will be one of arrogance and egotism. Yet, in truth, as the detention session wears on throughout the day, Andy quickly establishes himself as being an individual of far greater character, embodying the best aspects of good sportsmanship—fair play, even-handedness, and consideration for the needs of others.

Smartly turning audience anticipation on its head, Hughes gradually reveals that it is not Andy who has been obsessed with chasing glory, but rather his overbearing father who has been living his life vicariously through the attainments of his offspring. Though the other attendees at the detention gathering are aware of his reputation as a swaggering narcissist on the high school campus, leading in particular to conflict between him and Judd Nelson's rebellious John Bender, over time the full extent of Andy's personal frustrations is laid bare. While expectation suggests that his singular fixation on winning at all costs stems from his desire to retain his primacy within the school's social hierarchy, in actuality he has begun to feel suffocated by the obligations which have been placed on his shoulders. His drive to succeed is derived from his father's single-minded obsession with compelling him to ever-greater levels of accomplishment, though the increasing degree of personal sacrifice required to make this possible has caused him to rethink his own goals. Likewise, as the social conventions of his athletic peers are such that he comes under pressure to behave in a certain way towards classmates, he comes to regret a prank that he orchestrates against another student—the subsequent humiliation meted out against the younger teenager forces Andy to re-evaluate the nature of his behavior.

With *The Breakfast Club*, Hughes makes the point that participation is more important than winning, but he also accentuates the fact that we should resist the temptation to equate tenacious sporting ambition with unyielding self-absorption or a lack of consideration for others. Andy may enjoy a position of privilege within the school's elaborate social order, but it is one which is predicated upon living a rigidly orchestrated existence which seems more attuned to pleasing people other than himself. Ultimately, it is the gradual emergence of his independence and strength of personality that challenges this state of affairs, allowing him to break free of the shackles of parental expectation (a challenge which confronts each of the Breakfast Club's members, albeit in different ways) and more fully embrace his own personal code of ethics.

While Andy's cynicism and conduct under peer pressure do not necessarily paint a particularly flattering picture of the sporting fraternity of a typical high school environment, he eventually emerges as the very epitome of all that is affirmative and principled about team spirit. His virtues as an individual outshine the constraints placed upon him by his parents and fellow students alike; in his defense of Anthony Michael Hall's Brian and Molly Ringwald's Claire against the incessant, scornful provocation of Bender, the true quality of his moral integrity emerges, as is the case in his realization that his father's preferred direction for Andy's future is entirely at odds with his own. Every teenager who attends the Breakfast Club leaves the detention session changed as a result of the experience, and, in Andy's case, he emerges as no less talented an athlete, but as a much more rounded and contented individual.

Play Ball: Active Participation and Spectator Sports in *Ferris Bueller's Day Off*

If *The Breakfast Club* voiced some ambivalence towards high school sports, *Ferris Bueller's Day Off* (1986) was to nail its colors to the mast in no uncertain terms. The guilefully astute protagonist (Matthew Broderick) is largely contemptuous of high school customs at the best of times, but during his illustrious day traveling around Chicago he actually makes a point of mentioning the fact that—had he not decided to evade Ocean Park High School by faking illness—he would otherwise have wound up in gym class. So great is his disdain towards physical education that he views a sporting trophy not as a prized possession but as a useful counterweight on one of the jury-rigged devices in his bedroom. Yet while the more strenuous aspects of team sports may not appeal to Ferris or, by extension, his friends Cameron (Alan Ruck) and Sloane (Mia Sara), he is certainly not above enjoying sports as a spectator

Wrigley Field baseball park in Chicago, home of the Chicago Cubs.

pastime: a fact made clear by their visit to Wrigley Field, the famous home stadium of the Chicago Cubs.

Hughes makes the unambiguous point that sports have a highly beneficial potential to bring people together. Though Sloane is by no means the most engaged onlooker during the ball game, Cameron and Ferris both enjoy some male bonding over its familiar sporting conventions, with the latter even catching a baseball when it is hit into the crowd. The community aspects of sports are further stressed by the appearance of a "Save Ferris" notice on Wrigley Field's digital noticeboard; just one of many such notifications publicizing the legend of Ferris's supposedly ailing health, it demonstrates the efforts of the students and faculty of the high school to extend their donation drive in support of his recovery beyond their local neighborhood and into the wider Chicago area.

Acquaintance with the practices of baseball are also used in the film to signal a sense of communal belonging; while Ferris and Cameron share a chant on the bleachers, emphasizing their mutual rapport, their school's antagonistic dean of students—the fearsome Ed Rooney (Jeffrey Jones)—is shown to be wanting in his knowledge of the sport. On the trail of the absentee students, Rooney narrowly misses sight of Ferris on a television broadcast in a local bar; when the bartender explains that the game is currently at a 0–0 draw, the oblivious dean asks who is winning. His wanton indifference towards a recreation that has a proven ability to bring people together (as shown in the bonding between his wayward charges) only serves to deepen his position as a solitary outsider, out of touch with the social practices which help others to connect and relate to one another.

As Hughes makes clear with his inspired cut between Ferris's entertaining relaxation as a spectator and the sight of his out-of-breath classmates completing track and field activities, competitive sports may well have the capacity to forge understanding and accord when people participate in them, but this can also be true of witnessing a game rather than directly taking part. The distinction may seem relatively minor, but, for Ferris, it is fundamentally important; as with so many other aspects of his approach to life, he is able to reap the maximum reward while putting in the minimum effort.

The Sport of Kings?: Unconventional Applications of Sports in *Uncle Buck*

Not all of the sports explored by John Hughes's screenplays were to be quite as arduous as the team activities in his teen movies. The hunting and fishing pastimes explored by *The Great Outdoors* (Howard Deutch, 1988), for instance, serve mainly to highlight the conflict between its two central characters; while John Candy's family man Chet Ripley enjoys the activities as family-bonding pursuits, Dan Aykroyd's pretentious would-be socialite Roman Craig can see them only as competitive practices with the singular aim of proving his self-proclaimed superiority over others. However, the following year's *Uncle Buck* (1989) would see Hughes exploring a different social aspect of sports—and one which would be somewhat provocative in comparison to his earlier work.

The titular central figure of *Uncle Buck*, the laid-back Buck Russell (John Candy), is one of life's free spirits: unemployed in the long term, he manages to eke his way through life thanks to the occasional winnings from betting on horse races. But whereas gambling on games of chance is a common way of raising revenue, Buck's modest existence is entirely reliant on success in the bets he places, meaning that he eventually finds himself resorting to rather less sporting methods of ensuring that his goal is achieved. Though usually content to rely on his intuition, an encounter with old acquaintance and fellow gambler E. Roger Coswell (Brian Tarantina) alerts him to the presence in town of infamous race-fixer Jimmy Bean—a man who owes money to both of them. Aiming to make good on his debts, Bean has offered to illegally rig a forthcoming race in favor of one particular horse, meaning that all Buck and Coswell need to do is place heavy bets on the preordained winner in order to reap the rewards of the dishonest scheme.

As was often the case in a Hughes movie, cheats are seldom allowed to prosper, and even the lovable Buck cannot be allowed to succeed in participating in Bean's mendacious plans. When the time of the fixed race arrives, Buck instead decides to go in search of his niece Tia (Jean Louisa Kelly)—an even more pressing priority than his required presence at the race track, even though he stands to net an entire year's earnings as a result. However, the attack of conscience which accompanies him giving precedence to family loyalty eventually pays dividends of its own; realizing that his carefree existence cannot continue indefinitely, Buck comes to the conclusion that he must eschew a life that relies on random chance to cover his financial affairs and consider a more reliable (and honest) source of income in the future.

While Buck's easy humor and indefatigable good nature make him an appealing character, his willingness to compromise on personal ethics by debasing a time-honored sport for fraudulent ends leads to him paying a heavy price. For Hughes, pressing an unfair advantage in such a way is not only to corrupt a long-established pastime in a manner which would swindle any unwitting participants who would be taking part in it, but also to demonstrate a thoroughly un-American mode of behavior. The end result of Buck's attempted (but botched) involvement in the disreputable scheme, of course, is to see him forced to abandon a lifestyle based on luck and probability to instead seek income via more conventional, upright means. This takes the form of working for his girlfriend Chanice (Amy Madigan)—the owner of a tire service company, who aims to make good use of his hitherto un-channeled mechanical talents. Thus, honorable conduct is seen to overcome duplicity, and a new, more principled situation emerges as a result. Sports may not be the central issue of *Uncle Buck*, but they nonetheless form an important method of convincing an essentially unreliable figure to be true to his own nature and embrace domesticity and greater personal dependability.

Howe and Why: The Curious Case of Cameron Frye's Hockey Jersey

One sports-related question which has vexed many John Hughes fans is: Why does Cameron Frye of *Ferris Bueller's Day Off* spend most of the movie wearing a Detroit Red Wings ice hockey jersey when the action is situated in and around Chicago? Further deepening the mystery is the fact that the shirt is that of legendary Canadian player Gordon "Gordie" Howe (1928–2016), widely considered to be one of the finest ice hockey professionals of all time. Howe's career had started in the mid-1940s, but he reached his record-breaking prime throughout the fifties and sixties before retiring in 1971 (though he would make a short-term one-season return to the NHL between 1979 and 1980, where he played for the Hartford Whalers at the remarkable age of fifty-two). But why would a Chicago teenager choose to wear the jersey of a Michigan ice hockey team, especially when the city is so proud of its own Blackhawks?

The answer lay not with Cameron, as it happened, but rather with Hughes himself. Born in Michigan, he developed a deep affection for ice hockey in general and with the Red Hawks in particular. Howe had been one of the great sports heroes of his childhood, and though Hughes would later relocate to Illinois, he remained an ardent admirer of this towering figure's athletic prowess. Though he would attend Blackhawks games as he grew older, his appreciation of Howe's professional legacy never

Gordon "Gordie" Howe (1928–2016), one of the most successful professional ice hockey players of all time.

wavered, and following the eminent player's second retirement, Hughes was determined to include a tribute to this multiple award–winning legend. Thus, the appearance of Howe's famous Number 9 Detroit Red Wings jersey would forever be associated with Cameron for the duration of his day off with Ferris Bueller.

No explanation was given in the movie as to why Cameron had chosen to wear the jersey of an ice hockey team which had long been bitter rivals of Chicago's own side, though in recent years actor Alan Ruck has clarified—in retrospective interviews—that Hughes had carefully planned a backstory which never made the film's final cut. In this account, it would have been revealed that Cameron had spent time during his childhood with his Detroit-based grandfather, gaining affection for the Red Wings as a result. On his return to Illinois, he would have continued to express his support for the team, much to the chagrin of his Blackhawks-supporting father—a proud Chicagoan (with whom he was invariably in conflict). Thus, the jersey was initially to have been more than simply a curio, but rather a subtle symbol of defiance—an indication of Cameron's assertion of individuality against his father's attempts to mold him into compliant passivity. As it stands, however, that seemingly innocuous item of clothing remains one of the most iconic uniforms to appear in a film of the eighties.

9

Don't You Forget About Me

The Forgotten John Hughes Movies

As is made clear by this FAQ, many John Hughes features have become immortalized in popular culture. However, this was not always to be the case. Some movies featuring a John Hughes screenplay have, over the years, drifted into a state of relative obscurity in comparison to the big hitters of his filmography, being consigned to the murky depths of cinematic oblivion. But why were these atypical features doomed to such limited longevity?

A Class Act: *National Lampoon's Class Reunion*

John Hughes's first screenplay credit was for *National Lampoon's Class Reunion* (Michael Miller, 1982), a raucous and surprisingly ambitious movie which had been intended by the National Lampoon company to recapture something of the essence of John Landis's highly profitable *National Lampoon's Animal House* (1978). The earlier film's jubilantly anarchic campus comedy had proven to be enormously popular at the box office, and there were obvious commercial reasons why the company was keen to replicate its zeitgeist-driven mayhem for audiences of the early eighties. However, the bold attempt of *Class Reunion* to fuse the chaotic pandemonium of its lucrative predecessor with a less-than-subtle parody of the highly popular slasher horror subgenre—coming into the public awareness with the success of seminal features such as *Halloween* (John Carpenter, 1978) and *Friday the 13th* (Sean S. Cunningham, 1980)—was to prove slightly too ambitious.

National Lampoon's Class Reunion. Director: Michael Miller. Release date: October 29, 1982.

Set in the dubious surroundings of "Lizzie Borden High School" (actually filmed on location at the University of Pasadena campus), the film centers on a ten-year reunion of the school's graduation class of '72—an eclectic selection of blowhards, cranks, and the occasional shrinking violet. However, their celebrations are cut short by the escape of one of their erstwhile classmates from a mental institution, now unhinged and hell-bent on revenge for a prank perpetrated on him prior to graduation. As the murderer starts to pick off the partygoers one by one, longtime rivals are forced to band together in an attempt to identify the culprit and put an end to the rampage once and for all.

While the film contains some early flashes of Hughes's famous ear for witty dialogue, *Class Reunion* has little of the subtlety and assurance of his later screenplays. Hughes himself would later complain that the script he submitted had been greatly altered during its transition into the feature. The limitations of the movie's budget are apparent in the cheapness of its set dressings and flimsy props (such as the knife used by the murderer, Walter Baylor, which, in an early scene, is clearly constructed from tinfoil and cardboard). Likewise, the film suffers from a disappointingly linear structure; characters are given little time to develop, rapidly descending into caricature, meaning that their portrayal is largely dependent on Hughes's deft skill in crafting dialogic interaction to flesh out their personalities.

While *Class Reunion* was not a direct sequel to the earlier *Animal House*, quite in spite of audience anticipation to the contrary, it did feature the return of producer Matty Simmons (a longtime National Lampoon alumnus) as well as actor Stephen Furst—albeit in a quite different role this time around. The film performed poorly at the box office: a particular disappointment for National Lampoon given the meteoric profitability of its well-received forerunner. Reviewers were quick to identify the confused tone of the movie, which regularly veered between the understated and the outright absurd. Though a satire of the horror cinema of the time would, by necessity, be compelled to dispense with the tangible sense of threat which made so many other features of the genre so noteworthy, *Class Reunion*'s knowing surrealism was to eat away at even a nominal attempt to generate the kind of claustrophobia or peril that typifies so many horror narratives of the late seventies and early eighties. Yet, in spite of a few sporadic sparks of originality, including a surprisingly post-modern climax (the effectiveness of which is stymied only by some heavy signposting), the film was ultimately unable to transcend the increasingly well-populated field of horror spoofs, such as *Saturday the 14th* (Howard R. Cohen, 1981), *Student Bodies* (Mickey Rose, 1981), and *Pandemonium* (Alfred Sole, 1982).

Today, *National Lampoon's Class Reunion* remains recognizable among cineastes only for its status as John Hughes's debut as a screenwriter. In spite of a few cleverly rendered performances and a spirited cameo by music legend Chuck Berry, the movie has largely sunk without a trace, overshadowed by the cultural significance of *Animal House* and the forthcoming *Vacation* series. Hughes, however, would never again engage quite so closely with broad parody.

Booty and the Beast: *Nate and Hayes*

When John Hughes is mentioned in conversation, very few people are likely to correlate his name with swashbuckling adventure on the high seas. Yet with *Nate and Hayes* (Ferdinand Fairfax, 1983), he would engage in arguably the most atypical feature in his entire filmography. Though it emerged early in his career, the film diverged sharply from the family-focused comedies of domestic America that typified much of Hughes's initial output, switching briefly to the somewhat less familiar backdrop of the South Pacific Islands in the 19th century.

The historical action-adventure experienced a significant resurgence during the early 1980s, spurred on by the triumphant box-office success of Steven Spielberg's *Raiders of the Lost Ark* (1981). Several movies were to see release in the years following the debut appearance of Indiana Jones, though few would come close to reflecting the sheer refinement or high-budgetary values of Spielberg's smash hit. While Fairfax's *Nate and Hayes* could not hope to match the widespread appeal of *Raiders of the Lost Ark*, the film was to feature many stirring set-pieces, an arresting array of location filming, and some appealing performances from its cast.

Also known by its alternative title *Savage Islands* in international markets, *Nate and Hayes* formed a rare instance in which Hughes shares

Nate and Hayes. Director: Ferdinand Fairfax. Release date: November 18, 1983.

billing for a film's screenplay. The movie was co-written by David Odell (also the recipient of the movie's story credit), who had received an Emmy Award nomination for his writing for Jim Henson Associates' *The Muppet Show* (1976–1981). Odell's contribution to 1980s pop culture would be cemented by his screenplays for films such as *The Dark Crystal* (Jim Henson and Frank Oz, 1982), *Supergirl* (Jeannot Szwarc, 1984), and a cinematic adaptation of the popular animated series *He-Man*, entitled *Masters of the Universe* (Gary Goddard, 1987). The script Hughes and Odell crafted for *Nate and Hayes* is a fictionalized account of the adventures of real-life American-born pirate Captain William "Bully" Hayes (c.1829–c.1877), offering a highly embellished account of his piratical exploits, including the acquisition of his infamous vessel, the *Leonora*.

Nate and Hayes focuses on a Christian missionary named Nathanial "Nate" Williamson (Michael O'Keefe), who has been assigned to preach to the inhabitants of a remote island in the South Pacific. Williamson is accompanied on the voyage by his fiancée, Sophie (Jenny Seagrove), and the couple is ferried to their new mission on the sailing vessel *Rona*, captained by rough-and-ready adventurer Captain Hayes (Tommy Lee Jones). Shortly after their arrival, the pair's wedding is interrupted by a band of rancorous pirates led by the malevolent Ben Pease (Max Phipps), a slave trader who takes Sophie hostage. Thus, in spite of their shared suspicion of each other, Nate and Hayes have no choice but to team up in order to defeat Pease and rescue Sophie from captivity.

Filmed amid the stunning scenery of Fiji and New Zealand, the movie offers a greatly sanitized version of the historical Hayes, portraying him as a gruffly derisive, defiant, but generally honorable character. Hughes and Odell's screenplay maintains an affable, engaging approach to characterization which lent the action an agreeably knowing tone in places while retaining dramatic impact in others. As had been the case with so many films in the action-adventure genre, the believability of *Nate and Hayes*'s plotline is often willingly subordinated to attention-grabbing set-pieces and frenetic incident, though a talented cast of actors—most notably Tommy Lee Jones as the dryly caustic Hayes—make the most of their efficient dialogue.

Lacking much of the finesse demonstrated by Hughes's later work, *Nate and Hayes* is occasionally unevenly paced, with intermittently inelegant transitions between high drama and garrulous exposition, while some of the film's action sequences appear ponderous and blatantly flagged in advance. Yet the screenplay never seems to stray too far from its core aim of offering up competently presented escapism, and in fulfilling this purpose it almost always accomplishes its goal. But even with its flamboyant hero, entertaining villains, and a gleeful willingness never to let historical fact get in the way of a good story, *Nate and Hayes* was unprofitable in theaters, being completely overshadowed by the following year's blockbuster *Indiana Jones and the Temple of Doom* (Steven Spielberg, 1984). Though the film's critical reception was uneven, *Nate and Hayes* was to achieve an unpredicted cult longevity among its dedicated fan-base, which has seen it forge a modest place alongside other action movies of the time, such as *Romancing the Stone* (Robert Zemeckis, 1984) and *King Solomon's Mines* (J. Lee-Thompson, 1985).

For all its impressive cinematography, fastidious period detail, and pleasingly freewheeling wit, *Nate and Hayes* remains one of the most obscure features of Hughes's entire filmography. The movie did undeniably form an intriguing sidestep in his writing career, for he would not return to the historical action movie genre in later years and—while his distinctive aptitude for well-defined, shrewdly crafted dialogue was demonstrated throughout the action—*Nate and Hayes* was as conspicuous a departure from a "traditional" John Hughes film as can possibly be imagined.

Outlaws and Inmates: *Reach the Rock*

Reach the Rock (William Ryan, 1998) was one of the final movies to which John Hughes would contribute, and though the film has since become essentially disregarded by many on account of its restrained profile—both at the time of its release and in the years after—it has become an intriguing oddity within Hughes's wider filmography, which marked a sudden change in tone after a sustained run of family-oriented features throughout the nineties. Acting both as producer and screenwriter, Hughes's jarring departure from expectation confounded many critics but nevertheless signified a return to the more contemplative tendency of his mid-1980s output.

The film centers on the conflict between a troubled young man named Robin (Alessandro Nivola), who appears to deliberately bring about his own arrest in order to face incarceration in the police station of the small Illinois town where he lives. He is jailed by the ranking officer on duty, Sergeant Phil Quinn (William Sadler), who knows Robin due to a seemingly endless string of minor offenses. There follows an ever-increasing game of brinkmanship between the two men as Robin continues to bait the officer while Quinn reveals the fact that he holds the small-time offender responsible for the accidental death of his nephew. As the evening unfolds, the true reason for Robin's aberrant behavior is gradually revealed, raising questions along the way about the ramifications of individual choice and the nature of freedom in modern society.

Due to its stately pace, its focus on one main location, and the fact that the action unfolds primarily during a single night, many critics were baffled by Hughes's sharp deviation in approach. Although the unrequited love which is divulged to be the driving force behind Robin's dysfunctional viewpoint was a theme that had been explored at various points (and in different ways) throughout Hughes's 1980s features, less common was the sharp interpersonal conflict between the two central figures—a strategy which had been employed by Hughes for comedic ends, but rarely for dramatic objectives. The deliberately gradual exposure of Robin and Quinn's motivations led to a narrative tempo which was markedly slower than Hughes's earlier screenplays, meaning that the film's comparative leisureliness is something of an acquired taste.

Director William Ryan uses the limited number of locations throughout *Reach the Rock* to good effect, most especially the jail cell which forms the main focus of the movie's events, though his filming around rural areas of Illinois and Michigan also briefly but effectively showcases the off-the-beaten-track ambiance of the fictional community. Stars Sadler and Nivola engage admirably with their respective characters' multifaceted personal drives, highlighting their conflicts as well as their understated commonalities. The endgame of Robin's desperate if somewhat irregular scheme, once fully laid bare, is both poignant and thought-provoking, encouraging a careful re-evaluation of the delineation of

Reach the Rock. Director: William Ryan. Release date: October 16, 1998.

youthful romance that Hughes had explored in a number of his teen movies in the eighties. The film slyly interrogates the interplay between societal expectation of individual purpose and the manner in which people can be held hostage by their emotional patterns and dependencies, teasing out truths about the characters' lives as well as—by extension—commenting on the stresses of their responsibility to society in general. While Robin's cell turns out to be an ineffective means of incarceration, given his ability to remove himself from it and return at will, his restrictive personal mindset proves to be a far more efficient mode of imprisonment—albeit one over which he shows that he has limited control.

Reach the Rock is unlikely to feature in many personal top ten lists of John Hughes movies, and yet for fans of his filmmaking it is a genuinely unusual feature that stands apart from much else in his eclectic catalogue. While its dissimilarity to so many of his earlier films is likely to make it as divisive to modern viewers as it proved to be among contemporary critics, coming so late in his cinematic career it remains a suitably striking movie which forms a fascinating companion piece to his earlier teen cycle, presenting a starker and more uncompromising appraisal of the conflict which lies between the liberty of making individual decisions and the confining influence of external factors, both emotional and psychological.

A Stranger Here Myself: *Just Visiting*

French cinema and John Hughes may seem like an unlikely combination, and yet in 2001 Hughes was to contribute the screenplay to Jean-Marie Poiré's *Just Visiting* (known in the French market as *Les Visiteurs en Amérique*, and attributed to Poiré's pseudonym Jean-Marie Gaubert), a lively remake of well-received French time travel comedy *Les Visiteurs* (Jean-Marie Poiré, 1993). With Poiré's multiple César Award–nominated film proving to be a huge success among French audiences, later spawning two sequels (in 1998 and 2016), an English-language remake for the international market seemed like a solid commercial proposition.

Just Visiting retained the two stars of *Les Visiteurs*, Jean Reno and Christian Clavier, while adding to its cast several well-known American performers, such as Christina Applegate and Tara Reid, along with cult English character actor Malcolm McDowell in whimsical form as a wizard. Further adding class to the production are the mellifluous tones of Kelsey Grammer as the film's narrator. Moving the action from the 12th century France of the original to medieval England, the film closely reflects the premise of *Les Visiteurs* by using the plot device of a magical potion with unexpected properties to transpose the feudal protagonists into a modern setting—in this case, Chicago in the year 2000. There, main characters Thibault and André must contend with being anachronistic strangers plucked from their own time, with humor generated from the stark evolution in cultural attitudes which has come about in the intervening centuries. Not only must they overcome difficulties surrounding some unexpected romantic entanglements (often in surprising ways) and encounter some unanticipated descendants, they are also faced with the predicament of finding a way back to their own time when the odds appear stacked against them.

The work of screenwriters Christian Clavier and Jean-Marie Poiré, who had contributed the script for the original *Les Visiteurs*, was given a new and indelibly American angle thanks to the involvement of Hughes. Once again bringing his extensive knowledge of Chicago locations—and a still-obvious fondness for the city—to a screenplay, Hughes's participation was to add an intriguing dimension to the movie in that the characters' sense of disorientation was now no longer restricted to their extraction from their period of history, but also due to the culture clash that they encounter when removed from their Dark Ages–era English surroundings in favor of modern-day America. The film does explore the concept of universal equal rights in a laudable fashion, exploring the revolutionary nature of such fairness and egalitarianism through the eyes of protagonists who have only known the rigid class-based feudalism of medieval Europe. That the audience is able to interrogate the essential nature of impartiality and equality for all through the eyes of naïve cultural outsiders only heightens the importance the screenplay places on highlighting the need for collective parity for all individuals

Just Visiting. Director: Jean-Marie Gaubert. Release date: April 6, 2001.

within a just and unbiased society. For a fanciful comedy, the film makes this point in often surprisingly persuasive ways.

Just Visiting contains a number of intriguing visual reflections of not just Chicago, but urban America in general. At one point a city diner is deliberately shot to resemble Edward Hopper's 1942 painting *Nighthawks*, one of the most famous oil-on-canvas works in all of American art, and this conspicuous evocation of metropolitan life proves to be an effective shorthand for the film's broader strategy of juxtaposing the sophisticated bustle of the modern metropolis with the primitive existence of the central characters' lives of nearly a millennium beforehand. Poiré/Gaubert's direction, amply complemented by some eye-catching cinematography by Ueli Steiger, makes this comparison with both confidence and verve, underscoring the confusion of André and Thibault while also gradually investigating their ability to perceive the benefits of contemporary living. While the twelfth-century practitioners of the arcane arts may wield uncanny powers, the viewer is left in no doubt that the relationships playing out among the glass, steel, and concrete of a present-day municipality have an ability to contain magic all of their own.

Of all the screenwriting collaborations in which Hughes would take part, *Just Visiting* is among the most atypical. Yet the film contains much which situates it within the prevailing themes of his earlier work, such as an undeniable emphasis on self-determination and prizing hard-won individual freedoms. Although *Just Visiting* would not meet with the same level of critical or commercial success enjoyed by its illustrious predecessor, the movie did feature some appealing performances from its cast along with a charming depiction of Chicago as a city humming with energy and possibility. While it is by no means vintage Hughes, the screenplay for *Just Visiting* nonetheless echoes his infectious enthusiasm for urban Illinois and reiterated, with much dynamism, his desire to celebrate personal liberation.

10

They Just Don't Write Love Songs Like They Used To

Popular Music in John Hughes Films

I t is difficult to imagine the films of John Hughes in isolation from the music that was chosen to accompany them. Few aspects of Hughes's films are quite as important as the selection of music chosen to complement the action, and some of these tracks have become virtually synonymous with the movies in which they appear. Hughes was notoriously perfectionistic when it came to determining the correct tracks for a given film, drawing from a vast array of different artists and styles to ensure that each of his features was supplemented by an eclectic but always perceptive range of musical accompaniment. Hughes considered the choice of music for his films with the utmost seriousness, and even in movies where he was providing the screenplay but not in the director's chair, the musical decisions proved to be pivotal. It is difficult now to imagine *National Lampoon's Vacation* (Harold Ramis, 1983) without the strains of Lindsay Buckingham's "Holiday Road" and "Blitzkrieg Bop" by The Ramones, or *Home Alone* (Chris Columbus, 1990) without Macaulay Culkin exultantly miming to Irving Berlin's "White Christmas" (performed in that instance by The Drifters rather than the more famous Bing Crosby version).

Yet in movies directed by Hughes, his impeccable ear for music was never less than evident, and tracks by artists—both major and relatively obscure—were selected in an attempt to find just the right piece to augment his creative objectives. *Planes, Trains and Automobiles* (1987) features songs as diverse as Ray Charles's "Mess Around" and Paul Young's "Every Time You Go Away," while *She's Having a Baby* (1988) ran the gamut from

Kate Bush's "This Woman's Work" to Gene Loves Jezebel's "Desire (Come & Get It)." However, it is undoubtedly for his teen movies that Hughes's musical choices were at their most iconic, and during the course of these six films in the mid-eighties he was to prove just how vital the selection of the most effective tracks would prove to be in situating each feature within its particular place and time, showing them to be every bit as critical as any other stylistic aspect of the production.

Love Songs by Candlelight: The Music of *Sixteen Candles*

Sixteen Candles (1984) is forever associated with its use of Altered Images' "Happy Birthday"—an ironically upbeat choice, given the disastrous birthday of the film's protagonist Samantha Baker (Molly Ringwald). Scottish lead singer Clare "C. P." Grogan's buoyant, perky vocals contrasted perfectly with the melancholic dejection of a teenager whose parents have accidentally forgotten her sixteenth birthday, and perfectly epitomized Hughes's joyously caustic approach to this atypical coming-of-age tale. In many ways, this inspired choice would become even more concomitant with the film than the title track, The Stray Cats' "Sixteen Candles," in its establishment of Hughes's artistic *modus operandi*.

Billy Idol's "Rebel Yell," a defiant track from an artist conjoined with concepts of rebellion and individuality, appropriately accompanies the erratic driving of Anthony Michael Hall's nerdish "Farmer" Ted as he ferries Haviland Morris's worse-the-wear Caroline Mulford around the streets of their Illinois town in her father's Rolls-Royce. The juxtaposition is telling, for the unabashedly geeky Ted is just about as far removed from the traditional alpha male of the teen movie genre as it is possible to imagine. Likewise, the film's conclusion—sagely complemented by "If You Were Here" by new-wave British band Thompson Twins—was highly effective in its emphasis on Samantha's eventual triumph over adversity; not only does she finally receive the birthday cake that had earlier been denied her, but also the affections of her dream date Jake Ryan (Michael Schoeffling), whom she had previously considered to be entirely unattainable. The suitably uplifting song neatly encapsulates her sense of achievement in having succeeded in what had earlier seemed impossible, and against all odds.

As would be the case with his later teen movies, Hughes would supplement *Sixteen Candles* with tracks that would shine light on a character's personality or motivations (Ira Newborn and the Geeks' instrumental "Geek Boogie," The Divinyls' "Ring Me Up," and Tim Finn's "Growing Pains"), or provided an ironic commentary on the action (Darlene Love's "Today I Met the Boy I'm Gonna Marry," Annie Golden's "Hang Up the Phone," and Oingo Boingo's "Wild Sex in the Working Class"). He also exemplified the film's cultural credentials with a string of sagaciously chosen music from long-established stars such as David Bowie ("Young Americans"), Van Morrison ("Gloria"), and Frank Sinatra ("Theme from 'New York, New York'"), while other tracks were drawn from an array of

"Happy Birthday" by Altered Images. Release date: August 1981.

emerging 1980s industry talent, including Wham! ("Young Guns"), Nick Heyward ("When It Started to Begin" and "Whistle Down the Wind"), Paul Young ("Love of the Common People"), and Spandau Ballet ("True").

Hughes also accentuated *Sixteen Candles* with some witty, if sometimes unexpected, choices of music, including excerpts from Ray Anthony and His Orchestra's rendition of the famous theme from NBC's police series *Dragnet* (1951–1959) (originally composed by Walter Schumann, based in part on an passage from Miklós Rózsa's score for Robert Siodmak's 1946 film noir *The Killers*), Nino Rota's "Love Theme" from *The Godfather* (Francis Ford Coppola, 1972), Henry Mancini's theme from NBC's (later ABC's) crime drama *Peter Gunn* (1958–1961), and an uncredited incidence of Marius Constant's title theme from CBS's fantasy anthology series *The Twilight Zone* (1959–1964). Yet, strangely enough, the above selections—implemented for their sardonic commentary on the onscreen action—were far from the most unusual musical selections in a movie which pitched AC/DC's "Snowballed" against The Temple City Kazoo Orchestra's "Kazooed on Klassics," made Stevie Ray Vaughan's "Lenny" rub shoulders with The Premiers' "Farmer John," and coordinated The Revillos' "Rev-Up" with Night Ranger's "Rumors in the Air."

No High School Disco: The Music of *The Breakfast Club*

Simple Minds' "Don't You (Forget About Me)" is not only the song most closely associated with *The Breakfast Club* (1985); in many ways, it has come to be the most immediately recognizable piece of music to appear in any John Hughes movie. A Scottish rock band formed in Glasgow in the late 1970s, Simple Minds reached international recognition from the mid-eighties; Jim Kerr's distinctive vocals for this most renowned of teen anthems was played over the opening and closing credits of *The Breakfast Club*, accompanied by the sound of Charlie Burchill's inimitable guitar skills, and perfectly encapsulated the ethos of Hughes's core themes of authentic personal identity and belonging. The song charted at number one on the U.S. charts, and has become so innately connected to the teen movie that it has since featured in numerous later entries in the genre, including *American Pie* (Paul and Chris Weitz, 1999) and *Pitch Perfect* (Jason Moore, 2012).

While "Don't You (Forget About Me)" undeniably dominates the music of the film, it is complemented by an inspired range of tracks which similarly delineate the quandaries facing the characters, as well as their complex psychologies. Karla DeVito's "We Are Not Alone" is used to explore the subtly different creative engagement of the five teens in detention as they react to the music; Emilio Estevez's athletic Andrew Clark breaks into an air guitar riff, while Anthony Michael Hall's cerebral Brian Johnson dances like a middle-aged physics teacher at an end-of-term disco. As each of the students respond in different ways to the song, Hughes emphasizes the fact that while they all have radically different

"Don't You (Forget About Me)" by Simple Minds. Release date: February 1985.

dance styles, the nature of their shared passion and inspiration is essentially the same.

Wang Chung's "Fire in the Twilight" is used to present the action of the teens' ill-advised foray away from the library which forms the film's central location; as they traverse the deserted school corridors in order to pay a brief visit to a locker, the song typifies the conflict between the imperious authoritarian Assistant Principal Richard Vernon (Paul Gleason) and the group's most rebellious member, John Bender (Judd Nelson). "Waiting," by E. G. Daily, exemplifies the marriage of tedium and uncertainty which tinges the extended period of detention to which the students have been subjected, while Jesse Johnson and Stephanie Spruill's "Heart Too Hot to Hold" perceptively indicates a gradual thawing in relations between the mismatched quintet. While Joyce Kennedy's "Didn't I Tell You?" reflects some aspect of the teens' growing realization that their predicament is perhaps more multi-layered than they had initially appreciated, underscoring the significance of their new-found maturity and individual development on a personal level, some of *The Breakfast Club*'s most impactful musical moments are actually those which are unaccompanied by lyrics. Instrumentals such as Gary Chang's "Dream Montage" and Keith Forsey's "I'm the Dude," "Love Theme," and "Reggae" each form an important function within the film, enhancing the action while often simultaneously (and sharply) illuminating the individual quirks of the main characters.

Electrifying Beats: The Music of *Weird Science*

Oingo Boingo's title track "Weird Science" immediately draws the audience into this most fantasy-oriented of Hughes's teen movies, using its electronic ambiance, vaguely macabre synth, and evocation of classic monster movie soundscapes to set the scene for the film's action with great efficiency. Fronted by Danny Elfman, now an internationally acclaimed film composer, American rock band Oingo Boingo was formed in 1972 (originally as "The Mystic Knights of the Oingo Boingo") and went through a number of stylistic shifts during their active years before eventually disbanding in 1995. "Weird Science" has become, in the opinion of many, their most successful song, appearing on their studio album *Dead Man's Party* in 1985. (The song would also later be used as the title theme for the USA Network's television adaptation of the film, also entitled *Weird Science*, between 1994 and 1998.)

Weird Science (1985) has also become well known for its inspired reworking of Roy Orbison's "Oh, Pretty Woman" by hard rock band Van Halen, a thoroughly modern rendering of a recognizable classic which is used to highlight not only the beauty of Kelly LeBrock's Lisa but also her intellect and ingenuity. Playing against the action of a car chase taking place between Lisa and two high school alpha males named Ian (Robert Downey Jr.) and Max (Robert Rusler), the knowing older woman causes consternation among the tormentors of her two teenage creators by

"Weird Science" by Oingo Boingo. Release date: August 1985.

spurning the advances of the antagonists (against their expectation) and reaffirming her connection with their geeky competitors.

The film's premeditated entwining of technology and desire is reflected in many of the tracks chosen by Hughes to illustrate the action, such as Orchestral Maneuvers in the Dark's "Tesla Girls," The Lords of the New Church's "Method to My Madness," Kim Wilde's "Turn It On," and The Broken Homes' "Do Not Disturb (Knock Knock)." Other songs are clearly geared more specifically towards delineating the mindsets and behaviors of the characters, most specifically the two protagonists—Ilan Mitchell-Smith's Wyatt Donnelly and Anthony Michael Hall's Gary Wallace. These include Wild Men of Wonga's "Why Don't Pretty Girls (Look at Me)," The Del Fuegos' "Nervous and Shakey," Los Lobos' "Don't Worry Baby," and Cheyne's "Private Joy."

Weird Science's sense of cutting-edge digital modernity was further enhanced by the presence of such songs as Ratt's "Wanted Man," Taxxi's "Forever," Max Carl's "The Circle," and General Public's "Tenderness," though Hughes showed equal willingness to stray into less conventional territory with the inclusion of tracks including Wall of Voodoo's "Deep in the Jungle," "Eighties" by Killing Joke, and—perhaps most notably—Mike Oldfield's hugely influential "Tubular Bells." Also included, if somewhat ironically given the less than brawny stature of the two protagonists, is a brief burst of "Gonna Fly Now," the celebrated theme from Bill Conti's original score for *Rocky* (John G. Avildsen, 1976).

Rhapsody in Pink: The Music of *Pretty in Pink*

The Howard Deutch–directed *Pretty in Pink* (1986) contains no shortage of music to accompany Hughes's screenplay. Foremost among his selections is the track accompanying the film's climactic scenes, "If You Leave" by British electronic music band Orchestral Maneuvers in the Dark. Playing through the senior prom at the high school attended by the film's central love triangle—Andie Walsh (Molly Ringwald), Phil "Duckie" Dale (Jon Cryer), and Blane McDonnagh (Andrew McCarthy)—the song must walk a difficult tightrope between commiserating with

Duckie's heartbreak at losing his childhood sweetheart, and Andie's jubilation at the eventual validation of her relationship with Blane. The restrained energy of "If You Leave" makes its impact all the more potent, and the piece augments the film's emotional climax with both intensity and considerable verve.

Other important tracks to feature in *Pretty in Pink* include, notoriously, Otis Redding's "Try a Little Tenderness," to which Duckie mimes with much gusto (though with little attempt to match Redding's performance style). The scene does much to establish the character's zaniness along with his heartfelt desire to impress his old friend/potential love interest Andie, with the Redding song proving to be a surprisingly perfect

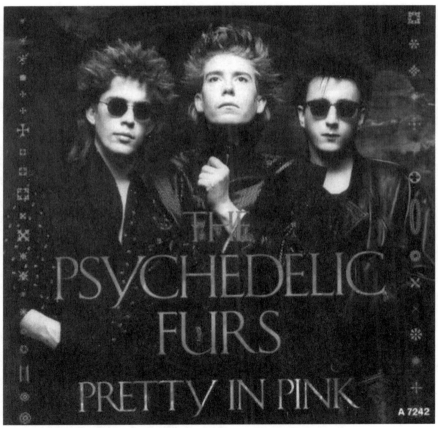

"Pretty in Pink" by The Psychedelic Furs. Release date: July 1981.

match for the occasion. Danny Hutton Hitters's "Wouldn't It Be Good," a cover version of the Nik Kershaw original, is used to establish the Trax record store managed by Andie's friend and mentor Iona (Annie Potts). The song not only sets up the character's buoyancy and bubbliness, but also the eccentricity of her distinctive music shop, which forms a background for some of the film's most significant scenes.

The title track, "Pretty in Pink" by the Psychedelic Furs, was not written for the movie but had in fact been released some five years prior. While a new saxophone intro was recorded for the film version, the majority of the song remains faithful to the 1981 original with the lyrics reflecting the movie's themes of the emotional difficulties of romance and the ambiguities of negotiating abstruse high school social strata. *Pretty in Pink* also featured a rendition of "Please, Please, Please, Let Me Get What I Want" by The Smiths, which would feature rather more prominently—albeit in an instrumental version—in *Ferris Bueller's Day Off* later that same year.

The movie would also include tracks by some major musical talents of the 1980s, in the form of Echo and the Bunnymen ("Bring on the Dancing Horses"), INXS ("Do Wot You Do"), New Order ("Shellshock"), and Suzanne Vega and Joe Jackson's "Left of Center." Music aficionados would also recognize tracks by other artists gaining widespread popularity at the time, such as the versatile Jesse Johnson's "Get to Know Ya," and "Round, Round" by Belouis Some.

The Slacker's Symphony: The Music of *Ferris Bueller's Day Off*

Ferris Bueller's Day Off (1986) is a veritable cornucopia of remarkable music; Hughes goes to exacting lengths to complement the film with a wide range of astutely chosen tracks, many of which made an instant impact on popular culture. Nominally the most immediately recognizable piece is "Oh Yeah" by Yello, a Swiss electronic band comprising musicians Boris Blank and Dieter Meier. The song accompanies Matthew Broderick's slick protagonist as he first sees the ostentatious 1961 Ferrari 250 GT Spyder California parked in his best friend's father's garage. The very deliberate and impassioned vocalization of the (very sparing) lyrics are perfectly suited to Ferris's overwhelming desire to possess the car for his own ends, even if only temporarily. With playful irony, Hughes reprises the song at the end of the film as the battered and humiliated dean of students, Ed Rooney (Jeffrey Jones), limps onto a graffiti-scrawled school bus, in need of a lift given that his own car has been impounded during his fruitless pursuit of the hooky-playing Ferris. The reprise stresses the gulf which lies between the triumphant Ferris and the thwarted Rooney, exchanging the rare and flamboyant Ferrari for the run-down public transport of which the aggravated dean is forced to make use. "Oh Yeah" was to be used again in eighties cinema and beyond, being heard in films such as *The Secret of My Success* (Herbert Ross, 1987) and *K-9* (Rod Daniel, 1989).

"Oh Yeah" by Yello. Release date: July 1985.

The many other prominent tracks in *Ferris Bueller's Day Off* include "Love Missile F1-11" by British new wave band Sigue Sigue Sputnik, an extravagantly bass-laden piece which attends Ferris's fourth-wall-breaking monologue on how to hoodwink concerned parents into believing the plausibility of fake illnesses in order to achieve a day free from high school. There is also quiet power in The Dream Academy's instrumental version of The Smiths' "Please, Please, Please, Let Me Get What I Want," a track which accompanies Ferris's visit to the Art Institute of Chicago. In a testament to the versatility of the music, Hughes uses the same piece to accompany Ferris's friend Cameron Frye (Alan Ruck) as he is mesmerized by Georges Seurat's pointillist masterpiece *A Sunday Afternoon on the Island of La Grande Jatte* (1884)—his close examination of the painting reflecting his own internal crisis and intense personal concerns—while in contrast, Ferris and his girlfriend Sloane (Mia Sara) share an affectionate kiss next to him, in front of Marc Chagall's enigmatic work *America Windows* (1977).

Other music in the film includes "Beat City" by The Flowerpot Men, a rousing piece which plays as Ferris and his friends approach Chicago in the "borrowed" Ferrari, and the inspired combination of Wayne Newton's "Danke Schoen" and The Beatles' "Twist and Shout" that can be heard as the titular hero energetically mimes to the well-known lyrics as he performs on a float during the Von Steuben Day Parade in the heart of Chicago. While some tracks exhibited relevance to Hughes's central themes of liberation and self-determination (General Public's "Taking the Day Off," Blue Room's "I'm Afraid," and The Dream Academy's "The Edge of Forever"), others were more eclectic in nature (Zapp's "Radio People," The English Beat's "March of the Swivelheads," and Big Audio Dynamite's "BAD"). Hughes also included a few discerning nods to pre-existing popular culture by including excerpts from "Jeannie," Hugo Montenegro's main theme from NBC's fantasy TV comedy series *I Dream of Jeannie* (1965–1970), and John Williams's instantly recognizable title theme from *Star Wars* (George Lucas, 1977).

Playing at the Heartstrings: The Music of *Some Kind of Wonderful*

Although sometimes unfairly overlooked, the music of the Howard Deutch–helmed *Some Kind of Wonderful* (1987) is a bravura example of a movie produced by Hughes wherein each individual track has been exactingly selected. Opening the film is one of its most memorable pieces, "Abuse" by German synthpop group Propaganda, an instrumental remix of their 1984 song "Dr. Mabuse." Accompanying the opening credits with much verve, and running alongside the spirited drum-kit playing of Mary Stuart Masterson's Watts, the track was curiously absent from the film's

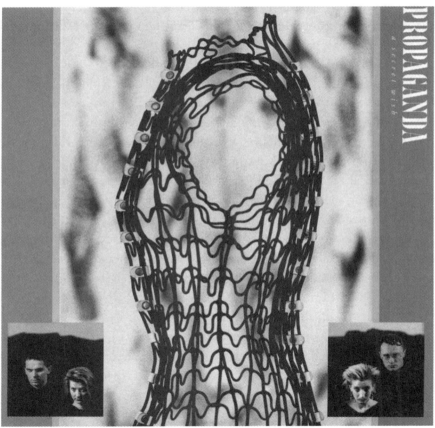

"Dr Mabuse" by Propaganda, as featured on their studio album *A Secret Wish*. Release date: July 1985.

official soundtrack album, but could still be found on Propaganda's studio album *A Secret Wish* (1985) and their remix album *Wishful Thinking* (1985).

The film's other key song is arguably Lick the Tins' "Can't Help Falling in Love," a rather inventive cover version of Elvis Presley's famous original, which featured a haunting flute and drum beat. The track plays as Watts and the film's protagonist, Keith Nelson (Eric Stoltz), finally realize their true feelings for each other, accentuating Keith's dawning comprehension of the depth of affection he feels for his long-standing best friend as well as articulating Watts's relief and joy at knowing that her love is not unrequited after all. The inclusion of the piece shares the effectiveness of the conclusion of *Pretty in Pink*, though its accompaniment to the deepening of Watts and Keith's relationship debatably has greater power due to the fact that—in this instance—the odds have been overcome to see the sensitive outsider winning the day over the more upwardly mobile potential romantic partner.

The aforementioned third point on the movie's central love triangle belongs to Lea Thompson's high-class Amanda Jones. Her appearance is complemented by the sound of The March Violets' "Miss Amanda Jones," a cover of a track by the Rolling Stones, though the original can also be heard later in the film as Keith gets ready for his long-awaited date with the hitherto-inaccessible Miss Jones. Perhaps appropriately, the party they attend is accompanied by Charlie Sexton's "Beat's So Lonely," perfectly evoking the isolation that is sometimes found when mingling in crowds—especially hostile ones.

As had become *de rigeur* for John Hughes teen movies, numerous tracks had been selected to give prominence to particular aspects of the main cast's personalities, heightening their sense of individuality. "Catch My Fall," by that unmistakable icon of rebellion Billy Idol, plays over the attempts of skinhead iconoclast Duncan (Elias Koteas) to provide unorthodox access to the local museum, as well as Keith's intentional plan to land himself in detention while at high school. Stephen Duffy's "She Loves Me" complements a scene wherein Watts gives Keith some lessons in effective kissing, leading her to realize her developing feelings for him (while he remains ostensibly oblivious to them). Keith's quandary in attempting to balance his attraction to Amanda with her unattainability due to the school's rigid social strata is communicated via Blue Room's

"Cry Like This," while the calculated scheming of Amanda's ex-boyfriend Hardy Jenns (Craig Sheffer) is expressed via the sound of Furniture's "Brilliant Mind," which accompanies the fruits of his malignant underhandedness, such as orchestrating Amanda's seclusion from her one-time friends.

Hughes also supplemented the film with numerous tracks from eighties bands, both well recognized and relatively unknown. Though Pete Shelley's "Do Anything" has become particularly associated with *Some Kind of Wonderful* due to its accompaniment of Watts showcasing her mechanical talents in a garage setting—one of the movie's most immediately identifiable sequences—there were numerous other songs which ably situate the feature within its time of production, such as The Jesus and Mary Chain's "The Hardest Walk," Flesh for Lulu's "I Go Crazy," The March Violets' "Turn to the Sky," and The Apartments' "The Shyest Time."

11

What a Funny Guy

John Hughes as Edmond Dantès

John Hughes may have been one of the most widely recognized screenwriting talents of the eighties and nineties, but—perhaps surprisingly—his output for the cinema didn't end with the scripts which emerged under his own name. In the later years of his career, Hughes occasionally penned screenplays and story treatments under the pseudonym Edmond Dantès. The protagonist from Alexandre Dumas's 1844 novel *The Count of Monte Cristo*, this multifaceted literary character was, much like Hughes himself, a character of complexity and significant contradictions. Hughes's choice of this particular pen name is not entirely clear. The Dantès of the Dumas text was a skilled and benevolent man who, following false accusations of criminality, eventually turns resentful and indignant. When in later life he achieves vast wealth, the literary Dantès embarks on an intricate course of action which sees him recompensing those who had remained loyal to him while admonishing individuals he considers culpable for his wrongful imprisonment. The elusive character has since become well known for his disguises and use of pseudonyms, such as Abbé Busoni, Sinbad, Lord Wilmore, and—most famously—The Count of Monte Cristo.

Though movies which featured Hughes's involvement under the Dantès alias often exhibited thematic similarities to his wider filmography, they are perhaps most interesting in the instances where his story treatments were developed into screenplays by other writers, shedding light on just how much of Hughes's artistic imprimatur survived the interpretation from outline to script. Like Dantès, Hughes could be an inscrutable figure, moving between genres in ways that were as unpredictable as they were inspired. His screenplays under the Edmond Dantès name may never be regarded as among his most instantly discernable works for the cinema, but they do add an interesting extra dimension to an already-prolific writing career.

A Shaggy Dog Story: *Beethoven*

Perhaps the most famous of Hughes screenplays to emerge under the *nom de plume* of Edmond Dantès was that of Brian Levant's *Beethoven* (1992), where the film's script was credited as a collaboration between Dantès and screenwriter Amy Holden Jones. The movie's plotline demonstrated many stylistic hallmarks of Hughes's later screenplays for family features, and would be very similar in terms of dialogue, characterization, and overall tone to subsequent films such as *Dennis the Menace* (Nick Castle, 1993) and *101 Dalmatians* (Stephen Herek, 1996).

While *Beethoven* featured a talented cast which included Charles Grodin, Bonnie Hunt, and Stanley Tucci, its true star is the eponymous St. Bernard dog who energetically drives the movie's action. A tale of a spirited puppy who charms his way into the Newton household, Beethoven (whose name is chosen when he barks in tune to Beethoven's Fifth Symphony) quickly wins over the hearts of his new owners but must overcome the sinister machinations of unethical veterinarian Dr. Herman Varnick—an admirably Machiavellian turn by actor Dean Jones—who seeks specimens of larger canine breeds for use in testing ammunition. The Newtons and their newest family member must fight against the duplicitous schemes of Varnick and his henchmen in order to save Beethoven from a grisly end, bringing the family closer as a result.

With a prominent subtext featuring animal rights and the moral imperative of ensuring the well-being of all creatures, *Beethoven*'s exploration of unscrupulous treatment towards domestic creatures in the pursuit of profit was largely in line with the promotion of ethical principles which would be established throughout many of Hughes's other screenplays for family movies; while bumbling criminal antagonists would be a common staple throughout numerous Hughes scripts of the early- to mid-nineties, from *Home Alone* (Chris Columbus, 1990) to *Baby's Day Out* (Patrick Read Johnson, 1994), the necessary integrity of the furtherance of scientific research would be touched upon again in films such as *Flubber* (Les Mayfield, 1997). In partnership with Jones, an experienced screenwriter who would develop scripts for movies as diverse as *Mystic Pizza* (Donald Petrie, 1988), *Indecent Proposal* (Adrian Lyne, 1993), and *The Relic* (Peter Hyams, 1997) during a varied career, the expected polish of Hughes/Dantès could be found in abundance throughout *Beethoven*. Given its focus on wisecracking children and cute, loyal canines, common sense may have suggested that the film would have been awash in schmaltzy sentimentality, and yet, in actuality, the end result is considerably more restrained. Special credit in this regard must go to leading man Grodin,

Beethoven. Director: Brian Levant. Release date: April 3, 1992.

who manages to layer his character—irritable patriarch George Newton—with admirable nuance, gradually revealing that the curmudgeonly father's antipathy to the lovable St. Bernard can be traced back to childhood heartbreak when his own dog, a beloved companion, was euthanized. Being a Hughes family film, of course, there is a happy ending: George is eventually able to overcome his long-buried psychological trauma to embrace Beethoven's status as a treasured pet, finally following the example of his rather more receptive wife and children.

Beethoven was a box-office success at the time of its release, proving especially popular among dog lovers, and would be followed by a staggering seven sequels. The first, *Beethoven's 2nd* (Rod Daniel, 1993), received a theatrical release, with the remainder being issued straight to video. The franchise also featured an animated spin-off series, *Beethoven*, which aired for one season of twenty-six episodes on CBS between 1994 and 1995. While Levant's original *Beethoven* movie is generally considered by critics to be the high point of the franchise, it is today more readily remembered for showcasing future stars David Duchovny and Joseph Gordon-Levitt in minor roles than it is for Hughes's involvement under his Edmond Dantès pen name.

Memories are Maid of This: *Maid in Manhattan*

Wayne Wang's 2002 film *Maid in Manhattan* was a popular romantic comedy which, though it sharply divided critical opinion, nevertheless proved to be a crowd-pleaser. Wang, whose creatively fruitful career had produced such wide-ranging features as *The Joy Luck Club* (1993) and *Smoke* (1995), brought a lightness of touch to the proceedings, lending a sense of fanciful whimsicality to New York City's famous urban sprawl. *Maid in Manhattan* was developed from an Edmond Dantès treatment, with the film's screenplay being authored by Kevin Wade. Wade was by then a veteran screenwriter with a career spanning back to the mid-eighties, which had included scripts for such high-profile movies as *Working Girl* (1988), *True Colors* (1991), and *Meet Joe Black* (1998). Using the Dantès story as the basis for his script, Wade was to engage with a number of themes which were recognizably Hughesian in nature.

The modern-day Cinderella tale sees senatorial candidate Christopher Marshall (Ralph Fiennes) falling in love with beautiful New York maid Marisa Ventura (Jennifer Lopez) after he confuses her with capricious socialite Caroline Lane (Natasha Richardson). The mistaken identity causes difficulty in the development of their relationship, further compounded by the markedly different life experiences of the hard-working, avowedly blue-collar single mother Marisa and the privileged, upscale career politician Chris. Although the path of true love proves problematic, the pair is eventually able to overcome familial discord, frenetic press

Maid in Manhattan. Director: Wayne Wang. Release date: December 13, 2002.

interest, and professional turbulence in order to forge their shared affection into a lasting bond.

While Wade's screenplay deviates from Hughes's original story in a number of ways (not least the fact that the action was initially intended to have been situated in Chicago rather than New York), the stimulating brew of star-crossed lovers and acute class consciousness bears more than a passing resemblance to *Pretty in Pink* (Howard Deutch, 1986) and *Some Kind of Wonderful* (Howard Deutch, 1987). Though the protagonists are most assuredly adults than the teenagers of Hughes's eighties heyday, there is still much that is familiar about a tale where a chance emotional entanglement proves powerful enough to overcome the obstacles of social status and peer attitudes. Like Steff McKee of *Pretty in Pink* and Hardy Jenns of *Some Kind of Wonderful*, Chris's political advisors disapprove of his fascination with someone they judge to be an awkward fit with the expectations surrounding his elevated position as an individual running for prominent elected office. And in the same manner as *Pretty in Pink*'s Phil "Ducky" Dale and *Some Kind of Wonderful*'s Watts, Marisa's down-to-earth family and friends express attitudes ranging from skepticism to outright hostility regarding her seeking a relationship with someone whose worldview and class status deviates so sharply from their own.

While an upbeat conclusion meets the pair after a long and arduous courtship fraught with difficulties and misunderstandings, the film ends on a thoughtful note which celebrates the unifying power of true love while similarly offering no solid assurances about their long-term ability to overcome the stresses which bear down upon their relationship. And yet, given the fairytale nature of the story, it provides just enough buoyant positivity to assure audiences that long-term romance may yet prevail against snobbery and social divisiveness—a classic Hughes motif, without question.

Wang takes considerable care to present New York through a lens of quirky imaginativeness, adding a sense of wonder and endlessly sanguine possibility to one of the world's most instantly distinguishable urban settings. The appealing principal cast receives stalwart support from actors such as Bob Hoskins, Amy Sedaris, and Stanley Tucci, and the movie also benefits from a spirited musical score from composer Alan Silvestri, which perfectly complements its air of engaging charm. *Maid in*

Manhattan was a popular comedy when released and, while it may have deviated from the fine detail of Hughes's original story, his influence on Wade's screenplay remains undeniable.

You Know the Drill: *Drillbit Taylor*

Another John Hughes script treatment under the Edmond Dantès name was to form the basis for *Drillbit Taylor* (Steven Brill, 2008), a knockabout comedy that was never inclined to take itself too seriously. Adapted into a screenplay by Kristofer Brown and Seth Rogen, the film was among the best known of Brill's directorial career at that point, following features such as *Little Nicky* (2000), *Mr. Deeds* (2002), and *Without a Paddle* (2004). While *Drillbit Taylor* was to meet with considerable skepticism among the critical community, it was a movie which nonetheless owed much to the slapstick charm of Hughes's early nineties output, thanks to its blend of oddball charm and the eventual triumph of its hopeless, nonconformist protagonist.

The plot of *Drillbit Taylor* is based around three less-than-athletic high school students—Ryan (Troy Gentile), Wade (Nate Hartley), and Emmitt (David Dorfman)—who rapidly find that their first week in class is made increasingly appalling due to the merciless ministrations of a obstreperous (and borderline psychotic) senior named Terry Filkins (Alex Frost). Soon deciding that enough is enough, the trio merge their comparatively paltry monetary resources and hire a bodyguard in the hope of staying safe from Filkins's increasingly sadistic wrath. However, their meager cash reserves lead them to the distinctly unrefined Bob "Drillbit" Taylor (Owen Wilson), a bargain-basement hired muscle who claims to be an elite military veteran but is, in actuality, a homeless drifter who is desperately trying to scrape together enough cash to move to Canada in the hope of better prospects. Soon, Drillbit is coaching the kids in increasingly implausible (and fictional) martial arts under the bold claim that they are clandestine black ops fighting skills. However, his best efforts to pull the wool over their eyes fall short when he encounters Filkins for himself and discovers that his "employers" are dealing with no conventional school bully, but a genuinely unstable and brutal individual. Thus,

Drillbit Taylor. Director: Steven Brill. Release date: March 21, 2008.

a series of unexpected strategies are launched into play as the boys and their unconventional bodyguard eventually manage to outmaneuver their manipulative enemy, gaining enough personal confidence in the process to begin enjoying school rather than simply enduring it.

In its emphasis on individual development and evolving to meet life challenges, *Drillbit Taylor* was most obviously indebted to Hughes's *Uncle Buck* (1989) and *Curly Sue* (1991), as well as his screenplay for *Career Opportunities* (Bryan Gordon, 1991). Drillbit is a likable but flawed figure, his tendencies towards duplicity and fraud tempered by a strangely fluid sense of personal integrity which usually leads to him doing the right thing—even if only grudgingly. Though his appreciation of honor is complex and somewhat multifarious, it makes him all the more interesting as a result. We discover, for instance, that some of his more outrageous deceit is often tempered by a grain of truth; while his claims of being an elite special forces operative is soon proven to be bogus, the audience later learns that he was indeed once in the employ of the military . . . only that he wound up going absent without leave after discovering that army life did not suit him. Likewise, his seemingly impressive nickname "Drillbit" comes not from his self-proclaimed prowess in combat, but because he injured one of his fingers with a drill while in high school.

As was so often the case in a Hughes film, by the conclusion Drillbit has overcome his propensity towards wrongdoing (he initially plans to rob the students, then later winds up overseeing the burglary of one of their houses) by reversing his unjust deeds and even making personal sacrifices to help protect his ill-fated paymasters. By the closing scenes the malevolent Filkins has been overcome, the trio has adapted to their situation with increasing self-assurance, and even Drillbit learns the necessity of abandoning his freewheeling ways in favor of a regular job and a constructive plan for his life.

Although the familiar Hughes themes were abundantly evident, the screenplay by Rogen and Brown was ultimately to divide reviewers when *Drillbit Taylor* appeared in theaters, and indeed the movie did not achieve commercial success. What Brill's film did accomplish, however, was the updating of classic tropes from past Hughes features into a thoroughly modern, 21st century setting. Although the later Edmond Dantès film credits would emerge sometime after Hughes had retired from screenwriting, the interest surrounding his involvement in the storylines of *Maid in Manhattan* and *Drillbit Taylor* proved beyond doubt that interest persisted in his contribution to the industry among critics and the general public alike. While there were many who may never have made the connection between Hughes and his Dantès pseudonym, for his many fans the enduring interest in his work continued to prove his cultural relevance even after his withdrawal from commercial filmmaking.

12

She Said We're Going Downtown

John Hughes's Chicago and Illinois

To anyone with even a cursory interest in the cinema of John Hughes, his love for the state of Illinois—and the city of Chicago in particular—has become the stuff of legend. Whether in the jubilant visual travelogue of *Ferris Bueller's Day Off* (1986) or his many cinematic visits to the fictional Illinois community of Shermer, John Hughes always displayed great affection for this famous northerly American state, with several of his films being set in and around the area.

While keen to emphasize the many virtues of Illinois, not least the unique urban landscape of Chicago, Hughes also employed the area as a kind of microcosm of American life in general, and much can be discovered about the characters of his various films by the way they regard and interact with the Windy City or its surrounding communities. Ranging from Jefferson "Jake" Briggs of *She's Having a Baby* (1988), who comes to feel suffocated by the social assumptions surrounding his white-collar existence in Chicago, to *Planes, Trains and Automobiles'* (1987) Neal Page, who spends the entire movie desperate to the point of obsession to return to the familiarity of the city and the comfort of his family home, Hughes delineates Illinois with great dexterity and considerable discernment, his screenplays reflecting a state of cultural richness and complexity.

Sweet Home Chicago: City Life in *Ferris Bueller's Day Off*

In the years since it was first enjoyed by audiences, *Ferris Bueller's Day Off* has come to be particularly renowned as a cinematic love letter to Chicago—a city that was always close to the heart of John Hughes. Even more so than many of his films, it makes extensive use of the urban sophistication and rural beauty of this sprawling metropolis, along with its surrounding communities. Many of the movie's most prominent scenes were filmed around famous landmarks, while others were to prove slightly different in reality than they would appear on-screen.

- It is heavily suggested throughout the film that the community in which the main action takes place is actually the fictional Shermer district which featured in many of Hughes's movies (most notably his canon of teen features), as is made explicit by Jeanie's questioning at Shermer Police Station during the third act. Ironically, the well-to-do Bueller family home was actually not to be found in Illinois at all—the house's exterior was really that of a private residence in California, on Country Club Drive within Los Angeles's Long Beach area. The same could not be said for the visually unique Frye home, which—as its leafy surroundings suggest—was based on an authentic Illinois location, in this case a privately owned house situated on Highland Park's Beech Street. The school attended by Ferris, Cameron, and Sloane, Ocean Park High School, was actually Glenbrook North High School, situated at 2300 Shermer Road in Northbrook. Having first opened to students in 1953, the institution came to be renowned for excellence in teaching standards, and paid host in 1997 to then-incumbent President Bill Clinton, who gave a widely reported speech on education policy during his official visit.
- One of the first locations encountered by the audience when Ferris and his friends arrive in Chicago is an unlikely landmark—a multi-level car park, where the expensive vehicle is safely stored (or so the protagonists are led to believe) while they explore the city. Later owned by General Parking Corporation, the car park was located on Chicago's West Madison Street & Wells Street. A rather more

recognizable sight of the city can be found soon after, when the characters visit the Sears Tower. Now officially renamed the Willis Tower (from July 2009 onward), the building stands 1,450 feet high, making it one of the tallest structures on the planet. In one of the movie's most thoughtful scenes, Ferris and his friends look down upon Chicago from the Tower's observation area, the Skydeck. The Willis Tower can be found at 233 South Wacker Drive in Chicago.

- Another famous Chicago landmark is to be found in the form of the Chicago Board of Trade, where Ferris and his companions witness (with some bemusement) the intense transactions taking place on the trading floor from the relative calm of its adjacent visitor's center. Located at 141 West Jackson Boulevard, the Chicago Board of Trade has been based in its current building since 1930 (though the organization itself was actually founded many decades beforehand, in 1848). Its distinctive architecture, imposing height (at an elevation of 603 feet), and National Historic Landmark status have made it a conspicuous sight within the Loop District of the city. A much less obvious location for Ferris would come in the form of the upscale Chez Quis restaurant—the exterior of which was, in actuality, never a commercial eatery but a private home in the central location of Chicago's West Schiller Street. The building had been extensively redressed for the scenes in which it had appeared, giving an impression of an appropriately high-class eatery. However, in the years since the release of *Ferris Bueller's Day Off*, the building has been significantly redesigned and now bears little resemblance to its previous form.

- Later in the film, Ferris and his friends are fortunate enough to enjoy a game of baseball at the famous Wrigley Field, official home of the Chicago Cubs since 1916. Situated at 1060 West Addison Street, Wrigley Field is one of the most instantly recognizable sporting venues in all of Chicago. Initially named Weeghman Park when it opened in 1914, it later became known as Cubs Park between 1920 until 1927, when it was eventually renamed Wrigley Field in recognition of William Wrigley Jr., the chewing gum magnate who attained control of the Chicago Cubs in 1921. It currently has a seating capacity of 41,268.

The Willis Tower (formerly the Sears Tower) in Chicago, currently the second-tallest building in the United States.

- The Art Institute of Chicago was an establishment that was greatly respected by Hughes, and as such it was only fitting that Ferris would visit its artistic treasures with Cameron and Sloane during their time in the city. The building is situated at 111 South Michigan Avenue, and is the second-largest art museum in the United States. Famed for its internationally acclaimed collection of Impressionist artwork, the museum holds an extensive number of exhibits which include works by Renoir, Seurat, Monet, Cézanne, and Toulouse-Lautrec. It is of particular interest to admirers of American artwork due to it being the home of Grant Wood's significant painting *American Gothic* (1930).
- Perhaps Ferris's most ostentatious decision during his time in Chicago was to hijack an impromptu part in the city's Von Steuben Day Parade, which traditionally takes place along Dearborn Street. Generally conducted midway through September, the carnivalesque procession was organized in commemoration of the life of Baron Friedrich Wilhelm von Steuben (1730–94), who had served as a major general in the Continental Army during the American Revolution. The event is conducted annually in many cities throughout America (including, notably, New York City). Chicago's parade is organized by the United German-American Societies of Greater Chicago; instituted in 1957, the

The Art Institute of Chicago, established in 1879 in Grant Park, Chicago.

pageant celebrated its fiftieth anniversary in September 2007. And if the arduous prospect of being involved in such a strenuous activity necessitated some subsequent rest and relaxation, participants may well have chosen to follow in Ferris's footsteps and unwind for a while at Cook County's scenic Glencoe Beach. A tranquil and picturesque North Shore beach, based in the village of Glencoe, this resort on the west side of Lake Michigan was the perfect place for one of cinema's most famous days off to wrap up before the truanting trio went their separate ways.

Home from Home: John Hughes and the Town of Shermer

Most obviously in his teen movies, though also evident in numerous other films, the action of Hughes's features often center around the fictional town of Shermer. An Illinois community which, it is heavily hinted, is located near the city of Chicago, Shermer is thought to be based loosely upon the real-life Chicagoan suburb of Northbrook in Cook County where Hughes had spent his teenage years. Significantly, Northbrook had initially been named Shermerville when founded in 1901, named in recognition of German immigrant farmer Frederick Schermer (1817–1901), who had donated the land upon which the town's first train station (Schermer Station) was constructed. Its current name of Northbrook was used from 1923 onward, and from its unassuming origins as a rural farming area it has gradually developed into a prosperous suburban community.

For Hughes, Shermer became a kind of shorthand for postwar America in general: a social melting pot where ambitious working-class determination and disaffected, affluent ennui clashed in often unexpected ways. Shermer High School first appears in *Sixteen Candles* (1984), where Samantha Baker's vexed student days were actually filmed in and around New Trier High School in Winnetka and Skokie's Niles North and Niles East High Schools, though by the time this venerable institution reappears in *Weird Science* (1985) it was represented solely by Niles East High School. Interestingly, while Shermer High's most prominent appearance was almost certainly as the setting for *The Breakfast Club* (1985), Hughes

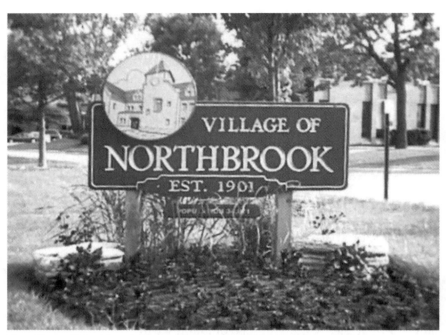

The village of Northbrook (formerly Shermerville) in Cook County, Illinois.

was to avoid the use of a conventional location to reflect the school's library (where the lion's share of the movie's action takes place), instead painstakingly constructing a set within the capacious gymnasium of Des Plaines's Maine North High School. John Bender's triumphant closing scene, however, was actually to be shot in Maine West High School's football field. A shift in venue would take place for *Pretty in Pink* (Howard Deutch, 1986), where Andie Walsh's place of learning was represented by two Los Angeles educational establishments—John Burroughs Middle School and John Marshall High School—whereas *Some Kind of Wonderful* (Howard Deutch, 1987) would instead use San Pedro High School as the backdrop for Keith Nelson's teenage anxieties. Thus, Shermer High School was to present many faces over the course of Hughes's teen movies, though, ironically, *Ferris Bueller's Day Off*—which was instead explicitly set around Ocean Park High School—was the only time in the cycle that Hughes would shift the filming location to his own real-life alma mater, Glenbrook North High School, which was to be found on Northbrook's Shermer Road. Confusingly, Ocean Park can briefly be seen to feature a "Go Shermer" poster in one of its hallways, which, puzzlingly, makes it look as though the institution is supporting a rival school in a sporting event.

Whether referred to overtly as Shermer or otherwise, the Chicago suburbs would loom large throughout Hughes's films, and many sights would be familiar to anyone who was acquainted with the North Shore area. From Glencoe Union Church, where Ginny Baker's wedding took place in *Sixteen Candles*, to the Northbrook Court Shopping Center, which featured briefly but pivotally in *Weird Science*, Hughes was never afraid to draw on locations throughout the region to add authenticity to his filmmaking. The suburbs also featured in movies as diverse as *National Lampoon's Vacation* (Harold Ramis, 1983), *National Lampoon's Christmas Vacation* (Jeremiah S. Chechik, 1989), *Home Alone* (Chris Columbus, 1990), *Career Opportunities* (Bryan Gordon, 1991), and *Dutch* (Peter Faiman, 1991), as well as Hughes's own *Planes, Trains and Automobiles*; *She's Having a Baby*; and *Uncle Buck* (1989). By contrast, the much later *Reach the Rock* (William Ryan, 1998) would take place in the similarly residential but considerably more subdued fictitious town of "Shermerville," which was to cast a shadier, more contemplative reflection over the comparatively upbeat depictions of the area in his earlier films.

Bright Lights and Big Dreams: Depictions of Chicago in American Cinema of the Eighties

While John Hughes's filmic output has become closely associated with Chicago and its surrounding area, most especially during the height of his popularity during the 1980s, his respect for the city was shared by many other filmmakers throughout the decade—often in some of the most culturally significant movies. While many of these features were mainstream comedies and dramas, many critics were surprised at how many teen-oriented movies were to emerge as the decade progressed, proving that the jewel in Illinois's crown was to inspire more than Hughes when it came to this ever-evolving genre.

Some of the most prominent films to feature Chicago throughout the eighties included legendary musical comedy *The Blues Brothers* (John

Landis, 1980), starring real-life Chicagoan John Belushi and showcasing many authentic locations in the city such as Maxwell Street and—in one standout scene—Daley Plaza, where automobile anarchy is brought to Chicago City Hall. *The Blues Brothers* not only highlighted numerous downtown settings throughout Chicago (a feat which *Ferris Bueller's Day Off* would replicate some years later), but also drew in nearby suburban locales, including Calumet City and Park Ridge—the kind of Illinois environs that Hughes would revisit time and again in his own work. Chicago landmarks also loomed large in *When Harry Met Sally . . .* (Rob Reiner, 1989), wherein the film's two protagonists meet at the University of Chicago and appear in scenes in Hyde Park and Lake Shore Drive, reflecting the city's verdant outskirts in ways that echoed much of Hughes's eighties output.

The city of Chicago: one of the most familiar skylines ever to appear in American cinema.

While Brian De Palma's acclaimed Prohibition-era crime thriller *The Untouchables* (1987) had highlighted numerous historic buildings around Chicago, including Union Station and the Chicago Theater, many other films with a significant public profile would feature prominent locations within the city and its surrounding area. These included Lake Forest in *Ordinary People* (Robert Redford, 1980), Marina Towers in *The Hunter* (Buzz Kulik, 1980), the Chicago Sun-Times building in *Continental Divide* (Michael Apted, 1981), the Green Mill in *Thief* (Michael Mann, 1981), and sites around the city's South and West Sides in *The Color of Money* (Martin Scorsese, 1986). Yet perhaps more germane to Hughes's work was the number of comedies and teen movies filmed in and around Chicago during the 1980s, such as *My Bodyguard* (Tony Bill, 1980)—a comedy with some barbed social commentary surrounding the lives of teens in the city's North Side, filmed at Lake View High School and featuring numerous scenes around Lincoln Park. With performances by numerous then-emerging talents such as Matt Dillon, Joan Cusack, and Jennifer Beals, the film's premise (a high school student is forced to hire a bodyguard to keep an aggressive antagonist at bay) would have some degree of resonance with the plot of *Drillbit Taylor* (Steven Brill, 2008) many years later. Likewise, one of the breakthrough movies in the early career of Tom Cruise—*Risky Business* (Paul Brickman, 1983)—would prove to be one of the most significant pre-Hughes teen comedies of the eighties. The tale of a freewheeling teenager who makes the most of his parents being out of town, only to meet with a catalogue of difficulties as a result of his revelry (not least his father's Porsche running into an untimely encounter with Lake Michigan, foreshadowing the fate of a certain Ferrari in 1986's *Ferris Bueller's Day Off*), the success of *Risky Business* would cement Chicago as being the perfect urban (and suburban) environment for the mélange of emotional commentary and gleeful chaos which so often go hand-in-hand with the genre.

Chicago also acted as a backdrop for *About Last Night...* (Edward Zwick, 1986), an account of young adulthood which advanced the Brat Pack from the late teen anxieties of *St. Elmo's Fire* (Joel Schumacher, 1985) to the possibilities of life as twentysomethings in an age of profound uncertainty. Starring Demi Moore and Rob Lowe, the screenplay was adapted from a David Mamet play and manages to transcend its stage

St. Elmo's Fire. Director: Joel Schumacher. Release date: June 28, 1985.

origins by drawing in various Chicago locations, including Grant Park and the Gold Coast. While the film's protagonists were slightly older than the characters in *Some Kind of Wonderful*, arguably the most tonally mature of Hughes's teen movie productions, the theme of harnessing the potential of youth by avoiding any risk of squandering its capacity for personal growth and development was mirrored in Zwick's energetic, often dryly witty approach. The responsibilities of young adulthood were also explored in *Nothing in Common* (Garry Marshall, 1986), which matched Tom Hanks (whose rise to worldwide fame was then still in its ascendancy) with industry veteran Jackie Gleason, to noteworthy effect. Concerning a young man who is forced to choose between a high-flying career as an executive and the needs of his ailing father, with whom he shares an often difficult relationship, there were obvious areas of overlap with Hughes's own frequently revisited preoccupation with the importance of the family unit and the need to ensure that personal advancement did not conflict with wider responsibilities to kith and kin.

As one of the great American cityscapes, Chicago would form the backdrop for many other movies that would be released throughout the 1980s. Films as diverse as *Pennies from Heaven* (Herbert Ross, 1981), *Class* (Lewis John Carlino, 1983), *Windy City* (Armyan Bernstein, 1984), *Raw Deal* (John Irvin, 1986), *The Big Town* (Ben Bolt, 1987), *Red Heat* (Walter Hill, 1988), and *Child's Play* (Tom Holland, 1988)—to name only a select few—were all to draw upon the city as the vibrant urban setting for their action. Yet, in spite of the dozens of movies which featured Chicago throughout the decade, it says something that Hughes's output which was situated in the area continues to resonate with audiences even to this day. From the metropolitan travelogue of *Ferris Bueller's Day Off* to the suburban ambiance of *Uncle Buck*, there was no disguising the warmth with which Hughes held Chicago to his heart, and the majority of his cinema continues to remain synonymous with the city among critics and the public at large.

13

Being Bad Feels Pretty Good

The Antagonists of John Hughes Films

I t is often said that the driving force of any dramatic situation lies in conflict, and over the years the screenplays of John Hughes would feature a stream of truly memorable antagonists, always ready to frustrate plans or disrupt lives for their own advantage or even simply for the sake of amusement. Hughes understood all too well that a truly compelling adversary could be credible yet wryly humorous, and that their opposition to the central characters had to be meaningfully constructed in such a way that the threat they posed was never entirely subsumed by their comic qualities. But how were the villains of Hughes's cinema framed by their nefarious motivations, and in what way did his protagonists manage to engineer the downfall of their bothersome adversaries?

Revenge of the Nerds: Geeks vs. Alpha Males in *Weird Science*

Rarely in a Hughes film were the lead characters quite as defined by their adversaries as in *Weird Science* (1985). Put-upon teenage boffins Gary Wallace (Anthony Michael Hall) and Wyatt Donnelly (Ilan Mitchell-Smith) find themselves under siege on two fronts: domestically, they face unrelenting ill-treatment from Wyatt's overbearing, militaristic older brother Chet (Bill Paxton); at school they are invariably in the sights of obnoxious bullies Ian (Robert Downey Jr.) and Max (Robert Rusler). Yet, while Gary and Wyatt are inevitably humiliated or otherwise undermined by their foes, it is in their eventual ability to rise above the intimidation posed by their detractors that they are able to discover additional internal resources and reach new maturity as a result.

The way the two protagonists initially react to their respective challengers explains much about their characters. Max and Ian are typical high school tormentors, capitalizing on the outsider status of geeky science enthusiasts Wyatt and Gary to isolate and irritate, and yet in spite of their endless flow of scorn and derision they are only too willing to lean on their victims when they think the pair's computing prowess can ingratiate them with the beautiful Lisa (Kelly LeBrock). By reluctantly agreeing to make alterations to the already-perfect dimensions of their computer-generated creation, the teens betray the autonomy of their unexpected mentor, showing only too clearly their willingness to jeopardize their bond of trust with Lisa in a desperate attempt to scavenge a degree of credibility among the school's mainstream, which until now has always rejected them. Their plans are thwarted at the last moment due to their lack of attention to detail, however, and Lisa reminds them that rather than bolstering respect among their persecutors, they have actually only laid bare their desperation for acceptance at all costs.

If Rusler and Downey Jr. present their characters as arrogant and unlikable, they are eclipsed by the home-grown menace of Chet, played to the hilt by a scene-stealing Bill Paxton. Cast somewhat against type in a comedic role—at the time Paxton was best known for performances in dramatic and action films including *Streets of Fire* (Walter Hill, 1984) and *Commando* (Mark L. Lester, 1985)—he clearly savors the repellent self-importance of this extortionist elder brother. Though his fashion style apes the armed forces, in fact Chet epitomizes the absolute opposite of military discipline: he is disruptive, intimidating, and self-serving, with no regard for family loyalty or the greater good. Paxton excels in delivering a performance which is equally comedic and entertaining, delineating this deeply unsympathetic oppressor with the aim of providing the perfect balance of coercion and pomposity. With his sneeringly exaggerated expressions and cavalier disdain for those around him, Chet appears to have next to no redeeming features whatsoever, thus making his eventual downfall all the more satisfying. When Lisa inexplicably transforms him into (quite literally) a new man at the film's conclusion, his plight seems all the more apposite for its comparison with the character development of Gary and Wyatt; whereas the two well-meaning geeks find personal evolution through their newfound ability to widen their social engagement and refusal to be strong-armed by others, Chet's combination of closed-mindedness and ignorance mean that the only way for him to find meaningful change is through drastic (if temporary) modification to his physical form, which subsequently allows his viewpoint to be similarly altered.

For all the movie's elaborate fantasy trappings, *Weird Science* is at heart a tale of individual development, witnessing the journey of two outcasts as they find respect and social acceptability by overcoming those who disparage them. Key to their building confidence, made possible through Lisa's wise ministrations, is Wyatt and Gary's realization that their antagonists are themselves insecure and vulnerable—to the unforgiving tenets of social expectation, to personal circumstance, or to forces outside their control. Rather than allowing themselves to be intimidated any longer, they are able to seize their own destinies rather than be subordinated to familial attitudes (as embodied by the tyrannical Chet) or the groupthink of their peers (represented by the contemptuous jocks Ian and Max). The capacity to transcend these restrictive forces is shown to be an essential step in their growing maturity as they edge towards the responsibilities of adulthood.

A Clash of Class: Snobbery and Aspersions in *Pretty in Pink* and *Some Kind of Wonderful*

Though Hughes's antagonists were often played for laughs, this was not always the case. With the manipulative adversaries of *Pretty in Pink* (Howard Deutch, 1986) and *Some Kind of Wonderful* (Howard Deutch, 1987), his screenplays would present unprincipled foes who would wreak havoc in the lives of his ill-starred protagonists, examining the motivations behind their intrigues as well as laying the groundwork for their own downfall.

In many respects, *Pretty in Pink*'s Steff McKee (James Spader) and *Some Kind of Wonderful*'s Hardy Jenns (Craig Sheffer) are characters cut

Pretty in Pink. Director: Howard Deutch. Release date: February 28, 1986.

from the same cloth. Both are defined by the arrogance of wealth and influence, so suffused with ennui that their devious toying with the lives of others almost appears to be a source of vague amusement to them. However, the roots of their antagonism actually run somewhat deeper than their initial offhanded cruelties may suggest, and the foundation of their malice actually turns out to be as much driven by social factors as it is by psychological ones.

Whereas Steff seeks to drive a wedge between his similarly affluent acquaintance Blane McDonnagh (Andrew McCarthy), the heir to a successful electronics company, and kindhearted working-class student Andie Walsh (Molly Ringwald), his impulse is driven as much by his own unreciprocated attraction to Andie as it is by a desire to ensure that the social boundaries of their high school are respected. A kind of mutual loathing has grown up within the student body between the well-heeled but disaffected on one hand and the hard-working, ambitious blue-collar classmates on the other. An invisible and yet seemingly impenetrable schism divides these two groups, and Steff uses this rift to great effect in his attempts to convince Blane that any relationship he might be considering with Andie has the potential to permanently damage his social standing. So convincing is Steff's line of argument that he nearly succeeds in derailing the nascent romance between the pair, though eventually true love manages to overcome class consciousness, ensuring that the scheme fails and leaving Steff on the receiving end of a crowd-pleasing revenge courtesy of Andie's doting childhood friend Phil "Duckie" Dale (Jon Cryer).

If anything, the conniving Hardy Jenns appears even more vindictive, precisely because the character proves himself to be so innately poisonous to those around him. While he shares the upper-crust superciliousness of Steff and similarly has a sense of social class–based aloofness in common with his predecessor, his antipathy somehow manages to run even deeper. He demonstrates unremitting callousness to his beautiful but less prosperous girlfriend Amanda Jones (Lea Thompson), constantly being openly unfaithful to her in order to ensure maximum humiliation and demonstrate his self-proclaimed sense of social superiority. When she finally reaches the point where she can take no more, instead succumbing to the romantic advances of the artistic Keith Nelson (Eric

Stoltz), Hardy determines to destroy both their reputations in the most demeaning way possible.

As with *Pretty in Pink*, the insidious plotting of the heinous Hardy does not go according to plan; the two films share a house party scene which lays bare the immorality of their central antagonist, and in *Some Kind of Wonderful* Hardy's plan to see Keith assaulted and degraded for his interest in his erstwhile partner is disrupted by the surprising encroachment of some unexpected guests—a group which most definitely does not feature in Hardy's elevated social circle. While he is unable to bring about his planned vengeance against Keith, Hardy is nonetheless able to engineer the expulsion of Amanda from his clique, ensuring that she becomes *persona non grata* among her peers at the high school; the fact that Keith later discovers that his true affections lie not with the would-be socialite but with his long-term close friend and ally Watts (Mary Stuart Masterson) only further increases Amanda's sense of social isolation. This intensifies the audience appreciation of Hardy's treachery, and yet such is Amanda's personal growth as a result of his conspiracies we are left in little doubt that she has discovered within herself sufficient strength of character to overcome the challenges that face her and move ahead towards a future that is driven by her own capabilities, rather than the social privileges of those around her.

Both Hardy and Steff represent the languid heartlessness of the idle rich, delineating extreme examples of an amorality that has been allowed to fester in the lives of people who have never wanted for material advantage or had to work in order to achieve their goals. Indeed, the sense of outrage at the circumvention of their schemes by people they consider to be socially inferior becomes almost tangible. For Hughes, quality of character invariably outplays inherited privilege, and in both *Pretty in Pink* and *Some Kind of Wonderful* we see the power of romantic love overcoming the machinations of the influential and powerful, even suggesting that the latter are not truly capable of a loving and mutually respectful relationship due to their egotism and self-absorption. These malicious antagonists may not have been successful in their plotting but, Hughes is quick to emphasize, they fail as human beings too; in their desire to control rather than cooperate, and in valuing coercion over mutual social collaboration, they distance themselves from the prospect of forming any interpersonal relationship of value, suggesting that they have rendered themselves almost as isolated within their community as their intended victims would have been.

Burglars and Bunglers: Hopeless Criminality in *Home Alone*

Sometimes the villains in a Hughes screenplay were more than simply counterproductive or spiteful; on occasion, they may even tip into the domain of outright criminality. Yet felonious intent did not necessarily call for a dark portrayal of such characters; *Home Alone* (Chris Columbus, 1990) owed part of its appeal to the ineptitude of its two ham-fisted housebreakers, Harry Lime (Joe Pesci) and Marv Merchants (Daniel Stern). While the prospect of two burglars intent on robbing a home which is being defended by a single adolescent may have seemed like a nightmarish scenario in other hands, Hughes presents these massively incompetent criminals in such a humorous light that it becomes almost impossible to take them seriously—even if their unlawful objectives proved to be anything but casual in nature.

Typical of a Hughes production, *Home Alone* contains many witty references to classic films, and to wider popular culture, which made clear his intent through indirect means. Pesci's hapless burglar Harry Lime shares his name with Orson Welles's famous character in Carol Reed's seminal Graham Greene adaptation *The Third Man* (1949), though Hughes's character proves to be the diametric opposite of ving to be humiliated and wrong-footed at every turn. Likewise, the old gangster movie so beloved of young Kevin McCallister (Macaulay Culkin)—the fictitious *Angels with Filthy Souls*—is an obvious pastiche of Michael Curtiz's *Angels with Dirty Faces* (1938), which starred James Cagney and Humphrey Bogart. That tale of gangland violence and armed robbery was every bit as grim and uncompromising as Harry and Marv's supposed reign of terror Welles's sophisticated, conspiring operative in the Reed movie, protranspired to be plagued with blunders and missteps. However, Kevin's familiarity with the classic *film noir* is just one factor which foreshadows his eventual ability to run rings around the interlopers later in the movie.

Part of the reason Harry and Marv make for such an effective pairing, quite aside from the perfectly pitched performances from Pesci and Stern, lies in the surprisingly delicate balance with which their characters are presented. The home-defense scenario which plays out at the film's climax, where Kevin relies on an inspired variety of jury-rigged traps to repel the intruders from his family's house, may well be considered the movie's defining sequence, but there was more to this pair of amateurish burglars than was immediately obvious from their relentless injuries at Kevin's hands. At times they employ unpredictably clever techniques, such as Harry infiltrating the McCallister home disguised as a police officer in order to gain the family's trust under false pretenses, thus discovering more about their travel plans (and, by extension, when the house will supposedly be empty for a prolonged period). Marv similarly has delusions of grandeur which extend beyond the pair's abilities, conferring themselves the flamboyant title of "The Wet Bandits" as their criminal calling card to enhance their notoriety—a moniker which he fastidiously puts into practice by flooding the homes of their victims following a successful burglary. (This conceit later backfires on them spectacularly, of course, linking them to the sites of all their previous crimes.) And at the conclusion of the movie, when the bruised and beaten Harry and Marv angrily advance on Kevin (whose abundant reserve of defense strategies has finally run dry), we see a suggestion of danger hitherto only hinted at—an indication that they might just consider more serious retribution for the indignities they have suffered, if their threatened reprisals were not so swiftly curtailed by the timely appearance of unexpectedly protective neighbor Old Man Marley (Roberts Blossom).

Kevin's constant aptitude in outmaneuvering the ham-handed adults is part of the feature's ongoing charm—Harry explicitly mentions that he never reached sixth grade at school, suggesting that in intellectual terms the pair has met their match in the guilefully inventive youngster. Yet on every occasion that Kevin manages to thwart the plans of the Wet Bandits, the more determined Harry and Marv become to successfully rob the McCallister home, until it eventually becomes a matter of professional pride (and personal obsession) to them. Here, as in his screenplays for the later *Home Alone* sequels, Hughes is able to blunt the potential edge of a scenario which places a minor in peril by frequently emphasizing the immaturity and sheer idiocy of the antagonists. Core to the movie is a focus on Kevin's craftiness over the burglars' greed and disregard for the common good, ensuring that the innocent and virtuous prevail over those with nefarious ends.

Hughes would engage with unskilled and incompetent criminals in numerous later screenplays, among them *Career Opportunities* (Bryan Gordon, 1991), *Baby's Day Out* (Patrick Read Johnson, 1994), and *101 Dalmatians* (Stephen Herek, 1996), where again and again these ill-fated antagonists would face off against more honorable characters only to wind up much the worse for it. In Hughes's cinema, crime most certainly did not pay, and a running theme throughout the presentation of his various antagonists pointed to harsh punishment (along with considerable discomfiture and, most likely, a great deal of physical hardship) for those who threatened individuals, communities, or society in general in order to further their own selfish ends. The antagonists in a Hughes movie may have been smart and malicious or dimwittedly venal, but they all ultimately faced the same fate: whether they opposed the happiness of others or the rule of law, eventually justice would triumph over adversity.

14

We'll Settle Down, Have a Couple of Kids

John Hughes Films and Parenthood

There are few duties in life quite so vital as that of parenthood, and as a committed family man nobody knew this better than John Hughes. The family unit is a crucially important issue in a great many of his films, and his treatment of parental responsibility is subsequently one which is situated front and center. While Hughes often held up the nuclear family as a kind of domestic ideal, over the years he would eventually develop a more nuanced theme: namely that the family unit is what its members choose to make it, rather than simply a structure into which they are naturally born. Always aware of the potential pitfalls of parenting, Hughes's screenplays explored many different ways in which his characters handled the obligations of guiding children into adulthood. Some were dedicated, others neglectful, and a few would prove to be outright eccentric in their parenting methods. However, Hughes understood that how people react to the concerns of being effective parents can say a great deal about their character and personality, and also underscores their own concerns about aging and placing themselves in the hands of a new generation.

Living Vicariously: When Parental Decisions Turn Bad

Ironically enough, the Hughes movie which seems most intensely concerned with the ramifications of parental influence is one that actually features parents in little more than fleeting cameos. *The Breakfast Club* (1985) is a thoughtful analysis of how teenagers come to be shaped by the actions and expectations of their mothers and fathers, and though the central premise of the film may have been that all five teen characters are wildly disparate in their views and personal styles, each and every one of them has been profoundly influenced by their parents in one way or another. Whether they have been subjected to parenting which is imperious, neglectful, or even abusive, the manner in which they have responded to the attitudes of their respective guardians is very telling in each case. Over the course of the film's detention period, we witness the ways in which a high-handed father compels Andrew Clark (Emilio Estevez) to conform to his every whim, how the mistreatment caused by a sadistic parent leads to the delinquency of John Bender (Judd Nelson), and why the hothousing instigated by Brian Johnson's (Anthony Michael Hall) father and mother leads to his social awkwardness and lack of self-esteem. In a similar manner, the audience is shown the telling contrast between the upmarket Claire Standish (Molly Ringwald), whose apparent confidence and sense of entitlement is undermined by the unrealistically sky-high expectations of her mother and father, and Allison Reynolds (Ally Sheedy), whose own parents' exploits have predisposed her to react against mainstream expectations by embracing the diametric opposite of conventional customs. (It is left to the viewer's own opinion as to whether Allison is attending detention simply because she has nothing else to do, given that she broke no school rules in order to be there, or if her presence is instead due to the reason that she is actively avoiding her domestic situation by spending as much time away from her family as possible.)

By the end of *The Breakfast Club*, all five students have come to the conclusion that the most effective way to attain the happiness they have been seeking is to be true to themselves, allowing their individuality to win out against the false image they have been trying (and largely failing) to live up to. In realizing that they must embrace their own unique qualities, rather than allowing others—whether peers or adults—to define them on their behalf, the teens each come to appreciate the fact that the only way they can take full responsibility for their life is to assert their own control over it. In this sense, Hughes makes the point that it is entirely possible for a parent to have the very best of intentions and yet still fail in their responsibilities, if their purposes are not backed up with the ultimate aim of helping their offspring to lead a life of autonomy, fulfillment, and self-determination.

The Breakfast Club was not the only time a Hughes screenplay would highlight a parent's shortcomings through their absence rather than their on-screen actions. *Weird Science* (1985) follows a more conventional teen movie format, with Mr. and Mrs. Donnelly (Doug MacHugh and Pamela Gordon)—father and mother of the film's protagonist, the luckless Wyatt (Ilan Mitchell-Smith)—fulfilling the traditional roles expected of the genre. Not only does Wyatt's older brother—Bill Paxton's arrogant, intimidating Chet—constantly threaten him with the prospect of revealing his indiscretions to their parents, thus portraying them in the light of oblivious but instinctive authority figures, but the ramifications of risking the disapproval of the Donnellys loom large over the film's climactic house party sequence. The latter could, in the grand tradition of so many teen movies past, only have taken place during the parents' temporary absence from their home—the time-honored point where raucous celebrations take place, and much anxiety is generated when it comes to restoring the family's abode to its previous state of repair before the return of the aforementioned householders. Naturally, Hughes, being more than aware of these clichés, was fully prepared to turn audience expectation on its head, ensuring that—while viewers may have predicted certain outcomes—the actual reality wasn't always quite what they would have anticipated.

Sometimes, absent parents simply had to make the most of a bad situation, such as Peter and Kate McCallister (John Heard and Catherine O'Hara) of Chris Columbus's *Home Alone* (1990). Though devoted guardians of a large family, the McCallisters' unfortunate lapse of attention leads to their accidentally leaving their son Kevin (Macaulay Culkin) alone at home while they jet off on vacation to France. In line with Hughes's established thematic concerns, their neglect of the family unit—no matter how inadvertent—leads to the total disruption of their intended plans, with the vacation ruined, Christmas compromised, and every member of the family being inconvenienced in one way or another until the McCallisters are reunited once again. Thankfully for the estranged Kevin, the local community is able to step in to ensure his safety during his parents' absence, even when the neighborhood is virtually deserted—Roberts Blossoms's Mr. Marley provides much-needed backup just when

Kevin's seemingly inexhaustible supply of resourcefulness appears to be on the verge of faltering.

On other occasions, even an absent father could cast a very long shadow. The unseen Mr. Frye in *Ferris Bueller's Day Off* (1986) quite clearly holds his family in the iron grip of autocracy, and while he never actually appears in person throughout the movie his influence is nevertheless unmistakable. His domineering and oppressive methods of parenting have left his son Cameron (Alan Ruck) a nervous wreck, filled to bursting point with neuroses and complex inhibitions. Over the years Cameron has become convinced that he is little more than a possession to his father—simply another addition to the older man's collection of fine

Macaulay Culkin (1980–   ), popular child actor and, later, a musician and vocalist.

objets d'art and vintage automobiles, though appreciated somewhat less than these prized material rarities. Cameron's youth and early adulthood have been strictly governed by his father's attempts to control how he thinks and behaves, leading to a kind of unthinking conformity which has presented him with a joyless and deeply unadventurous life. Only a slow process of realization throughout a day away from his everyday monotony, where he experiences the metropolitan vibrancy of Chicago and the invigorating liberation of true independence, leads him to shake off the shackles of his father's despotic influence. Though Cameron's future beyond the climax of the movie is left uncertain, there is a real sense that, just as he has finally broken free of his father's manipulations and emotional cruelties, he is finally discovering that his adult life is a blank canvas of unforeseen possibilities—the very opposite of the inflexibly regimented life that had been marked out for him by others.

Bringing Up Baby: The Agony and the Ecstasy of Parenting

While many of Hughes's depictions of parenting were positive in nature, that is not to say that they were entirely free from dysfunction. Even the most well-meaning of mothers and fathers could sometimes make questionable decisions about their offspring's development due to the many challenges involved in bringing up a child and, while many of these choices would lead to humorous outcomes, sometimes a more thought-provoking consequence would result.

Perhaps most memorably, the beleaguered Jim and Brenda Baker (Paul Dooley and Carlin Glynn) of *Sixteen Candles* (1984) are responsible for much of the angst suffered by their daughter Samantha (Molly Ringwald) due to an ill-fated lapse in memory causing them to entirely forget the celebration of her sixteenth birthday. Neither Jim nor Brenda are neglectful or unapproachable parents; their oversight has been brought about entirely by the many arrangements necessary for the fast-approaching marriage of their elder daughter Ginny (Blanche Baker), which has had the effect of consuming all of their attention. Samantha, already miserable due to an unwelcome concoction of unrequited attraction and having to fight off unwanted suitors, faces major existential introspection upon discovering that—rather than planning a surprise to mark her landmark birthday—her own parents have managed to overlook the date completely. On learning their mistake, both Brenda and Jim are mortified and promise to do everything in their power to compensate Samantha for the hurt that has been caused, and such is her maturity that she is able to appreciate their gesture for its sincerity rather than allowing resentment to linger. However, it is also a mark of her personal autonomy and strength of personality that the pinnacle of her belated anniversary festivities comes not in the form of any parental gift but rather in the satisfaction of knowing that a relationship she had previously thought impossible has come to fruition when she joins new boyfriend Jake Ryan (Michael Schoeffling) in a tête-à-tête that is bathed in the light of her overdue birthday cake's candles.

An entirely different father-daughter dynamic is to be found in *Pretty in Pink* (Howard Deutch, 1986), where the low-spirited Jack Walsh (Harry Dean Stanton) is considerably more reliant on his daughter Andie (Molly Ringwald) and her positive mental attitude. Jack is an attentive but essentially listless parent, struggling to cope with his life following the departure of Andie's mother some years prior to the movie's events. Though he has difficulty motivating himself to seek paid employment, much less actually finding a job, Andie's hopefulness and her practical approach to living helps to keep him battling onward. Stanton and Ringwald present a touching and highly sensitive portrayal of family life throughout the film; the quietly despairing, melancholic Jack clearly values his paternal dynamic with Andie, seeking to support her as best he can while remaining painfully aware of his inability to fully provide for her. Yet, while the bright, hard-working Andie eagerly seeks to attract the attentions of affluent classmate Blane McDonnagh (Andrew McCarthy), she never blames her father or their economic circumstances for her inability to afford a comparable lifestyle to those of her school's more prosperous students, and it is this unselfish and self-effacing attitude that wins over Blane (and the audience's sympathies) in the end. As Jack himself points out, his bond with his daughter is a rare and valued thing indeed; while other teens are entering a period of rebellion and self-assertion, Andie seeks to provide emotional support for Jack just as he labors to provide a stable and loving home for his daughter—irrespective of their relative lack of income or material comforts.

Similarly supportive are Cliff and Carol Nelson (John Ashton and Jane Elliot) of *Some Kind of Wonderful* (Howard Deutch, 1987), who assiduously seek to ensure the best possible future for their gifted but intense son Keith (Eric Stoltz). Here, Hughes used his screenplay to examine the age-old debate about the commercial value of artistic endeavor; Keith has undeniable creative talents in various fields including music and visual art, but Cliff is keen for him to focus more intently on practical skills and academic results in order to win a place in college. To this end, a fund has been set up to cover the costs of his first year in higher education, including Keith's wages from part-time employment, and Cliff is adamant that his son will succeed in graduating, thus securing a greater earning potential as a result. However, Keith perceives a different path to adulthood; though he has no desire to disappoint his father, he also understands the value of art for art's sake and feels confident enough in his abilities to envision a future where he can use his creative skills to make a living for himself. This clash between his father's well-meaning but unwittingly dictatorial approach and Keith's implacable independence of thought underpins the conflict which lies between them. While there is no denying the obvious respect and affection which defines their relationship, similarly Cliff's unintentional heavy-handedness sets in motion the events which lead to his willful, free-thinking son's eventual rebellion in using the cash from his college savings to purchase a pair of diamond earrings to win the affections of the good-looking and much-admired Amanda Jones (Lea Thompson), with whom he is deeply smitten.

Not all of Hughes's parent characters are quite as experienced in the responsibilities of raising a child, however. In his film *She's Having a Baby* (1988), he explores the extensive consequences the arrival of a new infant can have on both a relationship and the individuals within it, emphasizing not only the potential pitfalls but also the comfort and happiness that can be generated by the family unit. The college-educated, middle-class protagonists—Jefferson and Kristen Briggs (Kevin Bacon and Elizabeth McGovern)—are both employed in responsible jobs; he in the world of advertising, and she in the corporate sector. They have an attractive suburban home, a stable relationship, and a bright future.

Logically, parenthood seems like the next step in their marriage ... and yet the prospect fills Jefferson ("Jake" to his friends) with no small amount of alarm. Believing that the duties of fatherhood will be so far-reaching that he will be forced to abandon his dreams of writing novels—in the same manner that he was once obliged to sacrifice his master's degree to ensure greater income generation for the couple's domestic needs—Jake panics that his long-term literary ambitions will have to be surrendered. Kristen, on the other hand, frets more about the actual conception of the child when the process becomes more complicated than she had initially expected. In the end, however, both partners come to realize that far from being the threat to contentment that Jake had feared, parenthood actually strengthens their marriage and makes them consider anew the depth of their relationship. While Jake is forced to recognize that plans for the future only rarely run smoothly, he also discovers that sometimes the reality—while often unexpected—can actually prove to be better than anticipated.

In Loco Parentis: Surrogate Parents and Family Duty

If Hughes did not shy away from the complications that could be involved in ensuring the safe and meaningful development of a child's early life, similarly he was unafraid to observe the phenomenon of parenthood through the actions and viewpoints of characters who were neither mothers nor fathers themselves. This approach was often quite revealing, and—though generally played for laughs—the evaluation of figures who were unaccustomed to the obligations of acting as a guardian to children could also cast an interesting light on how their psychologies operated.

The most famous surrogate parent in Hughes's filmography was almost certainly John Candy as Buck Russell, the eponymous *Uncle Buck* (1989) who is forced to step in and care for the children of his brother and sister-in-law Bob and Cindy Russell (Garrett M. Brown and Elaine Bromka) when Cindy's father suffers a heart attack, necessitating a journey from Chicago to Indianapolis as they seek to support him during his convalescence. Suddenly left with parental responsibility for Bob and Cindy's three children, Tia (Jean Louisa Kelly), Maizy (Gaby Hoffman), and Miles

(Macaulay Culkin), the free-wheeling Buck finds himself thrown in at the deep end—a long-term bachelor used to taking care only of himself, he is now forced to find effective ways of providing effective care for two precocious adolescents and an obstreperous teenager. Though initially he is deeply skeptical about this accountability, Buck throws himself into the task with zeal, eventually winning over not just the perceptive Miles and Maizy but the irascible, independently minded Tia. However, the film is at its most discerning when investigating the way in which, having three young lives in his charge, Buck is forced to re-evaluate his priorities in life. After the travails of looking after youngsters, attending elementary school meetings, and fending off the attentions of Tia's disrespectful teenage suitor, Buck begins to realize that perhaps the idea of settling down isn't quite as daunting a prospect as he had once considered—a new awareness which paves the way to a thaw in relations between his brother and himself, as well as opening a new chapter in his relationship with long-term girlfriend Chanice (Amy Madigan).

Interestingly, when *Uncle Buck* was adapted as a television series on CBS in 1990 the central scenario was tweaked slightly, with Bob and Cindy being killed in a tragic car accident, and Buck (now played by Kevin Meaney) being named as the legal guardian of his brother and sister-in-law's children. This development allowed for Buck to remain in custody of the kids for a longer period than the temporary arrangement that was explored in the movie, though in actuality the series was only to run for a single season. A further adaptation appeared on ABC between 2015 and 2016, this time with Mike Epps in the role of Buck. The plotline of the more recent TV remake differed slightly from its predecessor in the sense that on this occasion, Buck's brother Will (James Lesure) and sister-in-law Alexis (Nia Long) have not been separated from their children at all, but rather are compelled to invite Buck to stay at their home as a kind of emergency babysitter.

Hughes would return to the premise of an unwilling or unconventional adoptive parent later in his career, most notably in Peter Faiman's *Dutch* (1991) and his own *Curly Sue* (1991). The former would see a clash of personalities between the easygoing freewheeler Dutch Dooley (Ed O'Neill) and the pretentious snob Doyle Standish (Ethan Embry), the adolescent son of his upmarket girlfriend he has offered to drive home to Chicago from his elite private school in Georgia for the family's Thanksgiving celebration. The glacial relations between the two eventually warm after their long and eventful road journey, largely because the straight-talking Dutch is able to identify the desperate sense of insecurity underpinning Doyle's snooty arrogance in ways that have long defied the boy's father, aloof socialite Reed (Christopher McDonald). Doyle's eventual success in overcoming Reed's machinations and eventually forging a new nuclear family is mirrored in *Curly Sue*, in which drifter Bill Dancer (James Belushi) finds that he is so eager to provide a safe and stable home for his young traveling companion, Curly Sue (Alisan Porter), that he becomes increasingly willing to seek out new strategies to ensure her long-term protection. Sue has her own thoughts on the matter, of course, and eventually Bill is forced to acknowledge the fact that if he intends to help her settle down in one place, he too must reject his itinerant lifestyle. Thus, when he enters into an unexpected romance with lawyer Grey Ellison (Kelly Lynch), this alternative family unit eventually conforms to the structure of the traditional nuclear model—thus bridging Hughes's strategies of celebrating the strength, support, and flexibility of the family while also recognizing that social expectations were changing with regard to long-established judgments of parenthood and domestic life.

Hughes may have examined many different aspects of modern parenting throughout his long screenwriting career, but at the heart of his work was always an appreciation of the fact that being a truly successful parent relied on more than the provision of a secure and comfortable home environment, but also on ensuring that children knew they were loved, accepted, and listened to. While his depictions of parenthood may have varied from the dramatic to the out-and-out comical, his message of mutual understanding and respect was never to vary.

15

Dodge City Was Enough Fun for One Day

John Hughes, Patriotism and the U.S.A.

John Hughes was a proudly patriotic American who regularly demonstrated unmistakable love and deep respect for his country. He knew that the United States remained a land of opportunity, where social mobility could be a real force for personal empowerment and where freedom of expression is a bulwark of social justice against the abuse of power. However, he was not oblivious to the huge issues which were affecting America throughout the 1980s and '90s, and the social commentary of his films often reflected these concerns via subtle and thought-provoking approaches. Hughes's consideration of the perennial American values of life, liberty, and the pursuit of happiness were often expressed through his screenplays, celebrating the hopefulness and progressiveness of the United States even in the most uncertain of historical periods.

What's Past is Prologue: American Culture Past and Present in *National Lampoon's Vacation*

Even when a John Hughes screenplay was openly satirizing American culture, there was still no denying his obvious affection for his country. In *National Lampoon's Vacation* (Harold Ramis, 1983), the journey undertaken by Chevy Chase's Clark Griswold contains numerous nods to the epic road trips of the Route 66 variety for which America has become famous. Yet one of the most intriguing aspects of the Griswold family's cross-country excursion is not necessarily the many strange incidents they encounter (and, on many occasions, directly cause), but the subtle observations that are made about the cultural phenomena which fall under the lens of Hughes's microscope.

Perhaps most telling of all is the family's visit to Dodge City—actually a set on the Warner Bros. backlot in Burbank which bears little visual resemblance to the real historical Kansas town. Initially, the sequence seems like a deliberate juxtaposition of the earlier scene situated in a rundown section of St Louis, Missouri (actually a set constructed elsewhere on the same backlot), where Clark asks for directions and meets with immediate hostility, followed by outright theft. This, he emphasizes to his kids, is the result of social troubles and deprivation affecting many inner-city metropolitan areas, encouraging them to take careful note of the differences in comparison to their own, comfortable suburban home in Illinois. In Dodge City, the situation is quite different—the Griswolds are met by tourist-friendly employees who urge them to soak up the historical atmosphere of the Old West. Yet while this deliberate contrast may seem like a premeditated strategy to differentiate between the problematic social issues facing modern society and the idealized, demotic assurances of historical romanticism, in truth Hughes has something rather more subversive in mind.

By calling upon the great American mythology of the Wild West, the screenplay suggests a highly recognizable period of the United States' history—the visual tradition of countless westerns past. Yet here, nothing is quite as it seems. The Dodge City that Clark and his family visit is a tacky, sanitized facsimile, with precious little of the rustic character of the real thing. Here, the gregarious tour guide portraying Wyatt Earp is so halfhearted in his attempts at authenticity that he is seen wearing anachronistic jogging shoes; the town's famous saloon has largely been given over to an ostentatious gift shop; and Clark manages to antagonize a cranky saloon bartender to the point that the man breaks character and fights back in the closest thing that this desultory replica comes to the best tradition of Boot Hill. In spite of Clark's indefatigable attempts to shore up his family's enthusiasm, the trip to Dodge City is a muted warning on Hughes's part about the dangers of glorifying the past. There never was a golden age, he seems to suggest; instead, every generation is free to fully embrace their own personal goals, with no need to feel constrained

National Lampoon's Vacation. Director: Harold Ramis. Release date: July 29, 1983.

by the expectancies surrounding what has gone before. For a land of boundless opportunity, where endless innovation is a safeguard against cultural stagnation, nostalgia may be a source of comfort but it is also potentially a counterproductive phenomenon in an uncompromisingly progressive world. Thus, while Hughes expresses no major objection to celebrating past glories, he does so with the caveat that the high point of American culture is not in its past, but actually unfolding all around it; in a country dedicated to renewal and self-determination, new possibilities are there to be embraced rather than simply compared to the pioneer spirit of times gone by.

National Lampoon's Vacation contains many such comparisons between an idealized cultural history and a more world-weary present day. These include Clark bringing his family to Kamp Comfort—a somewhat austere campsite exhibiting precious little similarity to the carefree summer camps of his youth—and a sequence set in Utah's striking Monument Valley, where a case of mistaken direction and mechanical troubles lead to the Griswolds' temporary separation from civilization. Faced with the practicalities of being lost in the great outdoors, Clark discovers the reality to be considerably less romantic than the prairie-roaming western genre of popular culture. Time and again, the film makes the point that the best way to enjoy any cultural experience is to leave expectation to one side and embrace each incident anew; the endless misfortunes accompanying the family notwithstanding, disappointment tends to be the result whenever Clark's elevated anticipation of a location clashes with a rather more mundane reality.

Even on arrival at Walley World—the sprawling fictional Californian funfair which forms the endpoint of their journey—Clark finds that his hopes of an authentic theme park experience are skewered by the fact that the entire establishment is currently deserted, having been closed for renovation work. This leads to his final, slightly alarming manic episode in which he hijacks a nervous security guard named Lasky (John Candy) and forces him to allow the family to enact the full Walley World experience in spite of the fact that the park is closed to all tourists. Only an encounter with the park's owner, the brazenly Walt Disney–like figure of Roy Walley (Eddie Bracken), can save them from prosecution (and being in the sights of a SWAT team) when Clark explains his desperate desire to keep his family happy—he successfully explains that he wanted to provide the kind of experience that his kids would find genuinely memorable, while ensuring that he and his wife can relive something of the innocent fun of their youth.

National Lampoon's Vacation may not have sentimentalized the past, nor was it entirely pejorative towards the present day. Clark's single-minded determination to ensure that the Griswolds enjoy every aspect of their road trip may well be motivated by the altruism of a dedicated family man, but in terms of his stated aspiration to introduce his children to new cultural experiences it succeeds in ways that he was unlikely to have anticipated, becoming unforgettable for all the wrong reasons. Yet, far from seeming inadequate in comparison to the glory days of family vacations past, the Griswolds come together precisely because of the offbeat qualities of their time on the road, proving that the endlessly adaptive nature of American culture—in all its variety and resourceful-ness—is still alive.

Renaissance Man: Economic Recession, Unemployment, and Reinvention in *Mr. Mom*

Though it may have appeared at an early stage in Hughes's career, *Mr. Mom* (Stan Dragoti, 1983) contained some of his most thoughtful social commentary on the subject of the changing face of employment. Just as trying economic times were exerting new pressures on the manufacturing industries of the time, so too were new career routes establishing themselves which deviated from long-held norms. The world was changing, and individuals had little choice but to find new ways to adapt their occupational goals. Yet while Hughes was all too aware of the many challenges that this environment had the potential to bring about for individuals and families alike, so too did he realize that such was the initiative and inventiveness of America and its people, such social trials also had the capacity to shake people out of their respective comfort zones and allow them to encounter new modes of personal development.

Mr. Mom's central figure, Jack Butler (Michael Keaton), is an engineer employed by a Detroit automobile manufacturing plant. Morale there is at

Mr. Mom. Director: Stan Dragoti. Release date: August 19, 1983.

rock bottom due to persistent rumors of redundancies, and, sure enough, Jack—in spite of constant reassurances that his job is safe—soon discovers that he is to be laid off but may be recalled to the company at some undetermined future date. Though highly trained, he and his colleagues (such as Christopher Lloyd's mildly eccentric Larry) find themselves unable to track down new employment, and they discover the duties of domestic life to be humbling and unexpectedly demanding. The rigors of childcare and housekeeping present new challenges to Jack's otherwise-methodical mindset, which is shaken by the lurch from an orderly professional life into the unpredictability of running a home. Yet just as his wife, Caroline (Teri Garr), undergoes a similar culture shock as she settles into a new position within a city advertising firm, Jack eventually understands the need to acclimatize to the demands that have been placed upon him, comprehending the manner in which he had previously taken Caroline's role as homemaker for granted. While their unanticipated reversal of responsibilities causes both of them to re-examine their lives and attitudes, the suburban backdrop which frames Jack's travails ultimately offers him a source of reassurance and reflection, just as the metropolitan milieu of Caroline's professional advancement exudes allure and opportunity.

Hughes would riff on various cultural phenomena in the screenplay of *Mr. Mom*, drawing attention to the decline of traditional manufacturing and the rise of the "yuppie"— namely young urban professionals, that most distinctive of 1980s figures typifying conspicuous consumption. Emphasizing the parity between the two spouses, Jack never stops hankering for his place on the vocational ladder even when the despondency of unemployment hits him hardest, while Caroline remains devoted to her family no matter how demanding her job becomes or how rewarding the fruits of her labors prove to be. Both must overcome antagonists who bring about challenges from higher up the corporate ladder—Jack's devious manager Jinx (Jeffrey Tambor), and the senior advertising executive at Caroline's agency, the scheming Ron Richardson (Martin Mull). These adversaries both seek to use their authority for personal ends, even extending to adultery in Richardson's case, but their intrigues are eventually overcome by the strength of the family unit which triumphs in the face of the corporate environment's essential instinct towards self-interest.

While both Jack and Caroline are forced to confront new and not entirely comfortable experiences as a result of their respective changes in employment status, similarly the pair comes to share considerable individual development as the movie progresses. The notion of making personal sacrifices due to economic necessity was one to which Hughes would return in later years, not least in *She's Having a Baby* (1988), wherein Jefferson Briggs is forced to abandon his postgraduate studies (and the improved prospects which would have accompanied his graduation) in order to seek a steady wage in the here and now. Yet for the Butlers, their efforts would eventually pay dividends when, by the film's conclusion, Jack succeeds in winning back his engineering job at the manufacturing plant; and Caroline—whose cross-media advertising campaigns have won her both praise and profitability at the agency where she works—finds that her career continues to go from strength to strength.

Not everyone who experienced the economic turbulence of the 1980s would have been as fortunate as Jack and Caroline Butler when it came to finding new employment, and yet Hughes maintains a persuasive subtext throughout the narrative which underscores the fact that people who allow themselves to remain adaptable to changing circumstances are more likely to acclimatize to new economic realities than those who are simply content to act rather than react. With the digital boom and the seemingly unstoppable rise in fortunes of the financial and service industries, Hughes knew that America was opening a new chapter which would bring with it many new opportunities as well as considerable issues, but with characteristic sanguinity he seemed eager to accentuate the view that for those willing to rise to the challenges which met them there could be rewards as well as difficulties.

Movin' On Up: Class Consciousness and Social Mobility in *Career Opportunities*

Although *Career Opportunities* (Bryan Gordon, 1991) may be one of Hughes's lesser-known screenplays, it is notable for its subtle commentary on class and social mobility in a period where the old political certainties of the Cold War were being swept away in favor of the New World

Order which lay beyond. While the movie is deeply focused on social preconceptions and cognizance of class issues, it also contains interesting overtones of the same conflict between artistic creativity and utilitarian practicality that had made the action of *Some Kind of Wonderful* (Howard Deutch, 1987) so extensive in its concerns regarding vocation and personal fulfillment.

Career Opportunities is a tale of two disparate people who, while seeming diametrically opposed in their worldviews, find they have more in common than they had initially realized. Slacker Jim Dodge (Frank Whaley) is derided by his peers as a naïve fantasist who is more concerned with spinning tall tales than he is with the necessities of working life. After a string of dead-end jobs have ended in ignominious failure, expectations of Jim's future are at rock bottom among his family and the denizens of his town. Conversely, the well-to-do Josie McClellan (Jennifer Connelly) seems to have it all—wealth, connections, and apparently boundless opportunity. Yet, unknown to the townsfolk, her father, Roger (Noble Willingham), is an abusive tyrant who torments and intimidates Josie at every opportunity, draining her of self-esteem and optimism. Thus, these mismatched young adults find that they are unexpectedly unified over the issue of long-term aspirations: the easygoing Jim is too lackadaisical to make any kind of constructive plan for the years ahead (either personally or professionally); Josie finds that her own needs and desires have become distorted by the treatment she has received from her father, causing her to consider her prospects in terms of opposition to Roger's own wishes regarding her life.

The two are thrown together when Jim, forced into another seemingly short-term job by his father, meets Josie in the least expected of ways—he is working after hours when he discovers her on the premises of the store where he is employed as a security guard. Josie has just tried and failed to shoplift some items as an act of rebellion against her oppressive parent. They soon learn that more connects them than divides them: Josie seeks to run away from home to embrace her own independence safely away from Roger's sphere of influence, while Jim seeks to break free of the small town that has for so long defined and disregarded him. Whereas Jim's father is judgmental and disapproving, Josie's is cruel and controlling. Their dual realization that their lives are essentially being stifled by

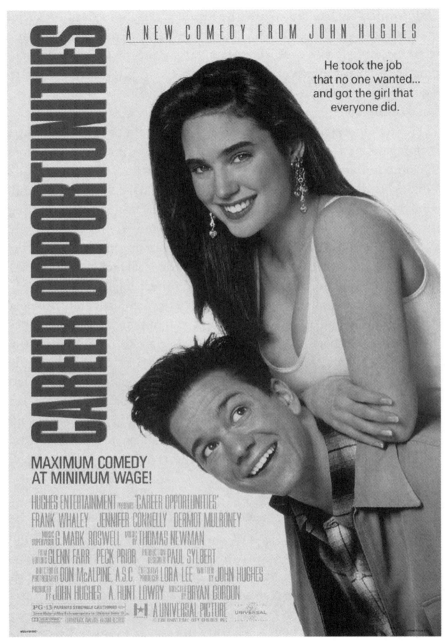

Career Opportunities. Director: Bryan Gordon. Release date: March 29, 1991.

the attitudes and actions of those around them lead to a course of action which sees them eventually managing—through a chain of unforeseen circumstances—to escape from the monotony and hypercritical atmosphere of their (fictional) small town in Illinois, heading instead for a new life in California.

A rare occasion in which Hughes would explore the darker side of the family unit, emphasizing the ways in which it can falter in its function when it fails to support all of its members, *Career Opportunities* nonetheless came with a positive message of self-improvement which gave proof that the American Dream was alive and well. The feckless Jim, whose indolence is matched only by a propensity for casual deceit that would have impressed even Walter Mitty, comes to comprehend that his worldview and appreciation of his own skills and talents have been unconsciously shaped by the uniformly low opinion of him which permeates the town. Similarly, Josie may well be regarded as popular and upwardly mobile by her peers, but she longs to cut loose from the assumptions surrounding her apparently perfect life while she remains miserable on account of her domineering father's machinations. Hughes uses their mutual plight to restate the point that America unwaveringly remains a country where personal determination can shape destinies provided individuals are willing to work towards a goal and have a single-minded resolve to reinvent themselves in order to fulfill it.

It is left to the audience to decide whether Jim and Josie's new life in Hollywood would prove to be sustainable, but, for Hughes, the upbeat conclusion to their tale reinforces the point that while Americans have an enshrined right to life and liberty, just as important is the pursuit of happiness. Like the Griswolds and the Butlers, who overcame adversity for the collective advantage of their families, the United States visualized throughout *Career Opportunities* was still a place which rewarded innovation and allowed for personal freedom, even when the burdens of everyday life seemed insurmountable. In this tale, everyone deserved a second chance at reshaping their existence for beneficial outcomes, and the self-improvement which resulted from this effort would prove that for Hughes, the Land of the Free would always retain its potent capacity for autonomy and regeneration.

16

A Neo Maxi Zoom Dweebie

Geekdom in John Hughes Films

In many John Hughes films, the ability to resist or even subvert conformity is held up as a virtue, and nowhere is this more clearly drawn than in his acclamation of geekdom. While the geek had long been a recognizable character archetype, the 1980s were a boon period for portrayals of the nerdy and unconventional. Characters such as Jaleel White's Steve Urkel on ABC's *Family Matters* (1989–1997), Marc Price's Erwin "Skippy" Handelman on NBC's *Family Ties* (1982–1989), Harold Ramis's Dr. Egon Spengler in *Ghostbusters* (Ivan Reitman, 1984), among many others, helped to ensure that the cult of geekdom erupted into popular culture to an unprecedented degree. Characters who are willing to overcome social expectation, or perhaps ignore it altogether, are often shown particular approval within a Hughes screenplay for their tenacious individuality, not least given his general tendency to celebrate those who are courageous enough to swim against the tide. While these characters often undergo major personal development in the course of the narratives in which they appear, their independence is inevitably reinforced rather than eroded by the process, and Hughes was to employ a number of methods in order to applaud, rather than humiliate, the underdog.

Big Man on Campus: "Farmer" Ted and *Sixteen Candles*

The geek, as a stock character, is often epitomized by certain stereotypical features. They may have a high degree of intellect, but find themselves outcasts due to an inability to interact with others on a social level—or, alternatively, being deliberately treated as pariahs by their peers when their skills or talent unintentionally lead to ridicule and derision. The uneasy relationship which exists between the geek and the mainstream (a desire to belong on one hand, yet a fundamental contempt for conformity on the other) was explored by Hughes in *Sixteen Candles* (1984) through Anthony Michael Hall's deeply idiosyncratic "Farmer" Ted.

Ted's self-appointed, slightly surreal nickname is never explained—he grudgingly says, after some time and to nobody's surprise, that he isn't really a farmer—but most telling is the fact that his character is simply credited as "The Geek" in the movie's closing credits. And yet, for all his function as a foil for Molly Ringwald's emotionally tempestuous protagonist Samantha Baker, the savvy Ted is never used simply as a straightforward target of anyone's joke. Rather, Hughes adeptly employs the character's relationships as a means to explore, via somewhat indirect methods, the tacit social structure which underpins high school life. Samantha—an intelligent, attractive, and independent young woman—desires Jake Ryan, one of the most popular and handsome students in town, but considers him vastly unattainable. Likewise, Ted—who is a complex miasma of false confidence and quick-thinking acumen—wants nothing more than to catch Samantha's eye, but knows that (by the standards of the system governing the school's social echelons) she is wildly out of his league. Thus, he embarks on a hopeless campaign of schmoozing and increasingly desperate chit-chat in his doomed attempts at winning her heart.

Though Hall was at the time best known for his appearance as Rusty Griswold in *National Lampoon's Vacation* (Harold Ramis, 1983), Ted was a world away from the weary traveler of the earlier film. A deeply inept lothario, the geeky Ted may at first have seemed like a victim of a deeply uncomplimentary system where submission to the conventions of the majority rules over all, but it is his knowledge of that rigidly codified structure (and presumably having fallen foul of it in the past) which leads to his ability to challenge expectations to his own advantage. While Ted fully expects to be abused by jocks and spurned by the popular, he still persists in furthering his ambitions regardless of his lack of success. But while he superficially appears to be a hormone-driven teenager, in truth Ted's gawkiness and character peculiarities are very efficiently counterbalanced by his more benevolent qualities. Genuinely empathetic and with a sincere ability to listen to the concerns of others, Ted reveals himself to be both a quirky, self-regarding geek and an oddly gallant figure; this duality is no more evident than during the movie's sequence at the auto shop, where Ted succeeds (and in an admirably brief period of time) to transform Samantha's sense of aversion and loathing towards him into an edgy but generally agreeable camaraderie. The way in which he puts this curiously compelling aptitude for persuasiveness into action is often surprisingly effective, not least when convincing Samantha to part with her underwear to allow him to triumph in a bet—a sequence which provides one of the movie's standout comedy moments (with the additional benefit of allowing Hall to deliver what is arguably the most surreal line in the entire screenplay: "Can I borrow your underpants for ten minutes?").

While the geeky outcast Ted and the much more widely accepted Samantha are initially cast as near-polar opposites, their trajectories eventually present themselves as surprisingly similar. Samantha's eventual romance with Jake is sealed not by her somehow being able to access his elevated social circle, but rather by him deciding that his feelings for her transcend the accepted conventions regulating who can date whom within the high school environment; in essence, the heart wins out over the unyielding bonds of social organization. But Ted's achievement seems all the more remarkable in that, through a chain of events that he could never have foreseen, he finds himself thrown together with Jake's former girlfriend—the glamorous Caroline Mulford (Haviland Morris)—who previously would never have considered being in the same room with him, much less be willing to converse at length. Though expecting to be rebuffed when she eventually shakes off the after-effects of too much alcohol, Ted is amazed when he discovers that his quick wit and compassionate manner sparks an attraction. In overcoming the strictures of the school's class system, his accomplishment (though unexpected) is arguably even more marked than Samantha's, and yet his romantic success somehow seems every bit as deserved as that of the movie's long-suffering protagonist.

While Ted's affiliation to geek culture is certainly more marked by his social inelegance than his academic prowess, his magnanimity and generosity of spirit prove that while he may not have conformed to the practices of the mainstream, he is still a companionable individual who strives to make the most of his rarefied status within the school's communal strata. Though he may have experienced an uphill struggle to achieve his goal of romance in spite of his outsider reputation, Ted nevertheless proves that, in a John Hughes movie, a sympathetic outlook and a skill for mental agility can triumph against both expectation and peer pressure.

The Awkward Fit: Brian Johnson and *The Breakfast Club*

Though only fifteen when he had portrayed "Farmer" Ted, Anthony Michael Hall's impressive comedic range was showcased still further the following year with his portrayal of bookish student Brian Johnson, one of the unwilling members of "The Breakfast Club" in Hughes's landmark 1985 movie of the same name. Cast into weekend detention as a punishment when a flare gun accidentally discharges inside his school locker, Brian soon finds that his reputation for academic excellence is no defense against the ire of Paul Gleason's fearsome Assistant Principal Richard Vernon, who views all of the students with collective derision. Yet Brian's range of pedantic interjections and a deep sense of insecurity within social situations forge the character into an intriguing complementary analysis of high school geekdom by Hughes, contrasting fascinatingly with the ostentatious showmanship and subtle self-doubt evinced in *Sixteen Candles'* Ted.

Perhaps of particular interest in a movie so acutely concerned with interaction between strangers, Brian's timid acquiescence quickly establishes the fact that he has major problems cooperating with—or relating to—students beyond his own self-restricted peer group. Interests and attitudes appear to be what divide the students, until they eventually discover an underlying commonality which brings them together and makes them realize their shared ground. But for Brian, who is already fighting the preconceptions that the others have about his geekiness and arm's-length approach to the school's mainstream, there is also a struggle to overcome his natural tendency to avoid socializing at all costs.

It soon becomes apparent that Brian's self-confidence issues have their root in repeated ill-treatment by the school's more popular denizens (evinced in the later confession made by Emilio Estevez's Andrew Clark, that the nerdy overachiever had suffered bullying as a result of his studious personality). However, as the detention session unfolds, it is also revealed that his strength of character has been all but subsumed by parental expectation and unrelenting pressure from within the educational establishment to put his academic prospects ahead of socializing and extracurricular activities. Hughes deliberately juxtaposes Brian's suppressed personality with the ultra-popular, opinionated Claire Standish (Molly Ringwald), whose snooty attitude masks a hidden desire to fully embrace her sense of personal individuality which has long been thwarted by her slavish compliance to the conventions of peer pressure within the school's social setup.

Because Brian's upbringing has brought little joy to his life, leaving him a virtual exile among the majority of his contemporaries, he is eventually forced to question how much of his scholarly manner is authentic, and to what degree it has become simply a persona he has adopted in order to satisfy the anticipation of those around him. Because the assumption is that someone with high academic ambition will conform to a particular set of recognizable characteristics, he has essentially sleepwalked into the very pigeonhole that his peers have prepared for him, allowing them to label and compartmentalize him to suit their own expectations. But Brian, of course, is much more than simply a walking collection of clichéd intellectual truisms; as the day progresses, his genuine character emerges more and more, eventually culminating in his being the member of the Breakfast Club who is chosen to pen the infamous short essay which is used by Hughes to open and conclude the film. This emblematic feature, which so ably typifies the movie's deep insight into the teenage psyche, was so much more than the ceaselessly emulated précis that it has since become. Though evocative of the students' recognition that they are each more than they thought they were, and also that they have discovered that more unites than divides them, it also clearly makes the point that Brian has finally found his own voice—no longer content to let others speak for him, he is now willing and able to put his talents for erudition to good use.

Brian was perhaps the most fully fleshed-out of all the geek characters to appear in Hughes's teen movies, and—although his story may have ended with less flourish than Ted's unexpected romantic success in *Sixteen Candles*—his personal growth was no less fulfilling. Indeed, while everyone who attended the Breakfast Club would find themselves altered as a result of the time they had spent in one another's company, Brian's gradual change of heart is one of the most poignant. As a result of the day's events, he is compelled not only to stand up for his own interests (in the time-honored tradition of other geek characters appearing in the teen movie genre), but he also learns to accept—and even enjoy—the company of others outside of his own narrow section of like-minded peers. There is a tangible, and pleasing, sense of someone beginning to emerge from a rigidly defined understanding of the world—governed by cerebral pursuits and unforgiving parental expectancy—to more fully comprehend the simple pleasures of friendship and social interaction. Perhaps most importantly of all, as Brian takes these first steps into a wider social sphere, Hughes makes clear the point that rather than eroding the distinctiveness of his personality, the once-meek student has begun to develop his worldview and his sense of belonging as he nears adulthood. This evolution is not simply a process of adaptation necessary to fit the new social reality that faces him, but an ongoing advancement in his attitudes that had lain dormant within him, merely waiting for the right conditions in which to flourish.

Together in Electric Dreams: Wyatt Donnelly, Gary Wallace, and *Weird Science*

For many modern audiences, the quintessential accoutrements of geekdom started to become widely available in the 1980s—namely digital devices such as the pocket calculator and the home microcomputer. In the sense that geeks were perceived to have a particular predisposition towards certain pastimes, and in many cases were typified by an in-depth knowledge of science, technology, and/or mathematics, the characters which most closely fit the mantle within Hughes's cinematic canon were the highly intelligent but socially inept Wyatt Donnelly and Gary Wallace (Ilan Mitchell-Smith and Anthony Michael Hall) of *Weird Science* (1985).

Though Wyatt and Gary's journey of personal self-discovery is discussed in detail elsewhere in this book, there is no denying that their geek credentials were most certainly in place and on display for all to see. Two well-meaning outcasts, their shared affinity for new technology and keen interest in science may have been a boon for their school grades, but their scholarly manner was anathema among their peers; cast adrift from the mainstream and unable to find romantic partners, they do at least have some solace in the fact that their like-mindedness has forged a strong friendship between them. Each understands all too well the other's frustration at being unable to integrate more comfortably among their fellow students, while their continued inability to attract members of the opposite sex ultimately leads them to find a scientific method of generating a girlfriend from nothingness, thus relying on technology to achieve what their ham-handed attempts at social interaction could not.

Many critics over the years have likened the events of *Weird Science* to a kind of teenage wish-fulfillment fantasy, and yet this would seem like a perfect fit for geekdom in general; in eighties popular culture, the geek was often to be found enthusing over fictional scenarios such as fantasy role-playing games, videogaming, and interacting over computer bulletin board systems (which in later years would evolve into home Internet access). Thus, escapism usually offered the geek a means of dealing with the world—if not necessarily reality—on their own terms, affording them an opportunity to establish a virtual persona which was bolder, more confident, and generally with a greater degree of social success than could ever be achieved in their actual everyday lives. Thus, when Kelly LeBrock's Lisa suddenly erupts into their lives, their initial reflex is to consider her a kind of simulacrum to be treated in the manner of a laboratory experiment—a grave error of judgment, which they soon realize when Lisa reveals that she is actually far wiser and more socially proficient than either of her unwitting creators.

Hughes deliberately contrasts his geek protagonists with Bill Paxton's pugilistic Chet. Arrogant, domineering, and forceful in all of his interactions, Chet makes his younger brother Wyatt's life a misery through his overassertive, boorish behavior, and in being situated as the movie's antagonist by Hughes it is easy to see why this bully was the perfect foil for the two meek central characters. While both Gary and Wyatt possess ample intellectual resources to outmaneuver the obtuse but muscular Chet, they live in fear of his constant belligerence and casual willingness to hold them for ransom with one threat or another, causing them to appear powerless in the face of his bellicosity. This was another steadfast trope of geek culture in the movies: namely, that geeks would generally be of weak physical stature and, in spite of considerable mental prowess, were in danger of being subjugated by enemies with less brainpower but greater physical strength. In Chet's case, however, his level of threat is accentuated by the fact that even the smart and emotionally aware Lisa is unable to change his behavior through reasoning or negotiation; it takes her to draw on her unexplained transformative powers to finally force him into a literal and psychological transfiguration.

Like "Farmer" Ted and Brian Johnson, Gary and Wyatt end the film with a considerable advantage: not only are they in a much stronger social position, with real partners rather than a technologically realized substitute, they have also retained all of the knowledge and skills that had marked them out as such formidable intellectuals in the first place. What Hughes is stressing, in effect, is that while intellectualism is of value in and of itself, without ample interaction with wider society it can become self-serving or redundant. Education and wisdom are two markedly different things, and only by working towards a life which combines learning with communication and collaboration can people get the most out of their talents and abilities. This theme may seem unusually profound when presented within a film driven by such knockabout fantasy, but considering Hughes's wider general preoccupation with community and cooperation, it was by no means out of place.

17

You Killed the Car

John Hughes and the Road Trip

Whether his characters undertake them intentionally or not, the road trip is a prominent fixture in several John Hughes films. While the Griswolds of the *National Lampoon's Vacation* movies were to take to the highways in a doomed attempt at finding recreation and relaxation, however, not all of Hughes's characters would prove to be quite so voluntary in commencing the epic treks which faced them. Featuring among them was the desperate cross-country journey of *Planes, Trains and Automobiles* (1987), which proved to be the antithesis of the carefree holiday meander, while the similarly Thanksgiving-themed *Dutch* (Peter Faiman, 1991) depicted a fraught, long-distance excursion that was typified by clashing personalities.

Yet far from simply employing the road trip as a straightforward plot device, Hughes approached the concept in a contemplative and multifaceted manner, reveling in the wide canvas of America's stunning landscapes while employing understated reflections on the characters who are traveling (and the locations they visit) with his trademark tongue-in-cheek restraint. For Hughes, the road trip was a means of broadening his characters' minds, as well as offering a chance to express his enthusiasm for lesser-seen parts of the United States.

On the Road Again: *Planes, Trains and Automobiles*

The film most closely associated with the Hughes road movie is *Planes, Trains and Automobiles*—a feature that did for long-distance commuting what *National Lampoon's Vacation* (Harold Ramis, 1983) had done for the family trip. The tumultuous but touching story of two totally dissimilar men who are thrown together during a disastrous journey from the East Coast to Chicago, *Planes, Trains and Automobiles* was to become one of the most beloved and immediately recognizable travel-based comedies of the 1980s. While much of its success lay in the beautifully observed performances of the mismatched protagonists (played with restrained sensitivity by stars Steve Martin and John Candy), Hughes's wittily insightful screenplay was at its best when depicting this peculiar journey as every seasoned traveler's worst nightmare, ensuring that everything that possibly could go wrong eventually does so, in one way or another.

The plot of *Planes, Trains and Automobiles* centers on the efforts of upscale advertising executive Neal Page (Steve Martin) to return from his office in New York City to his family in the Chicago suburbs in time for Thanksgiving weekend. What may seem like a straightforward task is immediately made problematic by an unexpectedly lengthy boardroom meeting, which delays his travel plans during one of the busiest times of the year. Missing his flight to Chicago, he is forced to book a seat on a later plane, but is less than enthused to discover that he is seated next to shower curtain-ring salesman Del Griffith (John Candy), an amiable but motor-mouthed traveling companion who soon drives him to distraction with his unremittingly prosaic attempts at conversation. However, bad weather forces the flight to divert to Kansas, leading the pair to find alternative transit via rail. But mechanical failure leads to their train breaking down in rural Missouri, so after being bused to St. Louis they are compelled to hire a rental car . . . only for that scheme to also go awry in the least anticipated of ways. Further mishaps await them as their agonizing journey brings them ever closer to their intended destination, but even at the conclusion of their unintended trek there is one last surprise for them to overcome—a hidden truth which leads the one-time antagonists to put aside their differences and, as a result of their shared ordeal, eventually become the closest of friends.

With astute and discerningly written dialogue, perceptive characterization, and many exceptional comic sequences (not least the desperation of Neal's profanity-ridden rant, directed towards Edie McClurg's disaffected car rental agent), *Planes, Trains and Automobiles* celebrated the best of America's "can-do" spirit by presenting situations which were unerringly relatable in order to delineate the relentlessly bad luck that plagues the main characters throughout their epic excursion. Just as the well-to-do Neal becomes ever further out of his depth, the endlessly sanguine and pragmatic Del somehow manages to pull increasingly innovative solutions out of his hat in order to drag them one step closer to home (albeit that his stratagems don't always go to plan, to put it mildly). While the film demonstrates considerable emotional heart, such is Hughes's lightness of touch that proceedings are never allowed to drift into out-and-out mawkishness. The friendship which begins to grow—albeit grudgingly—between the two is allowed to develop believably, remaining strangely affecting rather than ever seeming forced along to serve the purposes of the plot.

While the constant delays and diversions may make Del and Neal's journey an increasingly problematic one, they do at least allow Hughes and cinematographer Don Peterman to treat the viewer to some truly outstanding scenes. From the beautifully composed shots of rural Missouri's wide-open spaces to the frosty urban sprawl of New York, Hughes harnesses the wintry atmosphere of the Thanksgiving period with great assurance, making the two weary travelers' eventual arrival at Neal's welcoming Chicago home all the more satisfying as they finally emerge from the bitter cold into inviting warmth.

As the movie's title suggests, Hughes takes care to ensure that the action remains in constant motion, rarely lingering for too long in any one particular place. It is therefore creditable that Hughes's screenplay is able to constantly strike a careful balance between character-based comedy and genuine emotional gravitas, dispersing any pervasive sense of sentimentalism by concentrating—in the main—on the continuous erosion of Neal's patience and dignity on one hand, and the ineffably good nature of the endlessly practical Del on the other. As the plot unfolds, the audience gradually becomes aware that although these two men may seem vastly contradictory in their worldview, attitudes, and personalities, their goals exhibit more in the way of unity than divergence. Both are family-oriented and possess a compelling ethical core, meaning that even when they verge on the point of obsession in their efforts to reach Chicago by Thanksgiving, they never tip over into the realms of felonious or immoral behavior to achieve their ends. Similarly, Hughes slowly begins to build up the significance of the pair's efforts, forming the

Planes, Train and Automobiles. Director: John Hughes. Release date: November 25, 1987.

Herculean task of reaching the comfort of the Page residence into a rather eccentric form of quest narrative.

For all its emphasis on being separated from home and hearth in less-than-ideal circumstances, *Planes, Trains and Automobiles* rarely wavers in the warmth and geniality of its seasonal atmosphere, reveling in the down-to-earth levelheadedness of the great American public as the protagonists struggle against the clock to cross the miles which separate them from the endpoint of their journey. While the film gives Hughes an opportunity to progress his trademark theme of inclusiveness, underscoring Neal's eventual willingness to extend the bonds of his household to Del as an advancement of the Hughesian motif that the family unit has the capacity to extend beyond simple blood relations, we can also see elements of his premise that community spirit still had a relevant part to play in everyday life in the aggressively commodified 1980s. Whether in the presence of Del's network of friends and contacts encountered along this cross-country trip or in the good-natured targets of his resourceful and highly creative sales techniques, we are left in no doubt that the community-oriented America championed by Hughes in so many of his Illinois-based movies was here being extended across the United States, and with highly effective results.

A Turkey at Thanksgiving: *Dutch*

Hughes entered a particularly prolific phase of his career during the early years of the 1990s, but not all of his films during this period were to be equally successful with either critics or the public. The Robert Weissman–produced comedy-drama *Dutch*, which featured a Hughes screenplay, is generally regarded to be a rare misstep. And, indeed, the movie has come to be considered as something less than the sum of its parts.

On paper, *Dutch* looked like a sure-fire winner. Its director, Peter Faiman, had helmed the hugely profitable fish-out-of-water comedy *Crocodile Dundee* (1986) some years earlier, while the film's charismatic star, Ed O'Neill, had achieved considerable popularity for his role as the laconic, perpetually hassled family man Al Bundy in Fox Television's long-running situation comedy *Married . . . with Children* (1987–1997).

However, the film was subjected to the criticism which had accompanied some of Hughes's other movies at the time, namely that themes and plot devices familiar from his earlier screenplays were to re-emerge—albeit within different settings—in overly predictable ways.

Dutch concerns the travails of the cheerful but mishap-prone Dutch Dooley (Ed O'Neill), who travels to Atlanta, Georgia, in order to collect his girlfriend's obnoxiously snooty son Doyle Standish (Ethan Randall) from an exclusive boarding school and drive him home to Chicago to reunite with his mother for Thanksgiving weekend. This deceptively simple objective is complicated at every level. Doyle blames his mother, Natalie (JoBeth Williams), for the divorce from his father, Reed (Christopher McDonald), an aloof grotesque whose stuck-up pretensions have rubbed off negatively on his offspring. Thus, Doyle resents Dutch not only for his romantic entanglement with Natalie, but because the working-class values Dutch champions are anathema to the youth's ostentatious worldview. However, when Dutch's car is rendered un-roadworthy due to Doyle's machinations, the pair is forced to find alternative means of getting back to Chicago in time for the holidays.

Just as Hughes's script for *Career Opportunities* (Bryan Gordon, 1991) had been censured in some quarters for its thematic similarities to the central premise of the previous year's *Home Alone* (Chris Columbus, 1990)—the film's unlikely hero is forced to defend his workplace from inept burglars, rather than a lone child protecting his home from the same—so too was *Dutch* condemned by critics for the movie's many overt similarities to *Planes, Trains and Automobiles*. Whereas that well-received earlier feature had focused on the mismatched dispositions which existed between the aloof but successful businessman Neal and kindhearted traveling salesman Del as they are compelled to work together, *Dutch* placed greater emphasis on class conflict.

While the combination of O'Neill and Randall (now better known by the stage name Ethan Embry) was quite different in tone from the earlier acclaimed pairing of Steve Martin and John Candy, the film's similarities did little to rekindle the mix of interpersonal chemistry and inspired situations which had so distinguished *Planes, Trains and Automobiles*. The introduction of a somewhat unsubtle exploration of homelessness and the ability of extreme poverty to reshape life expectations and social

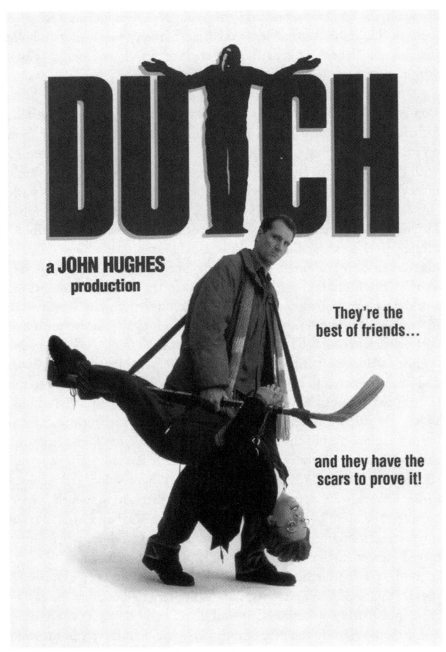

Dutch. Director: Peter Faiman. Release date: July 19, 1991.

relationships was widely disparaged for its heavy-handedness, especially coming at a period when the theme had already been comprehensively explored by riches-to-rags parables such as *Trading Places* (John Landis, 1983) and *Life Stinks* (Mel Brooks, 1991).

Though *Dutch* received the disparagement of reviewers for its main characters' general lack of likability, and indeed the unconvincingly abrupt conversion of the pretentious, high-and-mighty Doyle into a model of even-handed tolerance by the film's conclusion, the movie did achieve some muted approval for O'Neill's high-energy performance, which seemed to cover the entire gamut of human emotion throughout the narrative. *Dutch* may not be the best-regarded example of Hughes's filmmaking in the nineties, but it nonetheless retains a loyal core of admirers. However, due to the overwhelming and ongoing popularity of the earlier, near-identically themed *Planes, Trains and Automobiles*, the less well-known *Dutch* has since become something of a curio.

Burning Rubber: John Hughes and the American Road-Trip Movie in the Eighties

Road trips were big business in the 1980s, with travel forming the central theme in numerous movies, many of them very high-profile in nature. While the Hughes-scripted *Planes, Trains and Automobiles* and *National Lampoon's Vacation* would both become perpetually aligned with road-trip cinema, the eighties offered up a many-sided take on travel, which would see different genres such as comedy, science fiction, and emotional-drama tackling the issues presented by life on the open road.

Just as *Planes, Trains and Automobiles* had focused on the potential for a long journey to bring people together—even if the aforementioned travelers had been wildly antipathetic towards each other prior to undertaking the trip—so too were other road movies of the 1980s to consider the ability of dissimilar individuals to bond as a result of a difficult excursion. Movies such as the midlife-crisis comedy *Lost in America* (Albert Brooks, 1985), the musically themed *Crossroads* (Walter Hill, 1986), the coming-of-age drama *Stand by Me* (Rob Reiner, 1986), the romantic crime-farce *Something Wild* (Jonathan Demme, 1986), and fugitive comedy-drama *Midnight Run* (Martin Brest, 1988) all centered on the way in which characters who are in some way disparate or who demonstrate contradictory traits ultimately end up relying on each other to overcome the challenges presented by an eventful long-distance trek. Perhaps the greatest exponent of this type of film, beyond *Planes, Trains and Automobiles*, was Barry Levinson's Academy Award–winning *Rain Man* (1988): a tale of two brothers—played by Tom Cruise and Dustin Hoffman—who find that a fraternal bond grows between them as a result of an unanticipated cross-country expedition. The film did much to raise public awareness of autism, which until that point had been a poorly understood and rarely discussed condition, and won great praise for the subtlety of its characterization.

While more dramatic road movies were in evidence throughout the eighties—not least the harrowing emotional-drama *Paris, Texas* (Wim Wenders, 1984) and the disquieting portrait of drug-related crime-and-addiction *Drugstore Cowboy* (Gus Van Sant, 1989)—these were tempered by lighter approaches to journeying which blended offbeat wit with astutely rendered character interplay, such as Jim Jarmusch's thematically linked (yet stylistically varied) films *Stranger Than Paradise* (1984) and *Down by Law* (1986). Though the quirky chemistry of lead characters during a stressful trip would come closer to the underplayed depth of Hughes's work, the unabashed entertainment value of Hal Needham's knockabout comedy *The Cannonball Run* (1981) (and also his less critically lauded sequel, *Cannonball Run II*, in 1984) had more in common with the rambunctious chaos of *National Lampoon's Vacation* than the thoughtfulness and understated empathy of *Planes, Trains and Automobiles*.

Other road movies of the 1980s covered such seemingly incongruent ground as the romantic-teen-comedy *The Sure Thing* (Rob Reiner, 1985), science-fiction drama *Starman* (John Carpenter, 1984), and the Great Depression–era historical *Honkytonk Man* (Clint Eastwood, 1982). While at face value these films may have appeared to belong to very different generic traditions, all were unified by a common theme of overcoming differences in the pursuit of a shared goal. This premise was one Hughes would draw upon several times in his career, and not solely in films—such as *Dutch* and *Planes, Trains and Automobiles*—which dealt exclusively with travel-related concerns.

While the theme of overcoming adversity through mutual effort ran through much of Hughes's work, albeit often manifesting itself in very different ways, rarely was the sense of collective triumph over misfortune quite so acutely drawn as in his road-trip movies. In his high-profile engagement with the genre, he was to establish commonality not just with a long-running generic tendency in American cinema but also one which was continuing to prove commercially popular and critically successful in the film industry of the 1980s. This actually served as an interesting metaphor for his approach to movie production in general, namely his ability to create works that were simultaneously highly relevant to modern audiences and yet strikingly traditional in the basis of their subject matter. A Hughes road movie may have drawn on time-honored conventions of the genre, but they remained stylish and in tune with the eighties zeitgeist in ways which never allowed audiences to doubt their assertive modernity, not even for a second.

18

You Look Good Wearing My Future

Eighties Youth, the Cold War, and Uncertain Times in the Cinema of John Hughes

Teenagers in John Hughes's movies were growing up against a back-drop of shifting cultural mores, challenging economic conditions, and the atomic peril of the Cold War. It is not surprising, then, that the timeless anxieties which surround the inevitable act of growing into adult-hood seemed all the more immediate when playing out in this environment of uncertainty and geopolitical upheaval. Even Hughes's more confident protagonists, such as the urbane Ferris Bueller, were acutely aware that their future was largely at the mercy of powerful social and cultural forces they were incapable of reshaping, and their reaction to these influences affected their views on life in profound and wide-reaching ways. The manner in which the political environment of the 1980s influenced the characters of Hughes's films was frequently insightful, not least in his cycle of teen movies, and the techniques he employed to relate his protagonists and sup-porting characters to the erratic and unpredictable world around them were as subtle as they were reflective.

Living in the Shadow of the Bomb: The Cold War and the Cinema of John Hughes

Given the generally optimistic themes of mutual collaboration, family unity, and community cohesion which run through so much of Hughes's screenplays, it seemed almost ironic that so many of his best-remembered movies were produced within the precarious environment of a particularly glacial period of the Cold War. While the conflict had been running from the period immediately following World War II—epitomized by Winston Churchill's famed "Iron Curtain" speech in 1946—the Cold War entered a stage of renewed tension from the late 1970s onwards, and proved to be an issue of immense geopolitical importance for the presidencies of Jimmy Carter, Ronald Reagan, and George H. W. Bush in particular. While hostilities with the Soviet Union had fueled popular culture for decades, with stories of espionage and counterintelligence most prominently influencing the boon in spy movies throughout the 1960s and early 1970s, the deepening crisis of Soviet intervention in Afghanistan, and a sharp rise in military expenditure by both superpowers—particularly during the early years of the 1980s—caused a widening in the themes explored by Cold War cinema. Movies such as *Firefox* (Clint Eastwood, 1982), *Invasion U.S.A.* (Joseph Zito, 1985), and *Red Dawn* (John Milius, 1984) deal with familiar tropes of either intelligence gathering, surveillance within enemy territory, or a Soviet incursion of one kind or another onto American soil. However, there was also a resurgence in films dealing with the issue of nuclear conflict, including *WarGames* (John Badham, 1983), *The Manhattan Project* (Marshall Brickman, 1986), and *Miracle Mile* (Steve De Jarnatt, 1988), all examining the impact of atomic-attack scenarios—some narrowly averted; others shown in all their horror and devastation.

Until the fall of the Berlin Wall and the collapse of the USSR in the early nineties, the Cold War continued to cast a very long shadow over popular culture as much as it did on world politics, with the real and potential ramifications of the conflict winding through music, art, literature, and television just as much as it impacted on the world of cinema. Hughes was fully aware not only of the intensified friction of this ideological battle between the superpowers, but also realized all too well the effect that it was to have on the characters in his various movies. While explicit recognition of the Cold War tended to take a back seat in his movies, its presence was never entirely absent—as was, of course, the case for anyone who was living through the 1980s—and, as such, Hughes tended to deal with its effects in an indirect and often understated way.

For a filmmaker who generally advocated the virtues of overcoming problems by talking them through, and bringing people together in the furtherance of the common good, the apocalyptic potential of Mutually Assured Destruction seemed like anathema to his generally optimistic, upbeat worldview. But in an era when many teenagers were genuinely questioning whether they would live to see adulthood, Hughes seemed almost defiant in his depiction of young adults as witty, self-aware, and well-rounded, his carefully considered amalgam of youthful ingenuousness and worldly sophistication proving to be the ultimate expression of "life goes on," in spite of the dangers of atomic conflict, which seemed greater than at any point since the Cuban Missile Crisis of 1962.

No Tomorrow: Ambiguous Futures in *Ferris Bueller's Day Off*

While several of Hughes's teen movies considered the reactions of his characters towards the uncertainties of adult life, few would focus on the wistful contemplation of the ephemeral nature of youth more than was the case in *Ferris Bueller's Day Off* (1986). All the more noteworthy due to the film's general tone of lightheartedness and its themes of freedom and self-determination, the way in which Hughes expounds upon the reasoning behind Ferris's aversion to the hard work of high school—and the high value that the king of slackers places on the relationships which matter to him—is as remarkable as it is oddly poignant.

Running parallel to the slow-burning realization of his friend Cameron Frye (Alan Ruck) that his never-seen father has been a damaging and limiting influence on his life choices, Ferris's own ruminations on teen life are both enlightened and far-reaching. Whereas the opening scenes of the movie follow Ferris (Matthew Broderick) as he explains his life philosophy—which perhaps inevitably is framed by his pursuit of staying away from school as often and for as long as possible—the levity of his early musings about embracing the possibilities of life rather than mechanically conforming to the unthinking conventionality of society are sharply contrasted with his weightier considerations nearer the conclusion of the film.

Because the events of *Ferris Bueller's Day Off* focus largely on the attempts of Ferris, Cameron, and Mia Sara's Sloane Peterson to enjoy themselves on a barnstorming tour of Chicago, cramming in as many notable moments into a period of just a few hours, while trying to avoid the dogged pursuit of Ed Rooney—the school's fearsome but clueless dean of students—the unexpected tonal shift near the end of their journey seems all the more contemplative. As Cameron mentally works through his deeply rooted psychological issues, communicating the scale of his emotional problems to his two concerned friends, Ferris takes the time to explicate some difficult truths to the audience. Though he feels a moral imperative to make the most of the fading days of his teenage years, doing his level best to avoid the suffocating tedium of high school as much as possible, his efforts speak of a more innate need—one which will require greater determination than simply that which is involved in avoiding an obsessive high school administrator.

Reluctantly admitting to himself (and, by extension, to the audience) that he feels as though he must bear some responsibility for the discomfiting torrent of emotions that has bombarded Cameron throughout the day, given his insistence on borrowing the ultra-rare Ferrari owned by his anxious friend's tyrannical father and the internal turmoil that ensues as a result, Ferris feels certain that his freewheeling outlook on life is at least partly to blame for the turbulent end to his day off. However, the reason for his singular determination on having the day off—even in spite of an already-lengthy record of absence from school during the current term—is not simply a question of seeking to avoid a succession of tiresome classes and the wearisome delivery of uninspiring teachers. Ferris knows with painful clarity that such opportunities are soon likely to become few and far between; as only a few months of high school lie ahead before his graduation, there is a good chance that the bonds of friendship which connects him to Cameron—and his romantic ties to Sloane—are likely to be strained to breaking point thereafter. All of them are likely to apply for short-term jobs over the summer, and then Ferris and Cameron will be headed for college—with no guarantee that either of them will be attending the same institution, or that they will even be within easy traveling distance of each other. Likewise, as Sloane is a year younger, she has still to get through her senior year before she too can graduate; Ferris is

Ferris Bueller's Day Off. Director: John Hughes. Release date: June 11, 1986.

unsure if there is any way that even he, with his seemingly endless capacity for clear-headedness and inventive solutions, will be able to keep their relationship healthy while they are living so far apart.

This key sequence is of vital importance to the movie, as it is one rare occasion when Ferris admits (albeit grudgingly) that there are particular aspects of life that are beyond his ability to either outthink or stage-manage to his advantage. Throughout the film, we see him regularly manipulate and outsmart his parents, the school authorities, and even the public at large, but the inevitability of aging and the encroachment of adult responsibilities are unavoidable phenomena that cannot be outmaneuvered. Ferris understands all too well that there is a substantial risk that, in spite of his best efforts, he will drift apart from even his closest acquaintances as a result of the forthcoming new phase in his life—a development which rattles even the unflappable individualist with its threat of unfamiliarity. Instead of simply lamenting the inescapability of what is to come, however, he decides to make the more life-affirming decision to make the most of the time they still have in one another's company, in the knowledge that his friends will likely have drawn the same conclusions about the future as he has done.

While the uncertainties of the Cold War are never mentioned, a sense of social upheaval and cultural flux can be detected at a sparing handful of points throughout *Ferris Bueller's Day Off*. This is particularly evident during the Von Steuben Day Parade sequence, where Sloane and Cameron discuss their respective futures and come to the conclusion that the only assurance they can cling to is the prospect of college. But neither can settle on a subject that interests them enough to maintain their attention for the duration of their degree, and from this basis they both begin to question the validity and usefulness of a college education at all. In one seemingly lighthearted stroke, Hughes draws attention to the fact that the old certitudes of the postwar period were starting to be challenged by an aggressively postmodern culture of unpredictability which was being driven by technological advancement, economic and industrial changes, the early digital revolution, and, of course, the geopolitical tensions of the Cold War itself. Ferris and his friends are aware of the fact that they are growing up in a very different world to that which had been experienced by their parents, and in addition to the natural trepidation about emerging into adulthood they are also experiencing a sense of apprehension regarding the kind of shape their futures would take.

As the conclusion of the movie proves, Ferris's day off has a lasting effect on all three who take part in it. Cameron realizes that as a result of his actions in accidentally destroying his father's Ferrari, he must finally face up to the autocratic figure who has oppressed his development, ensuring that—whatever the outcome of that confrontation—his life has irrevocably changed. For Sloane, the prospect of ending her romance with her unique boyfriend encourages her to reaffirm their shared affection, turning his earlier off-the-cuff joke about marriage on its head by stating with considerably greater conviction that one day she really does intend to tie the knot with the impulsive Mr. Bueller. And Ferris himself, though having been forced to confess that even *he* lacks the capacity to wrangle his way out of everything that life throws at him, seems content to, at the very least, give it his best shot anyway—providing that his famous luck holds out.

The ability of Ferris and his friends to evade Ed Rooney and hoodwink more or less the entirety of their local community proved to be a potent mixture of inspired improvisation and blind luck, but the audience is left with the unshakable sense that if anyone can negotiate the uncertainties of a rapidly changing world then it is the savvy Ferris Bueller. Representative of a generational need to adapt quickly and convincingly to newly emerging situations, Ferris was not only the epitome of fast-thinking extemporization, but proof that while the future he faced was an ambiguous and unpredictable one, Hughes was nonetheless confident that there would indeed still be a future worth living in.

Light at the End of the Tunnel: Social Changes in *Pretty in Pink* and *Some Kind of Wonderful*

By the time of the late eighties, the climate of the Cold War was beginning to change. The appointment of Mikhail Gorbachev as the general secretary of the USSR's ruling Communist Party was to bring with it the introduction of various wide-ranging reforms, including *perestroika* ("restructuring") in 1987—an attempt to reorganize the Soviet Union's economy, including the arrival of private business ownership—and *glasnost* ("openness"), which heralded greater press freedom and loosened restraints on contact with other nations. Gorbachev's acknowledgment that the Soviet economy had essentially stalled by the mid-eighties, and that drastic measures were necessary to stave off existential threats to the USSR's very survival, eventually led to a period of rapprochement with the U.S., which would have seemed all but unthinkable a few years earlier. By the end of the decade, at the Malta Summit in December 1989, President Bush and Premier Gorbachev jointly declared that the Cold War was now at an end. Shortly afterwards, the Soviet Union would cease to exist as a political entity altogether.

While the hostile climate of the conflict had subtly influenced Hughes's filmmaking in the earlier half of the decade, so too would the change in temperature of the Cold War have an effect on the later features in his teen-movie cycle. The doubts and reservations voiced by the members of *The Breakfast Club* (1985) towards their collective futures would have resonance with teenagers of any recent generation, but the specter of nuclear conflict added a further degree of pathos to their considerations. Likewise, when the unexplained powers of Kelly LeBrock's Lisa transform Wyatt's living room into a silo containing a Pershing II intercontinental ballistic missile in *Weird Science* (1985), the presence of this nuclear weapon is used as a shorthand to delineate the gravest of danger; even in a comedic situation (appearing at it does at a raucous teenage party), the threat of atomic annihilation was never too far away.

While the two films in Hughes's teen-movie cycle to be directed by Howard Deutch, *Pretty in Pink* (1986) and *Some Kind of Wonderful* (1987), are most regularly considered in terms of their class consciousness, the approach of both features was also influenced by the gradual changes in cultural awareness of the altered trajectory of the Cold War. Like *Ferris Bueller's Day Off*, released in the same year, *Pretty in Pink* would emerge at a point between the heightened nuclear paranoia of the early eighties and the détente which marked the decade's conclusion; the characters were aware of the geopolitical climate and the insecurities surrounding its status, and were preparing for adulthood in the shade of bipolarity between two superpowers with diametrically opposed ideologies. Whereas Ferris Bueller was content to brush off topics such as European socialism as distant factors which were essentially irrelevant to his worldview (during a memorable diatribe while he showers), the oppressiveness of totalitarian communism was a rather more difficult phenomenon to ignore, and for wealthy characters like Andrew McCarthy's Blane McDonnagh and James Spader's Steff McKee, the opulent lifestyles they lead would have been unthinkable under the auspices of a Marxist-Leninist government. Indeed, in the case of the film's protagonist Andie Walsh (Molly Ringwald), her success in winning Blane's heart—in spite of the machinations of his snobbish friends, who oppose the relationship—is tacitly portrayed in terms of her social elevation. A hard-working and assiduous individual, Andie's job at record store Trax helps to support her family given the inability of her father Jack (Harry Dean Stanton) to find regular employment, and she counterbalances her part-time occupation with high school studies—a reminder of the traditional correlation between educational achievement and social advancement, which made the characters' cynicism of college in *Ferris Bueller's Day Off* seem particularly impactful.

We are left in no doubt that Andie's accomplishment at the end of *Pretty in Pink* is a distinctively American triumph. Her romance with Blane may well be an indicator of her social progression, but she succeeds only as a result of her industriousness, innovation, and virtues of character—all merits which had been hailed as defining American characteristics since the earliest days of the republic. Hughes's devoted patriotism was never in doubt, but when cast against the conspicuous threat of international communism (made all the more perceptible due to the Soviet occupation of Afghanistan throughout the eighties) his spotlighting of the kind of American freedoms and ambitions that could never have been possible under the restrictive state control of the USSR seemed all the more heartfelt.

While it is left to the viewer to decide whether Blane and Andie's love would stand the test of time, the fact that the relationship offered both partners an equal share in emotional fulfillment and economic prosperity seemed like the perfect antidote to the ominous political pressures of the Cold War. With the following year's *Some Kind of Wonderful*, however, Hughes's screenplay was to offer something quite different. As the Soviet

Union's isolationism and focus on brinkmanship was starting to wane, critics were tentatively beginning to question whether the decades-long hostility between the U.S. and USSR was finally set to become a thing of the past. While this invariably led to relief that a global nuclear exchange now seemed a less likely possibility, there were also reservations over the kind of shape that the world may take in the event that a conflict which had defined the latter half of the 20th century was set to come to an end. Although the constant threat of atomic warfare had injected a degree of insecurity into world affairs, the removal of the persistent hostility between East and West brought with it a new kind of instability; one which was to reshape international affairs for decades to come.

The characters of *Some Kind of Wonderful* are shaped by a quite dissimilar geopolitical climate; while the Cold War had not yet ended, its conclusion certainly seemed like a more plausible eventuality. The main players are therefore not as closely defined by the dynamics of the conflict as those of *Pretty in Pink*. Like Andie Walsh, protagonist Keith Nelson (Eric Stoltz) is creative and diligent. However, the fulfillment of his efforts differ from his predecessor in the sense that they are not reliant upon social advancement, but rather on a more complete understanding of his personal potential. By spurning Lea Thompson's Amanda Jones in favor of long-term platonic friend Watts (Mary Stuart Masterson), Keith essentially turns his back on the expectations of progression beyond his current situation within the class hierarchy, shunning any attempt to encroach upon the social territory of the conceited Hardy Jenns (Craig Sheffer) because he rejects any attempt to restrict himself within the confines of a classification that has been constructed by others. Yet while his father, Cliff (John Ashton), is firmly focused on encouraging Keith into college in the assumption that academic success will be the key to a more prosperous future, the younger Nelson is far from convinced that this is the case. Whereas the three main figures of *Ferris Bueller's Day Off* were skeptical of the merits of further education due to their sense of disconnection, Keith's cynicism seems to stem more from a sense that inherited privilege invariably undermines scholarly achievement, ensuring that the advantaged usually manage to stay at the top of the pack. Refusing to play their game, he calls upon like-minded people, such as

Watts and delinquent acquaintance Duncan (Elias Koteas), who are more motivated by the prospect of forging their own path rather than conforming to unthinking tenets of social expectation.

Although Amanda charts a similar course to that of Andie, in the sense that she hopes to improve her social prospects through a relationship with a more affluent partner, she fails where Andie succeeded due to the fact that Hardy does not share her affections and is content to embarrass and demean her for what he perceives to be her subordinate social status. She eventually proves her independence by abandoning him, considering the reputation of a pariah among the well-heeled elite to be preferable to his continued debasement. Yet while Amanda's determination to climb the social ladder ultimately does not succeed, like Keith she takes solace in knowing that she has reclaimed her dignity by embracing her blue-collar roots over the potential damage sustained by social-climbing affectations.

Because Keith, Watts, and Amanda all ultimately turn their backs on the orthodox manner of "getting ahead in life," preferring to mature and advance on their own terms, they can all be seen to embody a quite different take on youth anxieties than had been the case in the earlier *Pretty in Pink*. With the ideological standoff of the Cold War and the danger of thermonuclear obliteration now beginning to take more of a back seat in popular culture, with even the long-running James Bond film series moving away from the topic from the late 1980s onwards, certainties which had remained steadfast for several generations were now suddenly looking much less stable. Mirroring this ambiguity, Hughes's characters were themselves questioning the course of their respective adult lives, wondering how best to adapt to a world which was being reconfigured in challenging and often unexpected ways. He takes care to ensure that all of the characters' strengths—Keith's creativity, Amanda's strength of character, and Watts's can-do attitude—are all perennial assets which are essential in adapting to a society in flux. While there are no guarantees about their future success, Hughes still ensures that they are equipped for the unforeseeable in the best way they possibly can be.

The struggles of *Some Kind of Wonderful* reflected the unpredictability facing the globe in the face of a nascent, unipolar New World Order—a development which was to be revisited in the nineties, and reflected in the listlessness of later Hughes characters such as Jim Dodge in *Career Opportunities* (Bryan Gordon, 1991) and the troubled Robin in *Reach the Rock* (William Ryan, 1998). Those characters' personal insecurities and lack of focus in their life goals arguably had their genesis in the confusions of the main figures of *Some Kind of Wonderful*, each of whom were forced to deal with the unpredictability of a changing world whose challenges had ramifications for every aspect of their adult lives. While it is true that the Cold War was only ever a muted presence in Hughes's movies, it was nevertheless one which had an unavoidable impact on the way his teenaged characters thought, behaved, and planned for a future which was simultaneously tainted by uncertainty and filled with possibilities.

19

I'm a Kid, That's My Job

John Hughes and the Kids' Comedy Caper

With John Hughes's eighties comedies and cycle of teen movies likely to remain his most prominent achievement within the public eye, it is important not to forget that he was also responsible for providing the screenplays for many commercially successful family films throughout the 1990s which placed child protagonists firmly in the spotlight. Features such as *Dennis the Menace* (Nick Castle, 1993), *Baby's Day Out* (Patrick Read Johnson, 1994), *101 Dalmatians* (Stephen Herek, 1996), and *Flubber* (Les Mayfield, 1997) all either shifted their primary focus from teenaged or adult protagonists onto characters who were played by juvenile actors, or otherwise maintained a family-friendly emphasis which was much more determinedly child-friendly than had been the case with films produced in the earlier stages of his career. Understanding that child audiences are often among the most perceptive, Hughes retained his keen eye for characterization and sharp dialogue when crafting his youth-oriented films, and—while the result was often far removed from his adult comedies in stylistic terms— he remained committed to producing high-quality entertainment with an astutely contemplative edge.

From Ink to Hi-jinx: *Dennis the Menace*

Although Hughes had crafted the story for the crowd-pleasing *Beethoven* (Brian Levant, 1992) under his Edmond Dantès writing pseudonym, meaning that his involvement in the screenplay of that popular canine caper is sometimes overlooked, one of his most noteworthy contributions to the family comedy genre came about early in the 1990s with the release of Nick Castle's *Dennis the Menace* (1993). The movie was based on Hank Ketcham's long-running syndicated comic strip of the same name, which he drew from 1951 until his retirement in 1994 (though it would continue to be published thereafter, due to the creative input of Ketcham's assistants Ron Ferdinand and Marcus Hamilton). The comic centers around the adventures of a mischievous five-year-old named Dennis Mitchell, an essentially kindhearted child with a mop of blond hair and omnipresent red overalls who inadvertently causes chaos in the neighborhood where he lives. The movie was released under the title *Dennis* in Great Britain, due to the fact that there was another famous comic-book character in that country named "Dennis the Menace" which debuted in DC Thomson's *The Beano* weekly children's periodical in 1951. (The spiky-haired delinquent schoolboy Dennis, with his striped jersey and ever-present dog, Gnasher, has come to be beloved by generations of children in the UK but bears little resemblance to the kindergarten-aged all-American troublemaker of Ketcham's original comic.)

Though *Dennis the Menace* had previously been adapted as a live-action television series by CBS between 1959 and 1963, with Jay North starring as Dennis, Castle's film adaptation would be the first time the incorrigible youngster would make it to the big screen. Featuring an angel-faced Mason Gamble in the title role, the movie is a star-studded affair—Walter Matthau featured as George Wilson, Dennis's long-suffering elderly neighbor whose attempts to embrace the quiet life are invariably disrupted by the juvenile dervish next door, while his wife, Martha, was portrayed by award-winning British actress Joan Plowright. Dennis's parents were played by Robert Stanton and Lea Thompson, while Christopher Lloyd was cast as menacing burglar Switchblade Sam. (Thompson had previously played Amanda Jones in Howard Deutch's *Some Kind of Wonderful* in 1987, but was also highly recognizable in the popular culture of the time for her collaboration with Lloyd in Robert Zemeckis's iconic 1985 time-travel comedy *Back to the Future*, where they played Lorraine Baines McFly and Dr. Emmett Brown, respectively.)

Mason Gamble had to fight off considerable competition from thousands of other potential rivals when auditioning for the title part, but his cherubic appearance as the boisterous rascal divided critics with regard to his effectiveness in the role. Hughes's script itself followed the characterizations and comedic setups of Ketchum's original comic fairly closely, with only subdued embellishment to accommodate the time of production so as to preserve the fifties charm of the strip's early years. The innocence of youth is captured faithfully, with Dennis very much sketched out as a benign figure whose propensity towards pandemonium is generally explained by unanticipated situations or circumstances which quickly progress beyond his control. He is portrayed more as a catalyst of commotion than its willing initiator, and Hughes takes care to add a subtle level of depth to the character's portrayal by expounding upon his love-hate relationship with Matthau's Mr. Wilson, a curmudgeonly retired U.S. Post Office employee who is constantly aggravated by his unruly young neighbor and yet is secretly quite fond of the mischief-making scamp.

The movie's slender plot revolves not just around Dennis's various scrapes and pranks, but also the unexpected arrival of disheveled housebreaker Switchblade Sam—a ne'er-do-well who immediately strikes fear into the hearts of the local children as well as proving surprisingly adept at his criminal activities. Eventually, Sam receives his comeuppance, though only after some quick-thinking by Dennis and a collaborative effort which helps to bring the Mitchells and Wilsons closer together. The film met with a considerably mixed reception among reviewers at the time of its release, but its box-office performance proved to be convincing. While Hughes's general fidelity to the tone of Ketchum's source material was noted by some, others praised the attempts by Nick Castle to capture some aspect of the cartoon strip's visual flair in his live-action adaptation. Although the movie is unlikely to be considered among the most sophisticated of Hughes's many screenplays, its commercial accomplishment led to direct-to-video sequels, including *Dennis the Menace Strikes Again* (Charles T. Kanganis, 1988), which starred Justin Cooper as Dennis, and *A Dennis the Menace Christmas* (Ron Oliver, 2007), with Maxwell Perry Cotton in the title role.

Dennis the Menace. Director: Nick Castle. Release date: June 25, 1993.

Disasters in Diapers: *Baby's Day Out*

While the following year would bring praise for Hughes in the form of his screenplay for *Miracle on 34th Street* (Les Mayfield, 1994)—a remake of George Seaton's celebrated 1947 original—it was also to see his involvement in a rather less critically successful venture. *Baby's Day Out* (1994), directed by Patrick Read Johnson, has come to be regarded as a unusual slip-up in Hughes's filmography; a feature which was lambasted by critics and largely ignored by America's moviegoing public at the time of its release.

As had been the case with *Dennis the Menace*, Hughes shared production duties on the movie with Richard Vane while writing the screenplay himself. The film also featured a starry cast which included Joe Mantegna, Joe Pantoliano, Cynthia Nixon, and Lara Flynn Boyle. However, the winning formula which had attracted audiences to *Dennis the Menace* seemed to be essentially absent from *Baby's Day Out*, with the movie's various larger-than-life situations struggling to compete with the wholesome charm of its predecessor's comic-book-based antics.

The movie's plot is focused on the efforts of three criminals (played by Mantegna, Pantoliano, and Brian Haley) to kidnap the infant child of a wealthy family, with the intention of demanding a huge ransom for his safe return. All does not go according to plan, however, with the gang discovering that the baby—called Bennington Austin Cotwell IV, though nicknamed Baby Bink—has no intention of cooperating with their criminal scheme. Eventually, Bink escapes their clutches and goes exploring in the big city, his wanderings closely following the events of *Baby's Day Out*, a storybook that had been read to him. The kidnappers follow the infant's escapades but somehow always wind up one step behind him. Eventually, the child succeeds in evading their pursuit, leaving the crooks trapped at a construction site while he manages (more by good luck than judgment) to get himself recognized and returned to his family. But the perceptive juvenile eventually has the last laugh when he contrives a way of helping the FBI track down the criminals (themselves now the fugitives who are being pursued) and make them answer for their misdeeds.

Though *Baby's Day Out* featured some inventively shot sequences (a few of them featuring actor Verne Troyer as the stunt double for Bink), the movie is best-remembered for the winning portrayal of the runaway baby by Adam Robert Worton and Jacob Joseph Worton. The Worton twins were expressive performers who won the hearts of some viewers, but even their endearing presence did little to divert critics from the film's threadbare storyline and increasingly implausible events. While some reviewers did grudgingly admit that *Baby's Day Out* was more likely to appeal to youth audiences than it would to adults, the disdain of critics was to be mirrored in the feature's performance at the box office, where its domestic gross paled in comparison to its production budget.

Interestingly, while the film's lackluster economic revenue meant that no sequel would ever be forthcoming, *Baby's Day Out* became a smash hit throughout South Asia, generating considerable profits in such highly populous countries as India and Pakistan. It seemed ironic that one of the least commercially successful films to which Hughes would ever lend his creative involvement would ultimately become one of the most popular with some international markets, but in spite of its widespread approval with various overseas audiences it has since become one of his most obscure productions within North America.

Adapt to Survive: *101 Dalmatians* and *Flubber*

As the nineties drew nearer to their conclusion, Hughes's involvement with the family movie was to take a new direction with the production of two remakes of 1960s Disney films. The first—and arguably more critically successful—adaptation was *101 Dalmatians* (Stephen Herek, 1996), a live-action updating of the 1961 animated classic that had been directed by Wolfgang Reitherman, Hamilton S. Luske, and Clyde Geronimi (which in turn was based on Dodie Smith's 1956 novel *The Hundred and One Dalmatians*). While the prospect of updating such a well-loved Disney feature may have deterred many screenwriters, Hughes rose to the challenge with characteristic assurance, delivering a script which made the most of a talented cast from both sides of the Atlantic while retaining much of the original's charm.

Reflective of Smith's England-situated novel, the movie made use of some excellent British character actors, including Mark Williams, Tim

McInnerny, Joan Plowright, John Shrapnel, Hugh Fraser, and Hugh Laurie (many years before he hit the big time as the title character in the Fox Network's medical drama *House* between 2004 and 2012). Jeff Daniels and Joely Richardson provide engaging performances as the nominal protagonists of the film, and yet they are both surpassed by a scene-stealing Glenn Close in the role of villainess Cruella de Vil, appearing instantly

Baby's Day Out. Director: Patrick Read Johnson. Release date: July 1, 1994.

recognizable as the animated character while making the most of her every moment of screen time. The true stars of the film, however, were (debatably) the many canine stars of the title, who provided abundant charm for all pet owners in the audience.

For much of its duration, *101 Dalmatians* stays close to the storyline of the animated 1961 adaptation, with newlyweds Roger and Anita Dearly (Daniels and Richardson) fending off the increasingly sadistic attempts of fashion designer Cruella de Vil to obtain the litter of puppies that have recently been born to their pet Dalmatians. This is revealed to be due to a callous plan she has hatched to make clothing out of the distinctively spotted animals by skinning a sufficient number to craft a coat. Eventually, de Vil resorts to having the canines professionally dog-napped, leading to a desperate search in which it is eventually discovered that she has purloined no fewer than ninety-nine dogs from their respective families. Anita and Roger, with the help of the Metropolitan Police and Suffolk Constabulary, eventually manage to liberate the ill-starred pets from stately de Vil Mansion, and the Dearlys end up adopting the puppies themselves—which, in addition to their own two dogs, Pongo and Perdita, make up the hundred and one Dalmatians of the title.

Hughes's screenplay adds a few modern twists to the plot of the Smith text (for instance, Roger has computer-coding skills and develops a video game featuring the titular dogs), though he takes considerably greater care in evoking the charming English atmosphere which had been so faithfully conjured up by the original adaptation. Although *101 Dalmatians* did well at the box office, both domestically and in international markets, its critical reception was decidedly uneven. While some critics praised the performances and fidelity to the visual style of the sixties animated original, others voiced skepticism towards the occasional flimsiness of the plot and an over-reliance on slapstick humor, as well as criticism that Hughes was falling back on a storytelling approach that had been overused since the time of Chris Columbus's first two *Home Alone* films (1990–1992), and *Beethoven*. The commercial performance of the movie was, however, convincing enough to allow for the production of a follow-up, *102 Dalmatians* (Kevin Lima, 2000), which saw Glenn Close and Tim McInnerny reprising their roles. Hughes had no participation in the sequel (the screenplay of which was written by Kristen Buckey, Brian

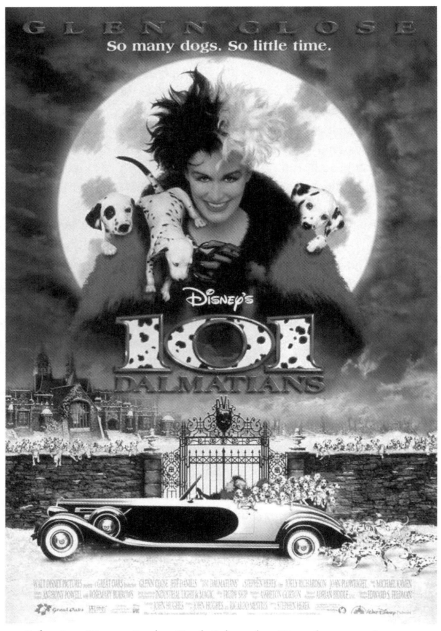

101 Dalmatians. Director: Stephen Herek. Release date: November 27, 1996.

Regan, Bob Tzudiker, and Noni White), but in spite of a widespread critical hammering it went on to considerable profitability following its release.

Hughes's involvement with Disney continued in 1997 with the release of Les Mayfield's *Flubber*. An energetic modernization of old family favorite *The Absent-Minded Professor* (Robert Stevenson, 1961), the movie saw the ever-popular Robin Williams assuming the role of protagonist Professor Philip Brainard—portrayed by Fred MacMurray in the original. Again, the movie featured unfaltering support from stalwart performers—which in this case included Marcia Gay Harden, Clancy Brown, and long-established Hughes alumna Edie McClurg—while Hughes and Mayfield worked in tandem to bring the events of the black-and-white original into the modern day. (Hughes also acted as the film's producer, along with Ricardo Mestres.)

Flubber concerns a good-natured but eccentric chemistry professor, Philip Brainard, whose scientific brilliance is matched only by his unconventionality and poor short-term memory. Having been so distracted by his research that he has forgotten to attend his own wedding not once but twice, his relationship with his caring, put-upon fiancée, Sara Reynolds (Harden)—who is also the president of the college where he works—is now in serious jeopardy. Things go from bad to worse when he inadvertently misses his third wedding due to the discovery of a remarkable new substance his robot assistant Weebo identifies as "flying rubber," leading Brainard to name it *Flubber*. However, the professor's unscrupulous former partner Wilson Croft (Christopher McDonald)—who had been responsible for stealing and exploiting earlier research from the oblivious scientist—is soon set on purloining not only the extraordinary Flubber, but the affections of the increasingly jaded Sara. With the aid of his robotic companion and the increasingly astonishing properties of his new discovery—which allow him to lend the ability to fly to everything from his vintage Ford Thunderbird to the college basketball team—Brainard eventually thwarts Croft's scheme, exposes the corruption of one of the establishment's wealthy sponsors (played by Raymond J. Barry), and finally succeeds in marrying his beautiful bride before any further mishaps can befall the star-crossed couple.

While *The Absent-Minded Professor* (along with its 1963 sequel, Robert Stevenson's *Son of Flubber*) had been warmly remembered by audiences from its sixties heyday, it had not received quite the same degree of cultural recognition as the highly successful *One Hundred and One Dalmatians*, meaning that Hughes had greater scope to craft an updated take on the original film's central scenario without the same risk of alienating purists. Many of the scenarios presented in the remake retained and embellished existing incidents from the Stevenson movie, with Hughes working closely from the events of the original Bill Walsh screenplay (which itself had its origins in "A Situation of Gravity," a short story written by Samuel W. Taylor). Many of the characters' names were changed, though their functions within the storyline remained largely intact, whereas various other flourishes were added to ground the film's events in the present day (such as the Model T Ford of Fred McMurray's professor being succeeded by the Ford Thunderbird so beloved of Robin Williams's iteration of the character). The outsmarting of affluent benefactor Chester Hoenicker, who is revealed to be in league with the scheming Croft, has resonance with the undoing of *101 Dalmatians'* Cruella de Vil and various other screenplays written by Hughes for family audiences, continuing the theme of the abuse of power and wealth being antithetical to the essential American virtues of honesty, community, and inventiveness: a conflict in which uprightness and integrity eventually prevail over malicious self-centeredness.

Critics differed sharply over the perceived merits of *Flubber*, with some praising Williams's hyperkinetic performance while others lamented the fact that in its assertive attempts at modernization the feature appeared to lose some aspect of its original charm. However, the uncertainty of reviewers did little to dent the movie's commercial fortunes; at the box office it proved to be a financial success both in the United States and in international territories. However, given its extensive production budget, the eventual overall gross did not prove adequate to encourage the development of any sequels, meaning that when Philip and Sara head off to Hawaii (by way of flying automobile) at the conclusion of the film, the characters were never to return for a post-honeymoon encore.

Hughes's Disney remakes may have been profitable projects, but they did little to endear him to the critical community. As had been the case

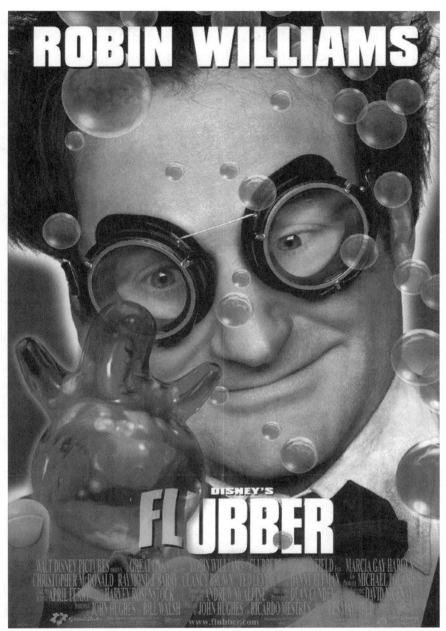

Flubber. Director: Les Mayfield. Release date: November 26, 1997.

with some of his other family-oriented features, many critics identified a tendency towards flimsy plotlines and strategies which had been recycled (sometimes rather blatantly) from his earlier movies. Nonetheless, the high profile which was afforded these films as a result of their financial success in theaters ensured that Hughes remained in the public eye as a producer and screenwriter, even at a time when the style and content of his output was becoming markedly different from the glory days of the mid-1980s to the early 1990s.

20

A First-Class Ticket to Nowhere

Authority and the Education System in the Films of John Hughes

High school life is a pronounced fixture in all of John Hughes's teen movies, with an education system that is generally populated by a mix of out-of-touch adults and overbearing authoritarian figures—an impersonal, monolithic structure that seems profoundly at odds with the hopes and dreams of the young protagonists who are forming the films' focus. Yet Hughes understood only too well the complex interpersonal politics which operate wherever teenagers congregate, and his features offer an engrossing mélange of intense, highly competitive conflict among societal strata and, conversely, insightful humor drawn from the unintentional absurdity of the relational struggles which often arise. Sometimes, high school staff members are condescending and imperious, whereas on occasion they are likable and sympathetic. However, one common factor between them is that they are all thoroughly relatable as human beings in their personal intricacies, merits, and imperfections. Hughes's take on high school life tended to be specifically examined from the perspective of the personal power-play and peer pressure operating in the 1980s educational environment, pitching inflexible authority against the uniquely teenage allure of emergent personal freedom and self-discovery, and his movies took into consideration not only the factors unique to the era but also those which have remained universal to the development of young adulthood.

Authority without Purpose: Assistant Principal Richard Vernon and *The Breakfast Club*

Almost certainly the most overtly antagonistic of public educators to appear in a John Hughes movie, Assistant Principal Richard Vernon of Shermer High School, is the absolute quintessence of a lofty, self-appointed judge of not only his students' conduct, but their future prospects in life. A disciplinarian with a rigidly strict attitude towards maintaining order, Vernon can barely contain his palpable contempt for the collection of weekend detention attendees. Yet while *The Breakfast Club* (1985) is predominantly concerned with the manifestly intricate relationships which form the social configuration of high school life, exploring the students' growing understanding that they share greater commonality than any of them may otherwise have realized, the belligerent assistant principal feels no similar ability to relate either to the teenagers or even to members of his own generation.

Vernon's attempts at repression are contrasted throughout the film with characters such as John Kapelos's Carl, the school janitor, who is able to offer advice to the students that is relevant and judicious largely because (although he may be employed by the same education system) he is not operating from a position of nominal authority over them. Carl remembers what it was like to be a teenager, confused by rapid changes in personal outlook and facing the future with a mixture of trepidation and expectation, and as such he is able to offer guidance which offers constructive counsel to the Breakfast Club's members. But Vernon makes it clear that he feels no such camaraderie, perceiving himself to be somehow superior to his charges both in terms of ethicality and institutional authority. Yet it is this professed sense of self-importance which isolates him not only from the students but the mainstream of society beyond the cheerless corridors of his workplace.

The late Paul Gleason had been a well-known face on television and in cinema since the 1960s, though the eighties would see him appearing in some of his most widely recognized movie roles, such as a detective in *Fort Apache: The Bronx* (Daniel Petrie, 1981) and shady uncover operative Clarence Beeks in *Trading Places* (John Landis, 1983). Though his appearances on television would be especially prolific, guest starring on successful series including *The A-Team*, *Cagney & Lacey*, *Remington Steele*, *Hill Street Blues*, *Magnum P.I.*, *Miami Vice*, and *Dallas*, among many others, his place in 1980s pop culture was cemented by his performance as the startlingly incredulous, by-the-book Deputy Police Chief Dwayne T. Robinson in John McTiernan's groundbreaking action movie *Die Hard* (1988). Gleason would also work again with Hughes later in the decade when he appeared as Howard, a supporting character in *She's Having a Baby* (1988). However, as Richard Vernon he was to make what was almost certainly his most noteworthy performance of the decade, and in one of the keynote roles of his entire acting career.

In spite of his bluster and arrogance, Assistant Principal Vernon is far from a contented man. Frustrated at his perceived inability to instill discipline among the student body, his response is not to attempt to better understand the teenagers within his professional remit but to crack down ever more harshly on their general behavior. His lack of personal fulfillment is further underscored by his exasperation towards the changing social attitudes of the time. Vernon blames what he wrongly believes to be an apathetic and excessively casual outlook on the part of the students upon an ineffectual system of educational discipline that has become unduly lax, unconscious of the irony that his generation was likely appraised in the same way during his own teenage years. Thus, he interprets a natural tendency to explore the boundaries of acceptable behavior, challenging the attitudes of his forerunners, as a direct attack on his personal authority within the school hierarchy, leading to a predictable clash of personalities.

Vernon's insecurities are most starkly delineated in his fiery conflict with the intelligent but openly insubordinate John Bender (Judd Nelson), whose own reputation as a rebellious firebrand hinges on refusing to back down in the face of the assistant principal's relentless hostility. Bender is somehow able to use just about every aspect of Vernon's authoritarian persona against him, from the senior teacher's cringe-worthy outfit to his overtly pompous mannerisms and turns of phrase. Yet while the behaviorally challenging Bender is a suitably defiant foil for the puffed-up Vernon, he eventually pushes the envelope too far and realizes that he has done so; finally, the assistant principal's professional composure cracks, and the middle-aged martinet leaves Bender in no doubt as to his

The Breakfast Club. Director: John Hughes. Release date: February 15, 1985.

feelings about the teenager's post-school future. Worst of all, in goading his charge to take a punch at him—knowing that nobody would believe the word of a known troublemaker over a senior educator—he exhibits a total lack of moral character, demonstrating that he cannot be considered a viable role model in any respect.

In his showdown with Bender (and, to a lesser extent, his interactions with Carl), Vernon inadvertently reveals the depths of his disillusionment concerning his own life and career. Clearly disappointed by the outcome of his professional trajectory, Vernon's disenchantment becomes all but palpable, and the audience gradually becomes aware of at least part of the reason he has become such an ominously malign presence within the school. From his supercilious bearing to his ostentatious clothing, Vernon is served up by Hughes as the kind of archetypal stuffed shirt who, with his killjoy attitude and sledgehammer teaching methods, is a relatable enough character to transcend generations precisely because he is a highly recognizable archetype in the eyes of just about anyone who has ever attended high school.

The consistently successful attempts by the Breakfast Club to outsmart, deride, and generally dodge Vernon throughout the course of their detention period are inspired, and yet conversely they also highlight the fact that Vernon is not simply a straightforward figure of fun. Given the overall message of the movie—namely that everyone is a unique individual, regardless of any assumptions that may be made by others regarding their place in the social order—Hughes makes a point of stressing that Vernon is no different from his students in this regard. He carefully applies an additional stratum of characterization to the assistant principal as the film progresses, emphasizing just how cynical and thoroughly disenchanted this strangely tragi-comic figure has become. The teenagers may well be bored and listless as a result of being cooped up in a school library for hours, but Vernon—in spite of his attempts to appear otherwise—is similarly burned-out, reduced to killing time in his office after a week's worth of teaching because no one else is willing to fill the same role. Thus, while it is made clear to the various members of the Breakfast Club that the punishment of detention lasts only for a Saturday, it becomes ever clearer that Vernon is similarly trapped—though in his case, his captivity is a self-made, lifelong commitment.

Losing His Faculties: Dean Edward R. Rooney and *Ferris Bueller's Day Off*

Like Richard Vernon, Ocean Park High School's dean of students, Ed Rooney (Jeffrey Jones), is a jaded disciplinarian who tries his best to rule over his institution with a rod of iron. As Cameron's panicked reaction during his fraudulent phone call suggests, Rooney's retribution is legendary—he is short-tempered, domineering, and has a hugely inflated idea of his own importance. Yet while so much of his sense of authority appears to be predicated on his overzealous preoccupation with maintaining order within the school, his dictatorial attitude is eventually revealed to be more focused on an underlying obsession with curtailing Ferris Bueller's sense of individual freedom than with ensuring the smooth running of the campus.

Throughout *Ferris Bueller's Day Off* (1986), Hughes goes to some length to emphasize the reasons Ferris and his friends are so desperate to evade school as often as possible. From Ben Stein's droning economics teacher, whose stultifyingly dull delivery has become the stuff of comedy legend, to the hypnotically monotonous discourse of Del Close's similarly unnamed English teacher, we are shown the high school experience at its most laborious; the learning process is far from entertaining, tedious bureaucracy trumps intellectual dialogue, and the teachers appear almost as bored as the students. It is in this kind of administrative environment that a character such as Ed Rooney thrives; he has crowned himself king of his own castle, and insists that his subjects pay homage to him as he sees fit.

The reality of the situation, of course, is that Rooney is far from being as secure in his position of authority as he would like to admit. While his students have little choice but to bow to his grandiose posturing, they do so not out of any notion of respect but because they have no desire to risk the prospect of detention, suspension, or worse. Similarly, while we see little of his interaction with other members of the school staff, his interactions with his ditzy personal assistant Grace (Edie McClurg) reveal that while she is willing to support his swaggering bluster and even play to his considerable ego, she stops short of taking him entirely seriously. Even more telling is his interaction with parents, whether real (Cindy Pickett's

Katie Bueller) or fraudulent (Alan Ruck's flustered improvisational phone call as Cameron impersonates Sloane's father is, in actuality, an imitation of stage and screen director Gene Saks). Rooney vacillates between taking a hardline, plain-spoken approach when he feels that he is taking the moral high ground, believing himself to be somehow superior to those he considers to be naïve or allowing themselves to be duped in some way, while instantly reverting to apologetic deference if he considers that his actions or attitudes may be subject to negative scrutiny.

Core to Rooney's character, of course, is the fact that he identifies Ferris Bueller as being the absolute antithesis of everything he stands for. While he may well be envious of Ferris's easy charm, popularity, and ability to influence those around him, the root of Rooney's antipathy lies in the fact that the wayward student effortlessly demonstrates the ability to outmaneuver the rulebook at every turn. Subverting authority to meet his own ends, Ferris shamelessly manipulates his parents, his fellow students, the school's staff, and even the local community at large—something which infuriates Rooney, whose own position is absolutely reliant on procedures and social etiquette being observed at all times. Yet while his stated aim is to expose Ferris's scams and even possibly forcing him to repeat a year of school to make up for his many absences, there is a mounting sense that Rooney has actually formed a personal

Jeffrey Jones (1946–   ), stage, television, and film actor, particularly noted for his performances on Broadway.

vendetta against the well-liked teen. Whereas Ferris is admired by his peers, Rooney is merely tolerated by the staff and student body alike—and while the despotic dean's status is contingent on maintaining a sense of authority and intimidation, his strong-willed student's influence is fostered by amiability and a seemingly sincere willingness to help others around him (if only to aid them in being able to undermine Rooney's draconian strictures themselves). Even the prospect of Ferris's imminent departure for college does little to soothe Rooney's antagonism, given his fear that the master slacker's popularity will lead to his producing an entirely new generation of similarly mutinous students in his wake.

At the time of *Ferris Bueller's Day Off*, Jones's reputation as a character actor was already well established through roles in movies such as Cold War thriller *The Soldier* (James Glickenhaus, 1982), where he played the United States assistant secretary of defense; a supporting part as Clive Barlow in James Signorelli's comedy *Easy Money* (1983), and as the mayor in horror-parody *Transylvania 6-5000* (Rudy De Luca, 1985). However, his breakthrough had almost certainly been his Golden Globe Award–winning performance as Emperor Joseph II in Miloš Forman's *Amadeus* (1984), which brought him into the public eye as never before. Following his appearance as Ed Rooney, Jones would perform in other high-profile roles, including Dr. Walter Jenning (a.k.a. "The Dark Overlord") in the divisive cult-comic adaptation *Howard the Duck* (Willard Huyck, 1986), beleaguered family man Charles Deetz in Tim Burton's supernatural comedy *Beetlejuice* (1988), and The Amazing Criswell in Burton's *Ed Wood* (1994). It was as Ed Rooney in *Ferris Bueller's Day Off*, however, that Jones was to be immortalized in the popular culture of the decade; the sneering, bridling dean of students is the very epitome of the kind of teacher almost everyone who has ever attended high school has encountered (and attempted to avoid) at one point or another, and in Jones's hands, Rooney was to become one of the most memorable of all Hughes's characters.

As Ferris outwits the boggle-eyed classroom tyrant at every turn, Rooney grows ever more frantic (and arguably unhinged) in his attempts to expose his student's scheming and disregard for the rules. However, the farther he strays from the school environment, the more hopelessly out of his depth the dean appears. Bereft of the wafer-thin patina of influence that his position lends him while securely within the institution,

Rooney is suddenly cut loose from his safety zone, winding up in surroundings where he is met with disdain and even open hostility. This
path eventually leads him into the realms of shameless lawbreaking
as he becomes ever-more desperate—determined to find any available
evidence to incriminate Ferris, he resorts to trespassing, housebreaking, and even an ill-considered assault on the Buellers' family dog in
his resolve to corner his prey. Not once does it seem to occur to him that
his illegal actions are considerably more serious in nature than those he
suspects Ferris of committing; the final insult comes when Ferris's sister,
Jeanie (Jennifer Grey), manages to thwart Rooney's apparent moment
of victory, not only providing Ferris with an alibi for his absence from
the family home but also revealing that she knows about the fanatical
administrator's numerous misdemeanors which have taken place on the
Bueller property—much to his horror. This leads to his greatest moment
of indignity when—beaten, bloodied, and unkempt—he is left with no
choice but to hitch a ride on a passing school bus, mortified as his uncharacteristically disheveled presence leads to a mixture of amusement and
incredulity by the students on board.

Rooney was notably described by the *New York Times* as resembling a
live-action version of Wile E. Coyote, the luckless character who—always
in pursuit of a guileful Road Runner in innumerable Warner Bros. *Looney
Tunes* cartoons—finds himself faced with endless injury and indignity in
pursuit of his objective, yet always seems to dust himself off and continue
towards his goal (even when faced with the stark reality of the utter futil-
ity of his actions). And certainly there is much to commend this comparison, considering the manner in which the dean is repeatedly humiliated,
injured, dirtied, and even attacked by a vicious guard dog . . . only to
continue in his ultimately fruitless quest to see Ferris brought down. For
Rooney, his aim quickly transcends the need to justify his administrative
authority within the school system; he finds himself fighting a figure who
opposes and contradicts virtually everything that he stands for. Ferris
is not only younger and cleverer than the dean, he also has an entirely
different worldview; the very personification of the old adage "don't work
hard, work smart," his actions throughout his day off make the point that
if authority cannot properly justify itself then it ceases to have validity,
and instead becomes a kind of aimless autocracy—a subtle but pervasive

system of personal oppression that is anathema to everything in which Ferris believes.

It is of little surprise that Ed Rooney has become one of the most striking of all antagonistic educators in John Hughes's cinema, but his actions and attitudes make for a revealing commentary on the importance of ensuring that the school system makes a constructive effort to connect with its students on something approaching their own wavelength. The eighties were a time of considerable cultural flux, and the values and certainties of Rooney's own youth were no longer necessarily as directly applicable to the generation of his students. With his quick, independent thinking, Ferris is a figure better suited to the age of unpredictability in which he was growing up, and the message he sent to the education system was clear—adapt to the needs of a changing world, or cease to be relevant to the new social reality that is gradually revealing itself.

You Tread on My Dreams: Assistant Principal Anita Hoargarth and *Uncle Buck*

Not all educational establishments to appear in Hughes films were high schools. With Suzanne Shepherd's fearsome Assistant Principal Anita Hoargarth, who rules over Maizy and Miles Russell's (Gaby Hoffman and Macaulay Culkin) elementary school with dispiriting oppressiveness during the events of *Uncle Buck* (1989), Hughes would make perhaps his most strident assertion of childhood freedom and creative liberty in the face of unthinkingly authoritarian bureaucracy. Protagonist Buck Russell (John Candy) is among the most easygoing and even-tempered of Hughes's characters, and yet when he encounters the formidable Ms. Hoargarth, he finds himself stirred into an uncharacteristically defensive stance—one which left the domineering educator speechless just as it encouraged approving cheers from audiences.

Buck's showdown with Ms. Hoargarth takes up only a few minutes of *Uncle Buck*'s screen time, and yet in its surprisingly impassioned vindication of juvenile innocence it remains one of the film's most arresting scenes. In the absence of the Russell kids' parents, Buck has been summoned to the school because Hoargarth has labeled Maizy as a problem student. He sits attentively as the assistant principal rails against the six-year-old, deriding her tendency to daydream and for her apparent lack of mental rigor. Then, incensed by her singular lack of humanity, he strikes back with all guns blazing. Buck immediately senses that Hoargarth is unthinkingly correlating imagination with idleness, and confusing a capacity for fun and play with a willing lack of conformity. He berates her for being so singularly out of touch after more than thirty years of teaching that she has completely lost sight of the importance of letting children be children. Trying to force young people into pigeonholes—convincing them from an early age that their opinion has no merit or that their lack of academic performance has branded them as failures—is, in Buck's opinion, deeply averse to positive personal development.

Suzanne Shepherd provides a superlative comic performance; with her haughty manner and hilariously fake mole, Ms. Hoargarth oozes condescension and a sense of utter conviction in her own superiority which makes the character instantly unlikable—all the better to emphasize Buck's spirited riposte against her tyrannical manner. Though at the time Shepherd's cinematic appearances had been limited to supporting performances in movies such as *Mystic Pizza* (Donald Petrie, 1988) and *Working Girl* (Mike Nichols, 1988), she would soon go on to greater success with a noteworthy role in Martin Scorsese's *Goodfellas* (1990) and most especially as Mary De Angelis in the award-winning HBO crime drama *The Sopranos* (1999–2007). She shows acute insight into the oddly complex balance required by the egregious assistant principal, alternating adroitly between the character's autocratic superciliousness and dumbfounded shock as her authority is undermined in the most unexpected of ways.

Although the sequence may not have taken place in a high school, the venue for which his eighties youth cinema debatably became best known, Hughes uses the confrontation between Buck and Ms. Hoargarth as a kind of microcosm of his acute concern over the potential abuses of the public education system. When teachers are nurturing and supportive, they are capable of awakening a lifelong love of learning in the students under their tutelage. By contrast, if they are singularly intent on railroading children and young adults into unthinking compliance and slavish convention, it is clear that they can do great damage both to their charges' personal confidence and ability to reason critically. Hughes takes care to present the fact that a vast gulf exists between knowledge and wisdom, using Buck's fervent counter-argument to demarcate the important line which separates intellectual curiosity from the mechanical process of absorbing facts so they can be repeated without question. Indeed, Buck makes the point of emphasizing that he does not consider himself an educated man, having never attended college (much to Hoargarth's predictable contempt), and yet he knows very well that the importance of having an inquiring mind transcends high school grades, certificates, and diplomas. To turn learning into a process of mindlessly accepting details, points, and statistics rather than encouraging students to think for themselves is, Hughes shows, an enormous waste of potential which impoverishes not just individuals, but society at large. Worse still, such an anti-intellectual approach is thoroughly un-American—a fact which would have especially concerned a patriot such as Hughes, who knew that the United States had been built upon independence of thought, the sharing of information, and the freedom to communicate ideas.

Because Buck Russell was one of Hughes's most congenial characters of the 1980s, the sudden ferocity of his attack on the bureaucratic methodology underpinning Ms. Hoargarth's approach to education seems all the more powerful. Yet Hughes, in employing such a tactic, succeeds in rolling Buck into the assistant principal's fastidiously organized office like a primed grenade, ensuring that his point was made with remarkable precision. In so doing, he manages to align Hoargarth with Richard Vernon and Ed Rooney in their shared contempt for the students under their authority, to say nothing of the characters' common disdain for youth issues (casually and somewhat conveniently ignoring the experiences of their own schooldays). With his distinctive call to make the most of life and respect the individuality of all, Hughes showed deep apprehension about the ability of the education system to wrongfully dilute or even deaden the creativeness of students, depriving them of resourcefulness and analytical thought processes simply by attempting to force them into conformity and submission. The subtle inference is that, rather than preparing students for the rigid nine-to-five rules of the workplace, encouraging unthinking compliance is actually antithetical to their future prospects in a world that was increasingly subject to rapid technological change, with an emergent digital economy that was relying more on innovation and creativity than on the repetitive systems of labor more familiar from years gone by. More importantly, Hughes saw that an erosion of critical thought impoverished society at large, bleeding inventiveness from a generation just when it was needed most. And this, more than anything, explains why Richard Vernon is left languishing in an unfulfilling job while John Bender strides forward into a more confident future, why Ed Rooney is continually humiliated by the quick-thinking Ferris Bueller, and why Maizie Russell is allowed to dream of reaching for the stars while Anita Hoargarth is left thunderstruck by her rigidly didactic philosophies being shaken to their foundations by a cheerful but strongly opinionated surrogate parent figure.

21

This Is a Really Volcanic Ensemble You're Wearing

Fashion in John Hughes Films

J ust as contemporary music and other modes of popular culture were remarkably important to a John Hughes movie, so too were the fashion styles adopted by the various characters. From calculated cool to effortless glamor, Hughes knew that fashion helped to define how audiences considered each of his characters; he was also aware that clothing often determined the way in which these figures viewed themselves. The appearance of Hughes's characters came to play an important function in how they are presented as people, and was an important aspect of how they were presented to audiences. These individuals were often distinctively dressed, and their choices of clothing could have both implications and consequences, depending on a given character and situation.

The Height of Fashion: Teen Characters and Costume Choices

If there was one thing that could be said for Hughes's teen movies, it was that he seemed intent on presenting young people as living, breathing, authentic individuals rather than clichéd stereotypes that had so densely populated the genre in years past. Working with costume designers including Mark Peterson, Marla Denise Schlom, and most especially Marilyn Vance, Hughes's cycle of teen features included characters who were never less than distinctively attired, and—such was the individualism of their appearance—many of their fashions have come to be fondly remembered and even celebrated in later years.

Though the wardrobe department of a John Hughes film is, like any other movie, indelibly situated in the time and place of its production—Ronald Reagan's America of the mid-eighties—there was a definite attempt to depict the youthful casts of his various teen movies as wearing the kind of clothing that would reflect the characteristic degree of care and attention that real teenagers would extend to their own appearance. Almost certainly the most prominent figure of fashion to emerge throughout Hughes's youth cinema was Molly Ringwald, who amalgamated an arresting range of apparel and accessories with perceptive, meaningful performances to create truly arresting figures. In *Sixteen Candles* (1984), *The Breakfast Club* (1985), and *Pretty in Pink* (Howard Deutch, 1986), the fashions embraced by Ringwald's very different range of characters always enhanced their depictions as unique, independently minded individuals who are never afraid to put their own personal stamp on their clothing. The various figures portrayed by Ringwald helped to popularize clothing items such as broad-brimmed hats and chunky bracelets, broadening their appeal from the mid-eighties onward. But because the characters she played in Hughes's movies were quite dissimilar in their attitudes and personal circumstances, so too were their fashion tastes subtly different.

For Samantha Baker of *Sixteen Candles*, her reluctant donning of a bridesmaid's dress made from pink chiffon (complete with sweetheart neck) and floral hair garland may have been the source of deep dissatisfaction at her sister Ginny's wedding, but her distaste was all the more tangible given the deep individuality of her day-to-day wardrobe. Her carefully accessorized array of cardigans, skirts, and dresses made her stand apart from the crowd due to her effortless collocation of the everyday and the stylish. This sense of experimentation and originality carried over to Andie Walsh, Ringwald's character in *Pretty in Pink*, whose social circumstances were considerably more straitened than those of the Bakers, but who was unwilling to let a lack of financial resources impede her sense of sartorial innovation. Andie had one of the most eye-catching wardrobes of any Hughes character, with her black wool fedora, arresting

choice of jewelry, and billowing skirts among her considered embellish-
ments. She bolstered awareness of her fashion prowess when, adapting
the fabric of two existing garments into one new dress, she unveiled the
pink, polka-dotted chiffon prom outfit (complete with shoulder cutouts)
which made her stand out among her high school peers in the movie's
closing scenes.

By comparison, the well-to-do Claire Standish of *The Breakfast Club*
had an outward appearance that spoke of her affluent background; her
diamond-solitaire earrings, baggy V-necked T-shirt, and stylish leather
boots were paired with a chic bomber jacket to create a highly effective
look. Like the other members of the misfit group of students in detention,
Claire's clothing reflected certain aspects of her personality—in her case,

Molly Ringwald (1968–   ), actress, dancer, and vocalist;
more recently, an author of fiction and non-fiction.

a desire to dress in a manner that was relevant and reflective of her prosperity. The athletic Andrew Clark (Emilio Estevez) dresses in sporty gear which highlights his muscular physique, while timorous Brian Johnson (Anthony Michael Hall) prefers a smart-casual ensemble that mirrors his uptight persona. But perhaps the most visually conspicuous of all the detained teenagers is Judd Nelson's rebellious, independently minded John Bender, whose fingerless gloves, jean jacket, white T-shirt, plaid flannel shirt, Doc Marten boots, and scruffy trench coat mark him as a defiant, iconoclastic figure who is not to be trifled with.

Ferris Bueller, who clearly is the kind of figure who makes a point of dressing to impress, chooses to wear a printed sweater vest, black beret, casual trousers, white oxford shoes, and a dual-color leather varsity jacket for his much-admired trip around Chicago in *Ferris Bueller's Day Off* (1986). And yet—in spite of his attention-grabbing appearance—his taste for fashion finesse is arguably eclipsed by that of Mia Sara's Sloane Peterson. Ferris's girlfriend can turn heads throughout the city with her outfit, which consists of a cropped and fringed white leather jacket, high-waist gray shorts, blue tank, and white boots. The couple's appealingly individualistic appearance is deliberately differentiated from that of their edgy friend Cameron, who opts for a hockey jersey, thin suspenders, a beret cap, and (appropriately, given his hypochondriacal nature) a T-shirt emblazoned with the caduceus medical symbol.

Hughes's teen characters refused to be ignored, and the uniqueness of their costumes—as well as the fine detail of their various adornments and accoutrements—is just one reason they continue to remain in the public consciousness.

Clothes Maketh the Man (and Woman): Changing Fashions and Character Development

On many occasions, the clothing adopted by particular characters in movies featuring a Hughes screenplay had an additional significance—the development of their fashion choices throughout the course of the film's events were used to chart a particular shift in attitude or circumstance. Though this may simply seem like part and parcel of everyday life, in fact the attire of Hughesian characters was chosen very carefully to reflect the course of their fortunes.

The deterioration of Jack Butler (Michael Keaton) from a dapperly dressed engineer to an unkempt slob in *Mr. Mom* (Stan Dragoti, 1983) was perfectly gauged to echo the deterioration of the character's self-esteem. Prior to his redundancy, Jack seems entirely comfortable in the sharp formalwear expected of his workplace, but his slow slide into casual (and, eventually, rather *too* casual) clothing parallels his unease at being cast adrift from regular employment. Now bereft of the regular pattern that had governed his life for years, he finds himself directionless and indolent, unable to motivate himself in undertaking the many tasks required for the smooth running of his household. By contrast, his wife, Caroline (Teri Garr), makes a seemingly effortless transition from informal clothing to the business attire required by her employment in a big-city advertising firm, signaling the way in which she conforms with relative ease to the responsibilities of this demanding new post.

A similar strategy is used in *Planes, Trains and Automobiles* (1987), wherein the profound differences between the movie's two reluctant travelers are immediately signposted by the way they both dress. Executive Neal Page (Steve Martin) is clothed smartly in an expensive business suit, matched with a high-quality hat and coat. His perfectly coiffured silver hair, immaculately shined shoes, and expensive watch (which eventually turns out to be of use as an item to trade during his fraught journey) all mark him as someone who takes fastidious care of his appearance. His high-class exterior is deliberately juxtaposed with that of chirpy salesman Del Griffith (John Candy), whose attire may not be quite as costly as Neal's, but which proves to be infinitely more robust. The mustachioed Del covers his comfortable cardigan and bow tie with a heavy winter jacket, matched with thick mittens, a warm cap, and ear-warmers. Whereas Neal's outfit is perfectly adequate for someone intending to catch a flight from New York to Chicago, it soon proves to be insufficient for the long, unexpected trek that lay ahead. As his initially spotless professional clothing eventually becomes stained and tattered, the ever-practical Del seems largely unscathed by the misadventures that befall

Steve Martin (1945–   ), actor and stand-up comedian who has
also been active as a writer, producer, and musician.

him, due to the fact that his own choice of layered apparel is considerably
better suited to the rigors of life on the road.

Sometimes a character's change in clothing would come about
through an alteration of worldview rather than external eventualities.
In *The Breakfast Club* (1985), nothing could better typify the transformation of Allison Reynolds (Ally Sheedy) from kleptomaniac loner into a
socially aware livewire than her sudden shift in wardrobe. First depicted
in head-to-toe black clothing, Allison's appearance at the end of the film
in a ruffled pink sleeveless dress—complete with white floral headband—
marks her emergence from intense inner conflict and self-examination,
signifying that she is finally ready to embrace life rather than continually

shying away from it. Intriguingly, a similar strategy was employed two years later in *Some Kind of Wonderful* (Howard Deutch, 1987), in which the protagonist Keith Nelson (Eric Stoltz) is forced to re-evaluate the way he views his best friend, the tomboyish Watts (Mary Stuart Masterson). Having favored accoutrements such as a leather motorbike jacket, driving gloves and dog-tags throughout much of the movie, talented mechanic Watts is the very epitome of utilitarian style; even her pixie cut suggests a no-nonsense attitude. Yet when she is suddenly dressed formally in a chauffeur's outfit at the film's conclusion as part of Keith's abortive attempt to romance Amanda Jones (Lea Thompson), the intended target of his affections, her shift from the functional practicality of her usual garb is just one facet of his eventual realization that his heart instead lies with his best friend and soul mate.

In other instances, a marked disparity in clothing style could denote an attraction of opposites. During *National Lampoon's Vacation* (Harold Ramis, 1983), Chevy Chase's Clark Griswold is the living embodiment of the suburban family man, dressing as sensibly as a vacationing corporate employee could possibly be expected to. Yet as his cross-country travels get underway, he begins to develop an obsession with a beautiful woman driving a Ferrari (Christie Brinkley) whom he encounters throughout his journey. This unnamed mystery female is dressed in figure-hugging, beach-style clothing, her long blonde hair and affable smile leaving Clark smitten at first glance. But what really becomes noteworthy is the veritable chasm that exists between Clark's archetypal married father attire and the faultless elegance of the Ferrari woman's outfits, both underscoring his fascination with her as well as signaling the doomed nature of the bumbling patriarch's ill-advised crush. By that same token, the stunning computer-generated Lisa (Kelly LeBrock) of *Weird Science* (1985) exudes effortless glamor in all of her costumes, not least her charcoal dress with plunging neckline and pink cocktail dress (complete with elbow-length black gloves), and yet her allure is further accentuated by the way in which her clothing is invariably the diametric opposite of that which is worn by her creators, gawky teenagers Wyatt (Ilan Mitchell-Smith) and Gary (Anthony Michael Hall). As her combination of sharp intellect and captivating magnetism turns heads regardless of her choice of attire, the two socially awkward teens are so intrinsically bound to their own, deeply unadventurous clothing conventions that they end up showering with her while still clad in shorts and footwear. Though Lisa eventually succeeds in injecting a modest degree of sophistication into their fashion sense, Gary and Wyatt's comparatively orthodox choice of apparel echoes the way in which they are under the ongoing tutelage of a wiser and more experienced figure whose independence is reflected in her unique sartorial tastes. (And the less said about their "ceremonial" decision to wear bras on their heads while conjuring up Lisa in the first place, the better for everyone.)

Fashion Victims: When Clothing Styles Go Bad in John Hughes's Cinema

While the most arresting fashions of Hughes's movies may well have been those to feature in his teen movies, not all of his characters could be a vision in taffeta and chiffon. Some of the most engaging of his creations became lodged in the public consciousness precisely because of the garishness or incongruity of their wardrobes. It is, for instance, next to impossible to imagine John Candy's Buck Russell without his shabby coat-and-hat combo in *Uncle Buck* (1989), or Cousin Eddie (as portrayed by Randy Quaid) of the *National Lampoon's Vacation* films being bereft of his tasteless leisure suit. Likewise, the style and glamor of Molly Ringwald's numerous costumes in *Pretty in Pink* were offset by the outrageous tastes of Jon Cryer's ostentatious Phil "Duckie" Dale, who is introduced to audiences bedecked in a bolo tie, hippie-style sunglasses, gray-checkered blazer, and a brown porkpie hat, among accessories galore. Duckie was clearly someone who was singularly unafraid to make a statement, and while his ensemble may not have been to everyone's taste, it was nonetheless very difficult to overlook.

Other characters who attempted but failed to impress with the impact of their outfit included Eugene Levy's hilariously insincere car salesman in *National Lampoon's Vacation*, whose flashy sport jacket was matched by a suitably kitsch necktie perhaps better suited to the worst excesses of the 1970s, whereas James Spader's arrogant socialite Steff McKee could be seen sporting an outfit of white linen pants and a royal blue blazer with shoulder pads which might have been an attempt to emphasize his affluent, country club background but only succeeds in making him look as snooty and distant from those around him as his supercilious behavior would generally suggest.

Teachers often have a poor track record of fashion throughout cinema history, and Hughes's selection of argumentative public educators was no exception. Ed Rooney, dean of students at *Ferris Bueller's Day Off*'s Ocean Park High School, starts his day in a respectable enough gray suit matched with a rust-colored necktie, but as his pursuit of his truanting nemesis commences, his attire slowly begins to disintegrate as his misfortunes mount, leaving his clothing in tatters as he limps towards home at the movie's conclusion. Rather more gauche was *The Breakfast Club*'s Assistant Principal Richard Vernon (Paul Gleason), whose weekend apparel consists of a wide-collared black shirt and a beige leisure suit which was well out of style by mid-eighties standards, leading to John Bender's memorable line inquiring if Vernon has, in fact, borrowed his outfit from flamboyant singer Barry Manilow.

Just as the inventive wardrobes of Hughes's teenaged protagonists were used to mark out their uniqueness and independence of spirit, so too were his less sympathetic characters bedecked in clothing which said something about their own personalities. Agreeable figures such as Samantha Baker, Duckie Dale, and Ferris Bueller were all very much individuals whose fashion sense exhibited their appealing, outgoing personalities, but authority figures generally tended towards more austere formalwear, while the geekier characters would usually fall somewhere between the two extremes, their more conservative attire showing only the occasional glimmer of eccentricity or personal expressiveness.

Because Hughes knew how vitally important fashion is to the lives of young people, he wasted no effort in emphasizing his characters' various qualities through their carefully chosen range of apparel. Yet he also realized that the same ability to make a statement through the chosen type and combination of clothing was equally applicable to his adult characters, meaning that a world of difference existed between figures such as Annie Potts's thirtysomething *Pretty in Pink*–style icon Iona, and Suzanne Shepherd's matronly, buttoned-down elementary school Assistant Principal Anita Hoargarth in *Uncle Buck*. For Hughes, the image that his individual characters chose to project to the outside world through the clothes they wore was of crucial significance to the way they related to (and interacted with) the world around them, and the care and attention that he and his production team expended on selecting just the right arrangement of apparel has meant that—even today—it remains one of the elements of his movies that is most regularly discussed.

22

You Have to Learn to Live in the Jungle

John Hughes's Love Affair with Suburbia

John Hughes often praised the virtues of suburban life in his films, holding them up as an unsung jewel of America. Yet he was not unaware of its drawbacks: the tedium and one-upmanship which sometimes underpinned the perfect lawns and white picket fences. Thus his movies, which often seemed to celebrate the suburban existence as a kind of family-oriented utopia which stood apart from the metropolitan sprawl of the city, were never blind to the nosiness, officiousness, and conflict which could taint community life. Hughes's characters were perfectly capable of recognizing the personal benefits of a comfortable family home in an outskirt community while simultaneously lamenting the meddlesomeness of prying neighbors, social climbers' irksome pretentions, and the weight of expectation surrounding social conformity. Thus, over the course of his career, Hughes was to develop an intricate relationship with suburbia, highlighting not only his affection for what such housing communities can represent, but also exploring his various notes of caution over the way in which their merits can often be counteracted by antithetical forces.

Beyond the Windy City: John Hughes and the Chicago Suburbs

While Hughes's engagement with suburban living generally tended to be life-affirming in nature, the manner in which his characters came to connect with their out-of-town existence could vary widely from movie to movie. Whereas Clark Griswold of the *National Lampoon's Vacation* cycle was the archetypal family man, cherishing home and hearth as he strove for a perfect existence that could truly never exist (or, as his predilection towards old home movies in *Christmas Vacation* suggests, had never really existed in the first place), *She's Having a Baby's* (1988) Jefferson "Jake" Briggs finds that he must first go through an inward-looking baptism of fire before he can fully accept his domesticated existence, lamenting the loss of his freedom as a single man and re-evaluating his literary ambitions before finally realizing that his love for his family outweighs his apprehensions of settling down. Thus, in time, he begins to appreciate that something he had initially come to regard as restrictive is actually a source of comfort and security.

For other Hughes characters, suburban Chicago forms a kind of domestic ideal; a goal which embodies the comforts of a secure and contented domestic life. Neal Page of *Planes, Trains and Automobiles* (1987) comes to view his upscale home on the city's outskirts as the one thing that keeps him going through the nightmarish journey he suffers from New York at Thanksgiving, little realizing that his traveling companion Del Griffith is seeking a rather less tangible goal—a loving wife and comfortable house that is now only a distant memory. When Neal overcomes his animosity with the good-natured Del and invites him to join his family, thus allowing him to avoid a Thanksgiving spent alone and miserable, he extends more than a hand of friendship. By making him an unofficial part of the larger family unit, Hughes employs the suburban environment as a means of fostering community spirit, emancipating Del from his undeserved outsider status.

The wily Ferris Bueller, with a talent for making the most of every situation, finds that both urban and suburban Illinois are places of infinite opportunity. The exuberance of his day off, and his attendant determination to squeeze every ounce of unfettered liberation out of the experience, marks him as the epitome of a Hughes teen protagonist: their suburban lives are both the basis of their personal journey of self-discovery and a launch-pad for the aspirations and dreams of adult life. Kevin McCallister of *Home Alone* (1990) is able to draw comfort from the familiarity and routine of his residential district when he is unexpectedly separated from his family, drawing on unforeseen support from seemingly sinister neighbor Mr. Marley when interlopers threaten the safety of his home. Buck Russell of *Uncle Buck* (1989) finds new potential for personal growth in the same practices and habits of suburban living; for him, the unpredicted break from his *laissez-faire* lifestyle in the city is the impetus he needs to reassess his life and correct his lack of direction.

For Hughes, depicting suburban Chicago was more than simply an exercise in nostalgia. As a means of supporting and sustaining the family unit, it was a method of celebrating the community at large, reacting against the faceless commoditization of modern life by promoting interpersonal encouragement and mutual inspiration. While not all characters were able to involve themselves with its capacity for development with equal success or enthusiasm, the theme which ran through each of Hughes's screenplays dealing with suburban life was that of the collective benefiting the individual rather than stymying ambitions, thus enabling new motivations and encouraging altruism for the shared advantage of all.

Hearth and Home: Suburban Family Matters in *Mr. Mom, Uncle Buck*, and *She's Having a Baby*

For many of Hughes's characters, life in suburbia was a complex duality which offered material comfort and a sense of community on one hand, but a sometimes stifling sense of social conformity and unwanted element of neighborly intrusiveness on the other. Never was this more manifest than in the lives of Jake and Kristen Briggs in *She's Having a Baby* (1988), wherein a newly married couple find themselves experiencing sharply conflicting emotions over their new life in suburbia. As their relationship gradually matures, they both become aware (albeit in different ways) that their suburban aspirations are symbolic of both the commitment of their new marital status and the subtle oppressiveness of a communal, societal orthodoxy to which they had previously been oblivious. Though their comfortable domestic existence initially seems idyllic, the responsibilities which come with their move also highlights the loss of the intoxicating freedom of youth—a factor which had seemed abundant

She's Having a Baby. Director: John Hughes. Release date: February 5, 1988.

during their years as unrestricted singles. Yet, whether facing the enormous responsibilities of new parenthood or the machinations of Jake's conniving friend Davis McDonald (played with gleeful deviousness by the charismatic Alec Baldwin), the Briggses' partnership holds together not because of the mutual sanctuary and financial security of their suburban residence, but because of the shared sense of love and respect which always manages to transcend their personal circumstances. The parity of this union—between two people who are intelligent, capable professionals with entirely reasonable and relatable concerns about their future—is able to survive precisely because of the way in which both partners look to each other, rather than the conflicting advice of others, to resolve their issues. Though the widely held assumption is that they should consider a home in the suburbs and an upwardly mobile, aspirational attitude to be driving factors towards greater prosperity and social status, it is only when Kristen and Jake overcome their anxieties about peer expectation and seek to forge a shared future that suits both of their needs, rather than remaining captive to the anticipation of conventionality, that they discover just how satisfying their lives, their marriage, and their growing family unit can be.

Anxieties relating to suburban life are also evident in *Mr. Mom* (Stan Dragoti, 1983), a rare departure from Hughes's perennial Illinois setting in favor of the outskirts of Detroit. Through the mishaps of newly unemployed Jack Butler (Michael Keaton), Hughes's screenplay celebrates the sense of community in suburban areas even as it laments its disadvantages. Like the Briggs family of *She's Having a Baby*, the Butlers are facing a kind of identity crisis—though, in their case, one which has been fueled by professional necessity rather than domestic expectation. Forced to acclimatize to the essential duties of running a home, from everyday housework to the round-the-clock care of young children, Jack soon finds himself re-evaluating everything he thought he knew about his suburban home environment when his wife, Caroline (Teri Garr), takes up a position in a city advertising firm. Bewildered at the sheer amount of housework that Caroline had regularly dealt with prior to his being laid off, Jack initially finds himself feeling restricted by the demands and confinements of his domestic existence, slowly slipping into a haze of trashy daytime soap operas and erratic drinking habits. However, as he is forced by necessity to take much more of an interest in the upbringing of his children Alex, Kenny, and Megan (an activity which had previously been curtailed by his work commitments) and encounters highly sociable denizens of his neighborhood, Jack begins to reconsider his misgivings. By arranging a weekly poker game with some of Caroline's friends who live locally, Jack inadvertently attracts the romantic attentions of the forthright Joan (Ann Jillian), seemingly oblivious to the fact that his change in professional circumstances has marked him as a potential new love interest. Compounded by his uncertainties over Caroline's highly successful performance at her new job, Jack's unwise extramarital temptations are stimulated by a need to compensate for his sense of powerlessness as a result of losing his job, but the restraints of a life spent largely within a suburban area also compound his sense of remoteness from the professional world. Thus, while suburbia is depicted as having the potential to bring people together, simultaneously Hughes draws attention to its occasional ability to isolate. Ultimately, Jack is able to overcome the enticement towards adultery—mirrored in Caroline's own struggle against the unwanted affections of her lecherous boss Ron (Martin Mull)—precisely because he comes to realize that his recent experiences have made him understand much more fully the often-unseen demands that had been continuously placed on his wife, making him appreciate their shared bond of affection and mutual respect all the more fully.

Hughes would revisit many of these themes some years later in the events of *Uncle Buck* (1989). The eponymous protagonist, freewheeling gambler Buck Russell (John Candy), finds his not-inconsiderable skills of improvisation taxed to the limit when he is called upon to look after his brother's three children on short notice. Taking up residence in their family home, the fiercely independent Buck has little choice but to make a psychological shift from the laid-back life he enjoyed in inner-city Chicago as he tries (with varying degrees of success) to adjust to an existence in the leafy suburbs. As he has no firsthand experience of raising youngsters, Buck is forced to undergo a crash course in childcare *in loco parentis*, but soon comes to comprehend that life in the well-ordered outskirts of the city is not quite so crushingly monotonous as he had anticipated. With no choice but to adapt creatively in order to meet each challenge that faces him, the gregarious bachelor soon attracts the interest of neighbor Marcie Dahlgren-Frost (Laurie Metcalf), albeit that he is unresponsive to her overtures—not least due to his existing long-term relationship with garage owner Chanice Kobolowski (Amy Madigan).

Marcie's advances do, however, provoke conflict between Buck and Chanice due to a misunderstanding that is deliberately concocted by obstinate teenager Tia (Jean Louisa Kelly). Yet far from ending the slow-burning romance, the quarrel—along with Buck's newfound experience of conventional domestic life—acts as a catalyst to tame his unsustainable bachelor lifestyle, making him realize that the time to settle down has finally arrived. Though his transformation from easygoing slacker to responsible family man is a gradual one, the unexpected appeal of his newfound suburban surroundings plays no small part in his dawning insight; deliberately cast in sharp contrast to his shady race-fixing dealings and rundown accommodation in Chicago, Buck finds his eyes opened to a new way of living and comes to understand that while unchecked conformity may be stifling, there are also many benefits to seeking a comfortable domestic existence.

Familiarity Breeds Contempt: The Highs and Lows of Suburbia in *Ferris Bueller's Day Off* and *National Lampoon's Christmas Vacation*

Hughes's underplayed juxtaposition of suburbia's ability to both insulate and integrate was a conflict he would revisit throughout his career. For Clark Griswold, of the *National Lampoon's Vacation* movies, for instance, a comfortable home on an upscale estate based on the outskirts of Chicago forms the epitome of contented family life. While Clark is regularly seen on the road as part of the travels which made the cycle famous, his obsession with providing happy memories and a stable domestic environment for his wife and children mean that even when he is at home there is still plenty of potential for wanton mayhem. In *National Lampoon's Christmas Vacation* (Jeremiah S. Chechik, 1989), the Griswolds' unconventional, sometimes fraught but ultimately sincere family camaraderie is pitched against the nominal antagonists of the film, his sneering neighbors the Chesters.

Margot and Todd Chester (Julia Louis-Dreyfus and Nicholas Guest) are rather cheerless, snooty social climbers who consider their well-to-do domestic situation not as a means to an end, but as a stepping stone to greater and more prominently displayed affluence. Considering Christmas to be little more than a crass commercial affectation, and having little interest in the celebration's spiritual underpinnings, the Chesters' total disregard for the festive season inevitably puts them in conflict with the relentlessly Yuletide-oriented Clark; initially contemptuous toward his unyielding efforts to provide his family with the perfect Christmas, their derision eventually turns to outright hostility when their increasingly unhinged neighbor's frenzied preoccupation with decorations and festivities sees their own property (and eventually themselves) suffering an increasing amount of incidental damage.

It is implied that while the Chesters see the Griswolds as a kind of vulgar irritant—a throwback to a more traditional age of altruism and family life, in a period that had become aggressively tooled towards commerce and commoditization—the real underlying issue is that they believe the seemingly upright, self-sacrificing Griswolds are lowering the tone of a neighborhood that the Chesters believe should be as pretentious and facelessly corporate as they. Although their proximate location forces the two families to coexist, albeit uncomfortably, their archetypal suburban environments are poles apart: Clark pursues a backward-looking idealization of his own cherished youth in a more innocent time; Todd and Margot lament the fact that community spirit and family values are allowed to persist in an age that they, and many fellow yuppies, felt should have long ago been left behind.

For the Bueller family in *Ferris Bueller's Day Off*, suburbia provides an unprecedented level of support following the advent of Ferris's faked and strangely ambiguous "illness." As Hughes displays throughout the movie, endless gifts, such as floral displays, are showered upon the family home, well-wishers constantly telephone to convey their hopes for a swift recovery, and fundraisers are being set up throughout the local high school he attends in order to meet his medical costs. While the crafty Ferris is, of course, able to use the outpouring of sympathy entirely to his own advantage, the way in which the community rallies around his "cause" is an unequivocal statement on Hughes's behalf that the warmhearted and supportive America of Clark Griswold's youth was still alive and well in the 1980s, emphasizing that the trend towards aggressive self-interest need not be considered the only option for society. Though much of the movie's action takes place in urban Chicago, the sequences in Ferris's neighborhood throughout the feature emphasize that while this classy suburban area is clearly no stranger to conspicuous consumption, the well-being of its various denizens is ultimately considered to be of paramount importance.

The suburban situations of *Ferris Bueller's Day Off* would be explored in more detail in the short-lived NBC spin-off of the movie, entitled simply *Ferris Bueller*, which was broadcast between 1990 and 1991. Hughes was not involved with either the conception or the production of the television adaptation, however. Taking its cue less from the film's inner-city Chicago sequences and more from the out-of-town circumstances which cropped up around Ferris's neighborhood (including the high school he attended), the action was transplanted from Illinois to the beachfront city of Santa Monica in California. Among the series' many fourth wall-breaking devices, the events of the 1986 film were referred to as a kind of metafiction, suggesting that the famous "Day Off" had merely been a fictitious representation of the lives of the sitcom characters. With Charlie Schlatter, Brandon Douglas, and Ami Dolenz taking up the roles of Ferris, Cameron, and Sloane, the cast received solid support from Jennifer Aniston in an early role as Jeanie Bueller, and Richard Riehle as the ever-inimical Ed Rooney. With a focus that was much more firmly rooted in Ferris's local community than the Chicagoan urban escapades of the Hughes film, the series had greater capacity to explore avenues that had been left largely uncharted by the original movie. These included Rooney's ditzy secretary, Grace (Judith Kahan), nursing an unrequited crush on the hapless dean of students, and a much more low-key examination of the thoughtful side of Ferris's character than the deep profundities that were occasionally in evidence throughout Hughes's film. In practice, however, the TV series owed less to the style of the 1986 feature and more to other early-nineties teen situation comedies such as Fox's *Parker Lewis Can't Lose* (1990–1993), featuring Corin Nemek, and NBC's own *Blossom* (1990–1995), starring Mayim Bialik. As had been the case with CBS's abortive TV adaptation of *Uncle Buck* (1990–1991), *Ferris*

Bueller suffered considerable critical hostility and was compared unfavorably to the source material, leading to its rapid cancellation.

Throughout his filmography, Hughes repeatedly returned to suburban settings, and while he was far from unaware of the interpersonal conflict and pettiness that could flare up within the confines of any community, so too was he quick to point out that the benefits of a responsive and responsible neighborhood inevitably outweighed the drawbacks of potential personality clash or divergence driven by variance over social attitudes. For Hughes, the suburbs at their best could be the very epitome of the American Dream—where personal development, family harmony, and social assimilation could intermingle in order to provide a model living environment which not only provided comfort and fulfillment in the present, but also supplied the foundation for a more affluent and ambitious future. Though this optimistic cultural appraisal may not have been a social blueprint that was particularly prevalent in the increasingly slick and often uncompromising filmmaking of the 1980s, the role of suburbia as a safe haven against the encroachment of a hard-edged and cynical age was emphasized by other films of the era, such as the thriller *Lethal Weapon* (Richard Donner, 1987) and the comedy-horror *The 'Burbs* (Joe Dante, 1989). While the geopolitical environment of the eighties may have been changing at a phenomenal rate, Hughes never lost sight of the fact that beneath the veneer of fast-moving current affairs and world politics the true heart of America lay not in its superpower status or cultural primacy, but in its people and communities.

23

Deliver the Kiss that Kills

Romance and Class in John Hughes's America

R omance is vitally important to many of John Hughes's films, but equally significant is the way in which he so often relates courtship and love to class consciousness. From the fraught love triangle between Andie, Duckie, and Blane in *Pretty in Pink* (Howard Deutch, 1986) to the longing and subtle cruelties witnessed by Amanda, Watts, and Keith throughout *Some Kind of Wonderful* (Howard Deutch, 1987), Hughes often emphasized the ability of social class to thwart romantic ambition and divide potential couples in spite of the best intentions. Sometimes these conflicts could be overcome, but on some occasions the indelible border lines would prove insurmountable. Hughes's complex and multi-layered approach to the conflict between socio-economic circumstances and romantic freedom is described through an exploration of the various relationships which arise routinely in his screenplays, investigating the numerous ways in which class and cultural attitudes can affect or even determine romantic involvement throughout the various fictional scenarios.

When Unity Overcomes Division: Negotiating Class Boundaries in *The Breakfast Club*

The Brat Pack titan that was *The Breakfast Club* is a film which is profoundly concerned with exploring the connections that exist between strangers—sometimes predictable, sometimes unlikely. While Hughes had an obvious interest in detailing the interactions between the "respectable" mainstream students and the rather more unconventionally minded outsiders, he also made the point that the divisions between them were based not only on cliques and particular attitudes, but also the relative prosperity of their parents which similarly informed their respective backgrounds. His earlier *Sixteen Candles* (1984) flirted with issues of social class, subtly acknowledging the fact that the attraction of Molly Ringwald's Samantha Baker for the handsome but unobtainable Jake Ryan (Michael Shoeffling) needed to overcome the obstacles not just of the school's rigid echelons of popularity and factions, but also the gulf which existed between her lower-middle-class background and his more well-to-do, determinedly white-collar family. But with *The Breakfast Club*, Hughes would expound on this issue with far greater clarity, drawing attention to the ways in which economic status had an incontrovertible effect on personal standing—and its ramifications—within a high school setting.

Hughes has won praise over the years for the ways in which his features depicted multifaceted characters who were quite different from the happy-go-lucky sybarites populating many other teen movies of the time, opting instead for a portrayal of teenagers who were both realistically rendered and ultimately relatable. Yet just as widely applauded has been his ability to introduce figures who are immediately recognizable as particular stereotypes familiar to the genre—the jock, the geek, the rebel, and so forth—in a manner which enables audiences to identify them without delay. Knowing that viewers will then instantly make specific assumptions about the personalities and qualities of these characters, Hughes is then able to skillfully undermine these expectations, challenging us to re-evaluate each individual by seeing them in a new light. In *The Breakfast Club*, he uses the elaborate but stringently followed system of popularity and acceptability which operates within a high school setting to offer an intriguing commentary on inter-class negotiation and mobility in the rapidly changing America of the 1980s.

This class divide was most prominently displayed in the seemingly improbable budding romance between Molly Ringwald's Claire Standish and Judd Nelson's John Bender; the pair overcomes their shared loathing at the beginning of the movie to eventually realize—over the course of a long day in detention—that not only do they face similar personal issues, but that their feelings for each other run more deeply than simply recognizing a profound commonality. Their early antipathy is fueled, in part, by the fact that their backgrounds could not be further apart. Claire's family is prosperous, whereas Bender's household is financially disadvantaged. As a result of this, Bender deeply resents Claire's superior attitude and position of privilege, while she regards him with disdain on account of his flippancy and disregard for the school's unwritten social system (which has elevated her to its apex). However, all is not quite as it seems. As the day progresses, Bender reveals considerably greater depth of character than the others had initially believed possible, his fellow students having regarded him as a disruptive influence simply because of his indifference towards his peers and his open contempt for authority. The audience learns of his troubled background, with an abusive father who regularly lashes out at him and has little concern for his well-being. Claire begins to realize that their domestic situations are not as different as she had supposed; although her own family is materially prosperous, any appearance of household harmony is deceiving. While money is no object to the pursuit of her lifestyle, Claire's parents are clearly too deeply involved in their own personal concerns to pay her much attention, and she often feels that her primary function is to act as a pawn in a tug-of-war between her mother and father. Only by comprehending that their situation at home is eerily similar, but for the superficial difference made by the relative affluence of their respective backgrounds, can the pair look beyond their preconceptions about each other and recognize that their shared personal experience transcends the social classes to which they belong.

Just as Bender's presumptions about Claire are disabused, the same is true of the audience's. While she may dress and behave in a manner emblematic of the high school "princess" (as she is termed), in truth she is battling to cope with the difficulties of her unhappy home life, the constant compromises surrounding her personal image (which are inflicted by peer pressure), and the stress of growing up in an age of great social and economic uncertainty. The same gap between perception and reality is true of all five members of the Breakfast Club, of course, from the near-suicidal anxieties tormenting Anthony Michael Hall's Brian

Johnson to the deep personal conflict that roils within Emilio Estevez's Andrew Clark. While all are initially considered to be representative of the particular cliques to which they belong, in actuality they are each individuals with complex drives who are subsumed by parental and social expectations. Both Andrew and Brian come from backgrounds which (it is inferred) are not quite as opulent as the Standish family, and yet they suffer from similar domestic disharmony—Brian's parents have pressurized the young scholar to the boiling point in their obsession with him obtaining the highest possible grades, while Andrew is locked in a damaging cycle of mutual hostility with his father, who demands peak athletic performance at all times. Yet arguably more striking is the slow-burning disclosure of the unusual situation surrounding Ally Sheedy's enigmatic Allison Reynolds, who is a compulsive liar and occasional kleptomaniac. Allison's family appears to be closer to Bender's on the socio-economic spectrum, and yet the abuse she suffers is of a quite different nature; her parents seem content to simply ignore her, discounting her views and consideration to the point that her behavior has become increasingly bizarre. Whether her unusual ways are a cry for help, or merely a byproduct of being so thoroughly overlooked that she attends a Saturday detention session for no reason other than that she has nowhere better to go on the weekend, her personal journey seems all the more poignant for the fact that—even more than the other students with whom she is sharing the day—her transformation is brought about solely by the fact that, for once, other people are actually listening to her rather than simply taking her presence for granted.

Hughes's point is that irrespective of the level of affluence enjoyed by the parents of his unconventional group of students, all of them are essentially facing the same difficulties intrinsic to being a teenager. They all undergo a struggle to throw off the shackles of their parents' influence, and eventually come to realize that they can relate to each other—in spite of the social chasm that exists between them—better than they can to their own mothers and fathers. It is ultimately left to the viewer to decide whether the friendships and nascent romances which are struck up throughout the detention session can possibly endure beyond the rarefied confines of that fateful Saturday. While the students' shared disciplinary punishment offers them an unexpected (and unprecedented) chance to encounter one another when the school's inflexible social structure would normally keep them apart, by extension Hughes offers a glimpse of how diversity is a strength rather than a disadvantage; the difficulties facing each of them may be essentially the same, and yet because the students are so different they are all able to bring a fresh perspective to long-running concerns. But while the reclusive, self-contained Allison's frisson with athletic extrovert Andy may have been poignant, it is the blossoming romance between the iconoclastic Bender and Claire, emerging from the restraints of smothering conformity, which really pushes the envelope of acceptability within the high school's social system. Their relationship is the very epitome of Hughes's prevailing theme that even the most seemingly incompatible people can somehow relate to each other under the correct circumstances, underscoring the point that love can prevail against even the most deep-seated assumptions about personal stereotypes and social boundaries.

While there are numerous profundities which manifest themselves throughout *The Breakfast Club*, perhaps the single-most unfaltering message to be delivered by Hughes is that if his characters are able to overcome social divisions and preconceptions regarding labels that surround particular groups, then the same must be true of the viewers themselves. Although there are no guarantees that the new bonds connecting the members of the Breakfast Club will endure, there is little doubt that every individual present on the Saturday detention setting emerges from the school library a palpably changed person, each with the power to overcome the self-limiting labels that previously defined them.

Putting the Class in High School: Problematic Class Divisions in *Pretty in Pink*

If *The Breakfast Club* had begun to explore the ways in which economic background had an impact upon the teenage experience, the issue would come to the forefront much more prominently in the following year's *Pretty in Pink*. As had been the case in the earlier movie, romantic desire and entanglement are used as a means to identify and interrogate issues regarding social division, though—in the case of *Pretty in Pink*—the emphasis shifts onto the way in which effort and aspiration can challenge a predominating but highly restrictive worldview which posits that wealth rather than moral virtue is a means of measuring success and influence.

Molly Ringwald's Andie Walsh is intelligent, creative, and attractive, but finds that her romantic pull towards handsome fellow student Blane McDonnagh (Andrew McCarthy) is blighted by a disparity in their respective backgrounds. Though Andie is more than aware of the challenges that are likely to face a nascent relationship when their high school is so fraught by social division, she underestimates the difficulties which are generated by the resentful, well-heeled Steff McKee (James Spader) in an effort to keep them apart. Steff desires a relationship with Andie himself, and seeks revenge for her spurning of his affections by threatening the social standing of Blane, knowing too well that his acquaintance would be damaged by the revelation that he is dating someone from a blue-collar neighborhood.

Though Andie is independently minded and far from naïve, she underestimates just how deeply hurt she will be by Blane's recognition that their romance has the potential to undermine his reputation among his peers. She already faces difficulties as a result of her father's (Harry Dean Stanton) depressive state of mind and inability to find gainful employment, supporting the family through working at a music store managed by her close friend Iona (Annie Potts). Steff plots to ruin Andie's chances with Blane, in spite of the deep affection which exists between the two, while also conspiring to compromise any chance she has of dating outside her own social group. Hughes takes care to contrast the role of friendship in both situations, highlighting the supportive and empathetic bond between Andie and her long-term confidante Phil "Duckie" Dale (Jon Cryer) while simultaneously underscoring the manipulative streak which taints the uneasy alliance between Steff and Blane. Yet he is also careful to avoid crude stereotyping; eccentric working-class hero Duckie is frequently jealous and conflicted, and while the well-to-do Steff is egotistical and overindulged, the similarly prosperous Blane is apprehensive and plagued by self-doubt.

Because Hughes treats the social issues of *Pretty in Pink* with genuine earnestness, his exploration of the stringently hierarchical structure which underpins high school life—and the way it so profoundly regulates and influences the formative years of young people—avoided any danger of the storyline being interpreted as a kind of straightforward "Cinderella story." While it is true that Andie's love for Blane eventually prevails, it does so at a cost—one which inadvertently breaks the heart of Duckie, who must come to terms with the fact that his lifelong crush on his best friend will always be essentially hopeless. Blane must accept that to follow the desires of his heart, he must risk the censure and alienation of his wealthy peers, but the focus is more squarely situated on Andie's success—as the viewer has witnessed her breadline domestic situation, her eventual capacity to surpass the restrictions placed upon her ambitions as a result of her social status seems all the more satisfying.

There is an undeniable sense of following the American Dream in Andie's ultimate accomplishment in using talent, hard work, and natural ability to enable her social mobility. Because she stays true to her emotional self, she overcomes Steff's malign machinations and Blane's indecisiveness to break through the obstacles of the social divisions which so overwhelmingly affect the high school experience—and adult life beyond it. Subtle hints are distributed throughout the film which suggest that the most bountiful monetary resources cannot solve every problem; problematic familial issues are hinted at in the case of both Blane and Steff, inferring that even their privileged backgrounds are not free from emotional difficulties, whereas Andie and her father, Jack, enjoy a close and mutually caring relationship in spite of their straitened circumstances. Yet perhaps the most prominent theme Hughes exposes and interrogates is that of the influence of the more affluent students; surrounded by a surfeit of material goods and suffering from the kind of ennui that can only be generated by having little to no restrictions on their buying power, they wield similar supremacy over the social strata of the school, ensuring that their exclusive coterie is jealously guarded at all times. That they are perfectly willing to estrange and isolate one of their own rather than accommodate the presence of someone beyond their clique presents an impression of an uncaring and often spiteful elite, which is far removed from the reciprocally supportive community of characters such as Andie, Jack, Duckie, and Iona.

Hughes often presented a clarion call for greater unity and collaborative effort, and throughout *Pretty in Pink* we witness the way in which protagonists working towards a common good are able to surpass the intolerance which forms the foundation of class prejudice. Though much effort is expended on the emotional hurt which can be caused by Machiavellian underhandedness and unfeeling compliance with the etiquette of social divisions, it is ultimately the message of hope which Hughes presents that lingers longest in the memory—that romantic devotion can prevail over damaging collective perceptions regarding class, and that sometimes it is better to risk isolation by standing up for something worthwhile than to live a life subjugated by the narrow-minded partialities of others.

True Love Defies Expectation: Subverting Class Preconceptions in *Some Kind of Wonderful*

While *Pretty in Pink* had celebrated the triumph of honest, working-class values over the callous plotting of a detached and hard-hearted elite, the movie's conclusion was not without its controversy. The original ending had Andie overcoming the hurt of Blane's rejection by defiantly reciprocating the affections of the adoring Duckie, but this conclusion had performed badly with test audiences, leading to the somewhat divisive climax to the film eventually released to theaters. The following year, however, Hughes would present another film—also helmed by Deutch—which would explore themes of social class from another perspective, resulting in a markedly different cinematic experience.

Some Kind of Wonderful depicts the trials of aspiring artist Keith Nelson (Eric Stoltz), whose industrious working-class family is dedicated to ensuring that he makes the most of his high school education in order to attend a good college, thus opening up new opportunities for his future adult life. But the headstrong Keith has plans of his own, not least the pursuit of the inscrutable Amanda Jones (Lea Thompson), a good-looking student who has managed—with no small amount of resourcefulness—to integrate herself with a group of popular, well-off students in spite of her own domestic background being little more prosperous than Keith's. The mutual attraction between the two angers the arrogant and well-to-do Hardy Jenns (Craig Sheffer), Amanda's boyfriend, who regularly treats her with casual contempt, humiliating her in the full knowledge that her social status within the school is dependent upon her relationship with him. Thus, Amanda finds herself torn between the thought of responding to Keith's steadfast interest in her on one hand, and the fact that the vindictive Hardy has the means of destroying her social credibility at any time of his choosing.

Conflict arises between Keith and his father, Cliff (John Ashton), when he uses the hard-earned money that has been saved by his family to pay his college fees in order to purchase a pair of diamond earrings to impress the target of his affections. The vengeful Jenns is eventually held at bay by Keith's unlikely acquaintance Duncan (Elias Koteas), an unexpectedly creative skinhead he befriends during detention, but the big date that Keith has long dreamed of ends on an unanticipated note when he discovers that the true object of his love is not Amanda at all, but his unstintingly supportive best friend Watts (Mary Stuart Masterson), who has been assisting him in the organization of the romantic rendezvous. Thus, Keith comes to realize that neither he nor Watts need to challenge the orthodoxy of the school's social system in order to bring their relationship into being, while Amanda—now cast adrift as a result of her severance from Hardy and his scheming associates—finds herself forced to re-evaluate her priorities in life, realizing how shallow the machinations of her erstwhile social group had actually been.

As with *Pretty in Pink*, the characters hailing from a blue-collar background are shown to have considerably greater solidarity than those with a more prosperous domestic situation. Keith, Watts, Cliff, and Duncan all provide support and encouragement for one another during the film's events, albeit in profoundly different ways. Amanda is forced to realize that the compromises she has been forced to make in order to enter the upper echelons of high school society have rendered her outlook inauthentic and her status unstable in the long term. Because her relationship with Hardy is volatile and lacking in substance, she is denied the kind of social mobility which opens up to Andie Walsh in the earlier film. Whereas Andie sought only to have her feelings for Blane returned, with his wealthy background merely incidental to her romantic ambitions, she succeeded in ways that are denied to Amanda simply because of the insincerity and essential hollowness of the latter's debased association with Jenns. While Hardy's machinations are very similar to those of Steff McKee, the gender-reversed nature of the film means that the dynamics of the love triangle are actually quite different—and the resolution correspondingly dissimilar.

Whereas *Pretty in Pink* had ended with the redemption of Blane— suggesting that not everyone at the pinnacle of the high school social system was entirely aspersive and profligate—there are no such assurances in *Some Kind of Wonderful*. Although Jenns and his cohorts retain their wealth and influence at the conclusion, the theme running through the movie is one of self-empowerment in spite of social circumstance. Watts and Keith come to comprehend that in order to achieve happiness, they must regard social mobility as an irrelevant consideration in their choice of romance, whereas Amanda, by contrast, is forced to appreciate (however painfully) that the price of her entry into the upper echelons of school society was too high, compromising her dignity and suffocating her sense of self-determination.

The tone of Hughes's screenplay for *Some Kind of Wonderful* is one of bold independence, laying emphasis on the point that social class is no indicator of either personal ethics or creative ability. Whereas in *Pretty in Pink* Andie discovers that her love for Blane is being interpreted as social climbing even when her ambitions are purely romantic in nature, *Some Kind of Wonderful* reconfigures this dynamic by positing the notion that autonomy of will is the foremost consideration in achieving true personal success. Keith's father, Cliff, is concerned about his son's direction in life not because he wants to stifle his artistic creativity, but because he considers a purely academic path to be a better guarantor of future prosperity. When Keith defies him, he does so not as a means of disregarding his paternal concerns, but because he has determined that in order to reach for success he must also risk failure—the choice is his alone to make. Yet in pursuing the popular Amanda, he is not attempting to raise his own social status within the school, but to make her come to terms with the fact that she does not need to affect the trappings of the more prosperous in order to advance her personal ambitions. Only by remaining true to herself can she hope to succeed on her own terms, beholden to no one.

Although *Some Kind of Wonderful* has a slightly darker tone than its predecessor (albeit that it is not entirely without humor), it is a film which is both hopeful and life-affirming. Whereas *Pretty in Pink* had been concerned with the negotiation of class boundaries, the later film was instead a rousing affirmation that sometimes they needed to be discounted altogether for the sake of greater considerations. Hughes does not play down the degree of influence which is wielded by those at the zenith of high school society, but, similarly, he makes the point that sometimes the search for prosperity and social elevation for its own sake can be a restrictive and even futile pursuit. Hughes's tales of love and conflict across social divisions may all have taken markedly different paths, but all point to the innovation and resourcefulness of the individual as the means to achieve lasting satisfaction in life. Those who are shown to succeed do so because they decide to draw upon their inner reserves of creativity and compassion in order to move towards adulthood with fulfillment and moral integrity. Characters who disregard these virtues in favor of social prominence and wealth are inevitably shown to be the lesser for it, bound as they are by the capriciousness of outside influences rather than the capacity of their own personal independence.

24

When I Get Older, These Kids are Going to Take Care of Me

The Role of Seniors in John Hughes Films

F or all the focus that has fallen on John Hughes's youthful characters, it is important not to overlook the fact that some of his most extraordinary creations have actually been in late middle age or older. Hughes employed senior citizens in his films for a variety of purposes: highlighting issues surrounding the generation gap, promoting responsible family values, and emphasizing that everyone should have the ability to feel a sense of belonging and relevance in a youth-oriented society—irrespective of age. Some of Hughes's more seasoned characters were treated with greater sympathy than others, but all of them had an interesting part to play in his wider commentary on society in general.

Mature Subject Matter: Grandparents in John Hughes's Teen Cinema

It is often said that children and grandparents are united against a common enemy. Yet in Hughes's movies, one intriguing factor is that while parents are sometimes shown to be out of touch with the worldview and ambitions of their children, grandparents almost always managed to be one step further removed from the outlook of the youth of the time. Never is this more evident than in *Weird Science* (1985), where Hughes introduced audiences to Henry (Ivor Barry) and Carmen (Ann

Coyle)—perhaps the most stereotypical grandparents ever to appear in any of his screenplays. In a movie that is passionately focused on the ability of people to adapt and evolve in order to better fulfill their personal potential, this archaic pair is still holding on to some kind of bygone age. The duo was perfectly cast. Henry, with his bow tie and slightly-too-neat mustache, was played by veteran Welsh character actor Ivor Barry—whose screen credits range from historical action-thriller *In Enemy Country* (Harry Keller, 1968) to wartime comedy *To Be or Not to Be* (Alan Johnson, 1983)—who beautifully articulated the older man's stuffy reserve. In a rare screen role for Ann Coyle, who was known in the eighties for minor roles in a 1982 episode of PBS's anthology series *American Playhouse* and *One More Saturday Night* (Dennis Klein, 1986), Carmen was brought to life with similar panache; with her outmoded dress sense and hopelessly naïve (but nonetheless rather admirable) assumption that maintaining a good relationship with his grandparents is a key priority for a teen-aged boy, she achieved a winning line in mortified indignation. During dinner at a genteel restaurant, Henry and Carmen make the unwittingly calamitous decision to pay an impromptu visit to their grandson Wyatt (Ilan Mitchell-Smith), knowing that his parents are temporarily away from home. Little do either of them realize that Wyatt is presently mired in (nominally) organizing a wild house party—the machination of his unexpected new mentor Lisa (Kelly LeBrock). Upon their arrival, the mature pair is outraged at sight of the upscale home being invaded by scores of rowdy teenagers. Although hopelessly out of their depth, they fight valiantly to restore order. As Henry irritably swats party guests with his endearingly anachronistic "Rex Harrison hat," the pair angrily confronts Lisa, disregarding her account of her recent creation (via a combination of technology, lightning, and possibly supernatural means) with the steadfast warning that they will never stand for "baloney." Sadly for them, their inflexibility in the face of the unfathomable scene proves to be their undoing; when they threaten to call the police, Lisa subjects them to her infamously uncanny abilities, which ultimately leads to both grandparents winding up, catatonic, in one of the house's closets. (Their appearance the next morning, still immobile and seemingly frozen in time, becomes the source of some perplexity for Bill Paxton's Chet.)

Although there is no doubting the good intentions of Henry and Carmen as concerned grandparents who are simply trying to protect the safety of their family's property, Hughes seems to derive great enjoyment from comparing the couple's mannerly, rigidly upright attitude to the raucous, Bacchanalian scenario which has been concocted by Lisa. The inference, of course, is that their attitudes are shown to be archaic by the standards of the modern day, a realization which would doubtless have remained a mystery to them had it not been revealed so thoroughly by their unexpected collision with youth culture and the strange powers of Lisa—both of which are phenomena so far beyond their ken that their subsequent comatose state seems to function as an allegory for their apparently thorough inability to process them in any kind of meaningful way.

During the previous year's *Sixteen Candles* (1984), Hughes had presented a rather different take on the role of the grandparent. In this scenario, Molly Ringwald's Samantha Baker found her life turned upsidedown by the presence of not one but two sets of grandparents, gathered for the forthcoming wedding of her sister Ginny. Though well-meaning and generally affable, these mature relatives soon become suffocating for Samantha, not least when they inadvertently begin interfering in her social life. Their interactions with her day-to-day activities are never maliciously meant—quite the opposite, in fact. However, what they perceive to be supportive helpfulness is often communicated as overbearing, meddling, and intrusive.

Making the characters appealing in spite of their low-key bickering and the occasional grumble about triviality is the fact that they are portrayed by familiar figures from stage and screen. "Grandpa" Howard Baker was played by Edward Andrews, at that point a highly recognizable character actor for several decades, starting from the 1950s and extending well into the 1980s. Andrews appeared in many television series and in numerous movies, including *Elmer Gantry* (Richard Brooks, 1960), *Tora! Tora! Tora!* (Richard Fleischer, Toshio Masuda and Kinji Fukasaku, 1970), and *Gremlins* (Joe Dante, 1984). His onscreen partner, Dorothy Baker, was depicted by actress Billie Bird; another prolific performer, Bird's television roles were plentiful, and she had made numerous cinematic appearances (many uncredited) from the early 1950s. Her film roles became more regular in the eighties, when she appeared in features as diverse as *Max Dugan Returns* (Herbert Ross, 1983), *One Crazy Summer* (Savage Steve Holland, 1986), and *Ernest Saves Christmas* (John R. Cherry III, 1988). The Baker grandparents' counterparts, Helen and Fred—the parents of Carlin Glynn's Brenda—were similarly well-known faces to audiences of the time. Carole Cook was a longtime actress of both stage and screen, especially well known for her Broadway appearances, while Max Showalter's long acting career saw his involvement in an abundance of film and TV credits from the 1940s onwards, with him becoming particularly well known for appearances in movies such as *Niagara* (Henry Hathaway, 1953), *Indestructible Man* (Jack Pollexfen, 1956) and *It Happened to Jane* (Richard Quine, 1959).

To today's audiences, the grandparents of *Sixteen Candles* may well seem hopelessly stereotypical. The characters tend to dress in a semi-formal manner that appears to be a style suited to people much older than the actors who are actually in the roles, and their squabbles and fixations appear to be straight out of some kind of clichéd senior citizens' handbook. Yet in truth, Hughes's characterization was simply reflective of the demographics of the time. In the 1980s, depictions of what might be perceived as "elderly" characters were quite different from those which are expected in more recent popular culture. Average life spans were shorter, and consequently the acknowledged demarcation lines of middle age were more likely to extend into the early thirties rather than, in the present day, the mid-forties or even early fifties. Thus, people who would today be considered to be middle aged were then more broadly deemed to be of advanced years, an expectation that was exacerbated by the fact that in the postwar years couples tended to have families much younger than has generally come to be the case. Fashion tastes have changed significantly, with older people more inclined to dress in a contemporary manner, and thanks to Internet access people of all ages have far greater off-the-cuff exposure to youth culture, allowing senior citizens to be more cognizant of the tastes of later generations. Similarly, since the 1980s there has been greater emphasis on diet and exercise to improve health and prolong life, allowing people to feel fit and "youthful" for much longer than may have been the case in previous decades.

Though some may consider them to be exaggerated parodies of older people, the grandparents of *Sixteen Candles* are relentlessly family-oriented and always try to act in the best interests of those around them. While their actions don't always match their intentions (consider in particular their alternating kindliness and rampant racial insensitivity towards Gedde Watanabe's weird-but-cordial exchange student Long Duk Dong), their presence signals a bulwark of reassuring normality among the torrent of uncertainty which assails the protagonist Samantha. As she faces the inner turmoil caused by young love, the sting of her parents forgetting her birthday, and the general anxiety of being a teenager at a high-stress point in her life (surrounded by the chaos of her sister's wedding and the grinding social insecurities of the school dance), the comforting—if sometimes disconcerting—company of her grandparents suggests a familiar Hughesian preoccupation with family solidarity, even in the face of upheaval and change.

Family is Relative: Grandparents and Domestic Conflict

Not all grandparents to appear in a Hughes screenplay behave quite as innocuously as those featured in *Sixteen Candles*. Throughout *National Lampoon's Christmas Vacation* (Jeremiah S. Chechik, 1989), the low-key conflict between two squabbling sets of grandparents form one of many problems to beset Clark Griswold (Chevy Chase) and his family during the festive season. Hughes's approach is very much based around providing a study in contrasts. Clark's parents, Clark Senior (John Randolph) and Nora (Diane Ladd), are largely affable and compassionate people who seem proud of their son's achievements and are determined (as far as possible) to involve themselves in the holiday spirit. By comparison, the parents of Clark's wife, Ellen (Beverly D'Angelo)—Art and Frances Smith—clearly disapprove of their daughter's choice of husband and are relentless in their disparagement of Clark's resolve to provide the perfect Christmas celebration. Thus, sparks fly as catty comments abound and subtle discord bubbles away beneath the surface—a dispute which seems all the more evident as a result of the otherwise-jolly Yuletide surroundings.

As had been the case with *Sixteen Candles*, well-known performers were cast in the roles of both the Griswold and Smith grandparents. As Clark W. Griswold Senior, John Randolph provided an air of quiet geniality to proceedings which seemed to transcend the underlying turbulence around him. A veteran actor from the 1940s onwards, Randolph was best known to audiences of the eighties for roles in films such as *Prizzi's Honor* (John Huston, 1985) and *The Wizard of Loneliness* (Anne Riley, 1988). Multiple-award-winning actress Diane Ladd played Nora Griswold, and would—shortly after—go on to be nominated for Academy Awards for her performances in *Wild at Heart* (David Lynch, 1990) and *Rambling Rose* (Martha Coolidge, 1991). Played with a pitch-perfect strain of curmudgeonly grumpiness, Arthur "Art" Smith is never less than entertaining in the hands of highly experienced performer E. G. Marshall. With a fruitful career on the big screen, Marshall is perhaps best remembered for his appearances in *The Bridge at Remagen* (John Guillermin, 1969) and as the president of the United States in *Superman II* (Richard Lester, 1980), though he would later appear in a high-profile role as John Mitchell in the controversial biopic *Nixon* (Oliver Stone, 1995). Marshall was joined by the polymathic Doris Roberts as his onscreen partner Frances Smith. A longtime TV and film performer (also an author, philanthropist, and political activist), Roberts won and was nominated for numerous awards in her extensive career, as well as appearing in regular roles in television series, including NBC's *Remington Steele* (1982–1987) and CBS's *Everybody Loves Raymond* (1996–2005). As might be expected from such a skilled lineup of experienced performers, comic timing and subtle character moments were to be found in abundance, with many gleefully observed situations of underplayed inter-family variance cropping up throughout the movie.

The conflict generated by the grandparents' presence is so effectively depicted in the Hughes script precisely because of its subdued nature. The two Griswold kids, teenagers Rusty (Johnny Galecki) and Audrey (Juliette Lewis), resent their private living space being hijacked by visiting relatives; Ellen intercedes, acting as peacekeeper, and yet is herself quite obviously being driven to distraction by the presence of judgmental busybodies in her home environment—especially at a time when there is already pressure on the family to appear suitably festive and cohesive. When Clark's ostentatious and hugely ambitious Christmas lighting display fails to work as intended, his in-laws berate him for his apparent lack of ability and the amount of money that has seemingly been squandered, while his parents protectively step in to defend his intentions. Sometimes, unexpected humor is derived from their bickering. When the Griswold and Smith grandparents first arrive to stay with Clark and Ellen, Frances makes a rather acidic comment that Nora appears to have visibly aged since she last saw her. (In fact, Diane Ladd was only in her early fifties when the movie was being filmed, meaning that she was only around eight years older than Chevy Chase, making him closer to the age of his onscreen mother than he was to the age of his onscreen wife Beverly D'Angelo.)

Given the vast amount of setbacks fired at Clark and Ellen during their Christmas vacation, bickering grandparents seemed to be among the least of their issues. Yet the low-level animosity that is generated by the two incompatible families who sometimes seem to be unable to stand the sight of one another, undeniably aids in presenting the kind of uneasy family environment which is bubbling beneath the veneer of festive jocularity. While it would take the later arrival of Randy Quaid's Cousin Eddie Johnson and his family to tip the scales into all-out domestic dissonance, Hughes employs the tit-for-tat point-scoring of the Smiths and the Griswolds as a subtle warning about what can happen to families in the event of a breakdown of communications and commonality. When the grandparents decide, on Christmas Eve, to pack up and leave rather than potentially suffer further catastrophes at the Griswold house, it is Clark who flatly refuses to allow them to depart, insisting that families must stick together no matter the circumstances. And sure enough, in true Hughes fashion this unity and mutual solidarity eventually wins out; following the unexpected turnaround of events which occur at the end of the movie's third act, the very relatives who were on the cusp of abandoning the family unit find themselves celebrating its redemption and eventual deliverance.

Only as Old as You Feel: Eccentric Aunts and Cantankerous Uncles

While grandparents may well have been the most prominent characters in the later years of life to appear in Hughes's cinema, they were not entirely alone. Some of his screenplays were to offer mature characters who, though related to the protagonists, were often far removed from the devoted family members who might have been expected from the more protective, encouraging individuals who were depicted elsewhere in his work. Perhaps the epitome of this later-life crankiness was Aunt Edna of *National Lampoon's Vacation* (Harold Ramis, 1983), played with wonderfully grouchy gusto by long-established actress Imogene Coca. Active in Broadway theater from the 1920s, Coca enjoyed an extensive career on television (and occasionally on film), being especially well remembered for her performances on NBC's *Your Show of Shows* (1950–1954) alongside Sid Caesar and Carl Reiner; NBC's situation comedy *The Imogene Coca Show* (1954–1955); and in an Emmy Award–nominated appearance in the "Los Dos DiPestos" episode of ABC's *Moonlighting* (1985–1989).

Though many of Coca's characters over the years had been quirky or gregarious, the acid-tongued Aunt Edna was anything but. Becoming an unexpected passenger on the inter-state road trip of Clark Griswold and his family, Edna's company is imposed on the hapless travelers at the least likely of junctures. During their visit to Cousin Eddie's home in Kansas, Clark and Ellen are asked to transport Edna to the address of her son in Phoenix, Arizona. This seemingly innocuous request becomes complicated by the discovery that Edna is extremely crotchety and far from complimentary towards the family—Clark, in particular. Her general mood becomes even worse when Clark accidentally forgets that he has temporarily tied the leash of her similarly irritable dog Dinky to the rear bumper of their car, the Wagon Queen Family Truckster, leading to the poor animal's eventual demise when he drives off. Incredibly enough, this cruel calamity is not the worst indignity to befall Edna during the journey; following a disastrous (and unanticipated) detour through the desert wilderness, the family discovers that she has died in her sleep.

Rather curiously for a Hughes screenplay, given the importance that he places on the significance of the family unit in general, Edna's fatality is played for dark comedy rather than the grief and shock that would, in reality, accompany such a startling trauma. True to their word, the Griswolds deliver her to the house of her son Norman—albeit strapped to the roof of their car with a piece of tarpaulin covering her body. On discovering that he is away from home, and realizing that they are already behind time with their itinerary, the Griswolds leave the corpse at the rear of Norman's property and rapidly depart before any questions are asked. (Interestingly, these actions don't appear to offend Cousins Eddie and Catherine who requested Edna's transit in the first place, as the situation is never referred to again.)

Perhaps surprisingly, given how memorably she articulates Edna's waspishness and argumentative nature, Coca reportedly found the character's overriding air of meanness unpalatable to portray. Her often-noted professionalism was also reflected in the fact that although she suffered a health scare during filming (thought to have been a minor stroke), she worked hard to re-memorize her lines such that as soon as she had been discharged from hospital, she was able to return to the production and complete her scenes as planned. For all her apparent unease with Edna's crotchety malice, Coca's depiction of the character became one of the comic highlights of the movie, and she remains one of the best-remembered (and most fearsome) of all the senior citizens to appear in a Hughes screenplay.

Characters of advanced years often found themselves on the receiving end of Hughes's barbed wit, and while *National Lampoon's Christmas Vacation* was noteworthy for its quarreling grandparents, it was similarly remarkable for its inspired double-act of Aunt Bethany (Mae Questel) and Uncle Lewis (William Hickey). Perhaps the ultimate in mismatched couples, the pair seems to be diametric opposites, with their advanced age and hearing difficulties being their only commonalities. Bethany is friendly and personable but also forgetful and easily confused, while the irascible Lewis is tetchy and ill-tempered, constantly frustrated by his wife's misunderstandings (and, indeed, with life in general). As was the custom with elderly characters in many Hughes-produced movies, Lewis and Bethany were portrayed by two well-established industry talents. Hickey had been active on stage and television since the 1950s, but also enjoyed a long career in cinema that endured until his death in 1997. He was particularly active in the 1980s, appearing in numerous high-profile movies which included *The Name of the Rose* (Jean-Jacques Annaud, 1986); *Bright Lights, Big City* (James Bridges, 1988); *Sea of Love* (Harold Becker, 1989), and—in an Academy Award–nominated performance—as Don Corrado Prizzi in John Huston's *Prizzi's Honor* (1985). Questel had been active in the entertainment industry for even longer, first appearing onstage from the 1920s and, from the 1930s onward, as the famous voice of Max Fleischer's cartoon character Betty Boop—a role she would reprise many times in her long career. Though best known for her voiceovers, she occasionally appeared on camera and in several Broadway productions. However, alongside Betty Boop she remains forever etched in the cultural memory for the distinctive tones of Olive Oyl, the object of Popeye's affections, and also as the voice of Casper, the Friendly Ghost.

From their earliest appearance in *National Lampoon's Christmas Vacation*, Bethany and Lewis manage to cause widespread mayhem (albeit not as a result of any premeditated intention on their part). First gift-wrapping their household cat, which gnaws on the cabling of the Griswold's Christmas tree and is promptly electrocuted, Lewis's everpresent cigar winds up setting fire to the aforementioned tree (and various living-room decorations into the bargain), leaving it as little more than an ashen husk. Yet what is perhaps most interesting is the way in which Hughes juxtaposes their competing qualities to both entertaining and humorous effect. Bethany is shown to be deeply patriotic, and bursts into the American national anthem at the drop of a hat. Even though she has major problems with her short-term memory, she remembers the lyrics of "The Star-Spangled Banner" with perfect precision. Similarly, she is such an agreeable presence that even her constant state of bewilderment isn't enough to stimulate serious irritation in anyone except her husband. Lewis, on the other hand, is in a permanently dark mood and liable to snap at anyone unfortunate enough to cross his path. He is cynical, domineering, and deeply sarcastic. However, Hughes is unwilling to let this tetchy complainer off with a free pass; Lewis's complete lack of repentance at burning down the family Christmas tree is later repaid when, still puffing on his trademark cigar, he accidentally ignites fumes from the storm sewer outside the Griswolds' home, causing an explosion and sending himself flying into the air with considerably less grace than any of Santa's reindeer.

Senior citizens received mixed fortunes in Hughes's writing; just as his long-running theme of strengthening familial bonds meant that elderly relatives often had a pivotal role to play in emphasizing the significance of kith and kin, similarly characters who disregarded the importance of the family unit or who disparaged their relatives risked meeting with unfortunate consequences. However, one thing which remained clear throughout his work was a desire to bring people together rather than divide them; he often stressed that good intentions had the ability to bridge the generation gap, accentuating the fact that compassion and empathy are noble qualities irrespective of someone's age, and underscoring the point that anyone should be able to remain relevant and useful in society as long as they are willing to acknowledge these same traits in others.

25

Don't You Want to Hear My Excuse?

Plot Holes and Narrative Inconsistencies in the Screenplays of John Hughes

Nobody can accurately claim to be absolutely correct all the time, and this was true even for noted perfectionists such as John Hughes. In his screenplays, Hughes always sought to present a robust form of internal logic which made even the most outrageous situations seem strangely plausible. However, even he occasionally offered up plot aspects which creaked under the strain of contradictions and narrative discrepancies. Similarly, the productions themselves—whether directed by Hughes, or with others behind the camera—were not immune from a random gaffe or technical glitch, such is the demanding and fast-paced world of movie production. In this section, Hughes's most credulity-stretching plot developments are placed under the microscope, as are the moments where continuity glitches and narrative contradictions came to light—often in the most eyebrow-raising of ways.

To Err is Human: Narrative Discrepancies

While plot holes were generally few and far between in a John Hughes storyline, sometimes they were so conspicuous that they simply couldn't be ignored. One such example occurs at the conclusion of *National Lampoon's Vacation* (Harold Ramis, 1983), when the accident-prone Griswold family finally reaches their destination—the expansive Walley

World theme park. Patriarch Clark Griswold (Chevy Chase) is incensed when he discovers that, in spite of his careful planning and their tortuous journey, Walley World has been closed to the public for two weeks in order for repairs and maintenance to take place. However, during Clark's subsequent meltdown—where John Candy's security guard Russ Lasky is effectively taken hostage and forced to accompany the Griswolds on the park's various rides—no cleaning staff or maintenance engineers are ever to be seen, and neither are there any tools or apparatus in evidence to suggest that work is even underway there. Similarly, the Griswolds appear to make full use of various rides at the park that would require supervision by personnel in order to be operated, not least for the sake of health and safety. Yet there, too, no actual members of the park staff are shown to be present, making it seem as though the equipment is somehow being automated. Even an interruption caused by bad weather is unlikely to be an excuse, given the sunshine that accompanies the family's arrival at Walley World—and considering the vast scale of the park, it seems even less likely that work would not be carried out around the clock in order to ensure that it would be reopened to the public as quickly as possible, to avoid unnecessary commercial loss.

Even the renowned *Ferris Bueller's Day Off* (1986) was susceptible to some narrative errors. Given that the storyline focuses upon Ferris's efforts to evade school, it is clear that the titular day off is taking place at some point during the work week. However, the Von Steuben Day Parade (which Matthew Broderick's Ferris gatecrashes as an impromptu musical performer) actually takes place in the fall, and on a Saturday. In part, this discrepancy took place because—while the movie is set during springtime—it was actually filmed much later in the year, hence the reason that in some sequences it is evident that tree leaves are beginning to take on autumnal colors. This was most obvious during scenes taking place at the Frye family garage, as the copiously windowed building is situated in a verdant area surrounded by trees, and yet some are clearly starting to turn golden with the changing season, necessitating various trees to have their leaves carefully hand-painted in a more spring-like hue of green by the production team for the sake of realism.

A strange glitch in continuity also surfaces during *National Lampoon's Christmas Vacation* (Jeremiah S. Chechik, 1989), when one event seems to momentarily take place out of sequence. During Clark Griswold's test of his home's copious exterior Christmas lights, an aerial shot shows an unannounced RV parked in the driveway of the house. Though this has not yet been explained at this point in the proceedings, the unfamiliar vehicle actually belongs to Kansas-based cousin Eddie Johnson (Randy Quaid) and his wife, Catherine (Miriam Flynn)—but the characters have not been introduced, or even mentioned. Once the lights have been extinguished, another shot from street level reveals that the same patch of driveway is now vacant, with no sign of the RV. But a few moments later, when Clark again manages to turn on the lights, the aerial shot again reveals the mysterious vehicle is back in place outside the house. Only at the end of the sequence is it revealed that the Johnsons have arrived, unannounced, to share Christmas with the family, and that they have arrived in the thus-far-unexplained RV.

One of Hughes's most baffling narrative goofs was revealed in *Home Alone* (Chris Columbus, 1990). Early in the movie, it is established that the telephone lines are inoperative throughout the neighborhood where Kevin McCallister (Macaulay Culkin) and his family live near Chicago, heightening the drama as, of course, this development means that his parents are unable to call him and check on his safety when they realize that he has been left alone at home while they have flown to France on vacation. Yet in spite of the fact that the lack of telecommunications is a plot point that is continually emphasized throughout the movie, there are a number of occasions where internal logic is somehow circumvented altogether. Kevin manages to order a pizza to be delivered to the door of the McCallister house without any explanation of how he managed to do this without the aid of a functioning phone line, and yet there is no indication of the telephone company having reconnected the house as Kevin's father, Peter (John Heard), is seen attempting and failing to call him from Paris directly beforehand. Similarly, during the Wet Bandits' climactic invasion of the house, Kevin somehow manages to call the police from an extension line in the master bedroom where his parents usually sleep. Again, there has been no suggestion that the functionality of the telephone line has been restored. Although the plot conceit of the disconnected telephone line worked well in the days immediately prior to the omnipresence of cellphones, it would otherwise seem strangely convenient that absolutely no family acquaintances are left in the Chicago area to check on Kevin, or—distraught by the prospect of being completely alone for so long—that even the most independent of adolescents would be able to resist the temptation to call on one of the few remaining non-vacationing neighbors for help (or even to find a nearby call-box and telephone the police in search of security). But such is the charm of his screenplay, Hughes somehow manages to keep the overall tone so blithe and upbeat—largely due to Culkin's captivating lead performance—that the audience is never allowed time to consider the grave implications that so easily could have befallen a child who had really been left alone in a similar situation.

If It Ain't Broke: Technical Goofs

While the magic of cinema is invariably fueled by suspension of disbelief, every now and again the complex machinery which lies behind the making of a movie is accidentally exposed, to jarring effect. This was no different for films which featured a John Hughes screenplay, and such inadvertent mistakes were especially evident in *National Lampoon's Vacation*. When Clark opens the door of the Wagon Queen Family Truckster in the moments following the inflation of the vehicle's airbag, a fair amount of production equipment can be seen reflected in its wing mirror. Similarly, at the point where Ellen Griswold (Beverly D'Angelo) says a prayer for the recently departed Aunt Edna (Imogene Coca), a boom mic briefly strays into the shot—a fact made all the more obvious when it momentarily distracts the gaze of Dana Barron, who is playing Audrey Griswold. Camera equipment and production crew members can also be fleetingly glimpsed at the end of the movie, when the family members are taking part in the various rides at Walley World. And during his trek through the desert, Clark is alarmed when he stumbles across a skeleton—presumably an earlier traveler whose journey had similarly gone awry. However, a metal spring can be seen in the rear of the skull to keep the jaw in place, which may well be common practice for skeletons in museums or teaching institutions but is highly unlikely to occur in someone who, we are led to believe, has died of natural causes and been abandoned to the wilderness.

The Griswolds' later travels were also not exempt from technical glitches. During their stay in a cramped London hotel room during *National Lampoon's European Vacation* (Amy Heckerling, 1985), an unfortunately considered pan by the camera momentarily reveals the behind-the-scenes apparatus which is holding the set's ceiling and walls in place. Later, when Clark carelessly traps the leg of the hapless English bike rider (Eric Idle) in the panels of a revolving door, Idle reacts in agony before the door actually makes impact—a preemptive response so obvious that it renders the scene amusing for all the wrong reasons. A similar blunder takes place in *National Lampoon's Christmas Vacation*, when Ellen angrily slices through a cabbage with a sharp knife in response to her mother, Frances's (Doris Roberts), incessant nagging. The sound of the knife striking the chopping board beneath the vegetable can be heard long before the blade has actually reached the surface. Later, Clark slices off the newel post at the top of his home's stairway with a chainsaw in a low-key fit of pique, but it is clear that there is no chain fitted to the tool and thus the amount of sawdust produced by the slicing motion is inaccurate. Strangely, during the squirrel attack near the end of the film, the newel post has mysteriously reappeared in its original place. And there is never an explanation of why, when the Griswolds live in the outskirts of Chicago—a city where temperatures regularly plunge in the winter months—that there is no insulation in their attic to conserve heat (as seen when Clark is accidentally trapped there while hiding gifts for his family).

There are also technical glitches to be found in movies directed by Hughes himself. During a conversation between Samantha Baker (Molly Ringwald) and her mother, Brenda (Carlin Glynn), in the family kitchen in *Sixteen Candles* (1984), a boom mic casts a shadow on one of the room's cabinets. In *Ferris Bueller's Day Off*, Cameron Frye (Alan Ruck) is pulled out of a swimming pool by his best friend, Ferris, who fears that he is drowning. However, as he is dragged to the surface a weight is temporarily visible, having been used to "anchor" Ruck to the floor of the pool. The graphic equalizer on the music system in Ferris's bedroom seems to have its settings altered from shot to shot, without any reason being given. In perhaps the most famous school-set sequence of the movie, the students attending the economics class are shown wearing watches that show a time of 6:25, though this would be too early for school and clearly it can't refer to the evening as it is implied to be the first class of the day. Even more curiously, while the economics teacher (Ben Stein) expects Ferris to be present for the class, the computer system in the office of Dean of Students Ed Rooney (Jeffrey Jones) displays Ferris's student timetable and yet economics is not one of the subjects listed on the screen.

A surprising number of technical errors to occur in movies that featured Hughes's creative involvement were to center around travel and transport. During the Griswolds' appearance on the *Pig in a Poke* TV game show in *National Lampoon's European Vacation*, an announcer proudly declares that a Honda 750 motorbike has been won as a prize, and a Honda Rebel 250 motorcycle is shown instead. Near the climax of *Ferris Bueller's Day Off*, as Cameron, Ferris, and Mia Sara's Sloane desperately attempt to reduce the figures on the odometer of Mr. Frye's Ferrari, the car is held in a stationary position while being reversed. However, this should mean that the tires should be moving in a backwards motion, and yet the wheels at the rear of the vehicle appear to be spinning forward. There are also numerous transport-related oddities situated throughout *Planes, Trains and Automobiles* (1987). The rental car used by ill-matched travelers Neal (Steve Martin) and Del (John Candy) is subject to all kinds of abuse during the movie, causing various continuity issues. Hubcaps are detached from the car and yet bizarrely reappear later as though nothing had happened, while Del accidentally bends the vehicle's steering wheel out of shape, only for it to be returned to normal in later scenes. Neal's briefcase is driven over by two consecutive New York taxis, visibly damaging it, and yet it later appears to be inexplicably as good as new. Perhaps most perplexing of all, Neal and Del leave New York on an American Airlines twin-engine aircraft, which is made clear when they board the plane at the airport. Yet once they are in flight, the plane has changed to a Boeing 707, which has four engines rather than the two which were evident earlier. A similar mistake takes place in *Home Alone*, when the McCallisters are seen departing Chicago O'Hare Airport in a three-engine McDonnell-Douglas DC-10 aircraft and yet touch down in Paris Orly Airport aboard a two-engine Boeing 757.

Here, There, and Everywhere: Geographical Illogicalities

Though Hughes's movies were famous for usually taking place in and around Illinois, this was not always the case, and sometimes a slip-up occurred which exposed the fact that not everything was quite as it seemed in a particular location. On many occasions this was something that was not immediately apparent, such as in *Mr. Mom* (Stan Dragoti, 1983), where Detroit-based supermarkets are seen to be selling C&C sodas when, at the time, the principal retail area for that product was solely in the Northeast of the U.S., meaning that they were very unlikely to be distributed in Michigan. Similarly, when the Griswolds are posing for a family photograph in *National Lampoon's European Vacation* in front of a Parisian fountain, Ellen can be seen holding up a tour guide, which is presumably supposed to be in the national colors of the French flag (blue, white, and red) but actually bears those of the Republic of Ireland (green, white, and orange).

Other geographical anomalies are a little more difficult to ignore. While *Weird Science* (1985) is set in Hughes's usual fictional locale of Shermer, Illinois, a sequence shows Gary (Anthony Michael Hall) and Deb (Suzanne Snyder) being pursued by an LAPD interceptor police car. A similar issue occurs in the later *Pretty in Pink* (Howard Deutch, 1986), where, at one point, Phil "Duckie" Dale (Jon Cryer) can be seen riding a bicycle past a number of cars, all of which bear Californian license plates in blue, in spite of the movie's Illinois setting. On the subject of travel, when Kevin McCallister departs Chicago O'Hare Airport in *Home Alone 2: Lost in New York* (Chris Columbus, 1992), his destination is announced simply as "New York," with no indication of which of the city's various airports (including JFK and LaGuardia) the plane is set to land. Also curious is the fact that although Kevin has been established as a keen viewer of movies and very culturally savvy for his age, on arrival in New York he seems oblivious to his location in spite of the fact that he has spotted the Empire State Building, one of the most iconic structures in the city. A slightly different transport-related discrepancy takes place in *Planes, Trains and Automobiles*, where Del and Neal are stopped in their heavily damaged rental car by a concerned Wisconsin State trooper (Michael

McKean). However, as it has been established that the pair is supposed to be driving directly between St. Louis, Missouri, and Chicago, Illinois, driving anywhere near Wisconsin would mean that they had taken a highly circuitous route, which would make little sense given their self-professed need to reach their destination as quickly as possible.

Another Wisconsin-based oddity takes place in *The Great Outdoors* (Howard Deutch, 1988), where John Candy's Chet Ripley and his family are vacationing in the rural locale of Pechoggin (though actually filmed on location in California). Throughout the film, a mule deer and a grizzly bear are both featured, and yet neither animal is likely to be found close to the Wisconsin area. No explanation is given as to their presence. But animals weren't the only things to be found out of place in a production that featured a Hughes screenplay. In *National Lampoon's Christmas Vacation*, it is shown that the Griswolds' home is situated next to a wet barrel fire hydrant, though due to the very low temperatures that are regularly experienced in Illinois during the winter months it would be impractical for such a hydrant to be used in this location due to the risk of freezing. Instead, a dry barrel fire hydrant would be more likely to be used in such an area, with wet barrel models being reserved for warmer regions.

Out of Order: Continuity Errors

No movie is entirely insusceptible to the occasional glitch in continuity, and this also was true of productions featuring a Hughes screenplay. Oversights can be found in various films which featured Hughes's involvement, ranging from the innocuous to the somewhat glaring. For instance, simple spelling errors crop up from time to time, including Samantha Baker of *Sixteen Candles* completing a study questionnaire which is marked *Confidentail* instead of *Confidential*, a sports-page article in the opening credits of *The Breakfast Club* (1985) misspelling Andrew Clark's surname as *Clarke* (when the movie's closing credits instead spell the name correctly), and a sequence in *National Lampoon's Christmas Vacation* where the illumination of the Griswolds' festive decorations prompts a nearby power station to switch their supply over to *Auxilliary*

Nuclear instead of the more accurate *Auxiliary Nuclear*. Yet other production incongruities were rather more noticeable in nature. At the beginning of *National Lampoon's Vacation*, and throughout much of the movie, Anthony Michael Hall's Rusty Griswold is shown to be around the same height as his mother, Ellen (Beverly D'Angelo). Yet during the concluding scenes at the Walley World theme park, he suddenly appears to be conspicuously taller than she is. This was explained by the fact that, as this climactic sequence was chronologically among the last to be filmed, the teenaged Hall had undergone a rapid growth spurt. Throughout *The Breakfast Club*, the distinctive eye makeup of Ally Sheedy's Allison changes randomly between scenes, while the hairstyle of Claire Standish (Molly Ringwald) puzzlingly shifts around from sequence to sequence. Perhaps the most noteworthy change in appearance to take place in any film featuring a Hughes screenplay is at the end of *Pretty in Pink*; when an unfavorable test screening led to the conclusion being reshot, the actors involved were recalled to film the new climax. While Molly Ringwald and Jon Cryer both had similar appearances in the roles of Andie and Duckie, Andrew McCarthy had been performing in John Pielmeier's Vietnam War–themed stage drama *The Boys of Winter* (1985) at the Biltmore Theater in New York—a role which had required him to slim down substantially and shave his head, as he was playing a U.S. Army recruit. Thus, while his hairstyle could easily be replicated with a wig, there was no mistaking the fact that his face was drastically leaner, which must have been jarring to viewers at the time.

Other goofs included issues with continuity regarding the state of the Wagon Queen Family Truckster in *National Lampoon's Vacation*. The car is damaged at various points throughout the movie, and at one stage is covered with spray-paint graffiti on both sides. Yet the damage, once incurred, seems to appear and disappear at random—in some cases, dents and scratches will look as though they have been repaired, only to reappear at a later point. Similarly, the graffiti mysteriously vanishes from Clark's side of the car while remaining on Ellen's side. Another vehicular anomaly occurs when the family's road trip begins; the Truckster is shown to have no luggage on the roof-rack, and yet when Clark accidentally reverses, the audience is shown bags and other luggage being pushed from the roof of the car after they collide with the open door of the garage. Even before the vacation has started, there is a strange inconsistency to be found when Clark uses an early games console to chart the route of the forthcoming journey on the family's TV. The console can be seen resting on top of a coffee table in the living room, and yet it goes missing between shots before finally returning to its original place.

Even some of Hughes's most celebrated movies could not entirely escape the occasional random continuity oddity. In a scene where Paul Gleason's Assistant Principal Richard Vernon is venting his frustrations with Carl (John Kapelos), the school janitor, safely away from the gaze of the five detention attendees in *The Breakfast Club*, Carl's position changes from shot to shot every time the camera cuts away from him. His arm is either on top of a filing cabinet or inside one of its drawers, but there is never an obvious movement from one to the other, creating an awkward effect. Likewise, when the rebellious John Bender (Judd Nelson) starts tearing pages from books in the library, it is obvious that the pages he is ripping up are simply plain paper, and yet when he eventually tosses the book at Anthony Michael Hall's Brian Johnson the pages suddenly have printed type and illustrations. The fearsome Ed Rooney also falls foul of continuity peculiarities; when staking out a bar in search of Ferris, keen to bust the wayward student for skipping school, he singles out a figure who is wearing a similar jacket to the one Ferris wears. However, Rooney's only glimpse of Ferris (though he does not realize it) was when he had picked up Sloane while disguised as her father in a long overcoat, hat, and dark glasses, meaning that he would be oblivious to Ferris's real outfit that day. Rooney realizes to his horror that, rather than apprehending Ferris, he has actually insulted an adult woman who is deeply unimpressed by his bravado. To show her contempt for him, she sucks in a mouthful of cola and sprays him with it through a straw, but Jeffrey Jones appears to recoil well in advance of her actually soaking his face and suit. Rooney also smugly uses the French expression *"les jeux sont faits,"* which he translates as "the game is up," but, in reality, the term is more accurately translated (as in casino parlance) as "the bets are made." When Jeanie (Jennifer Grey) is being followed by the police as she drives home at the conclusion of the film, the patrol car seems to disappear without any reason. Perhaps most curiously of all, when Ferris races home in an attempt to reach the house before his parents, his footwear changes three

Dan Aykroyd (1952–   ), actor, comedian, screenwriter, as well as a producer, musician, and businessman, seen here on location during the production of Howard Deutch's *The Great Outdoors* (1988).

times during the sequence. Strangely enough, this inconsistency is reflected in a later goof; as Ferris jumps back into his bed, planning to hoodwink his parents that he has never left the house while they were away, he kicks off shoes not twice (as might be expected) but on three separate occasions.

Among other oddities are the Griswold family name being wrongly spelled "Griswald" throughout *National Lampoon's European Vacation*, and the fact that—though only apparent to the most attentive viewers—Clark is holding his *Pig in a Poke* touring brochure upside-down on the flight from the U.S. to England. At the conclusion of *Planes, Trains and Automobiles*, as he finally reaches his home, Steve Martin's Neal can be seen holding the handle of a suitcase which he didn't appear to have with him at the start of his journey in New York, and which has never been seen belonging to either Del (John Candy) or himself at any point in the film. Following the unfortunate aftermath of Candy's Chet Ripley eating the formidable "Old 96er" steak in *The Great Outdoors*, Dan Aykroyd (in character as Roman Craig) can quite clearly be seen cueing the other performers to depart the scene—this gesture was presumably intended to take place off-camera.

In *National Lampoon's Christmas Vacation*, a swarm of Ford police vehicles can be seen racing to the Griswolds' home in order to free Frank Shirley (Brian Doyle-Murray) from his supposed kidnapping, and yet when the cars are later seen in stationary positions outside the house they have perplexingly become Chrysler models. When Buck Russell (John Candy) of *Uncle Buck* decides to cook up a culinary treat for his nieces and nephew, he can be seen adding ingredients to a huge pancake which is being cooked in a similarly vast frying pan. Yet a few minutes later, when he flips it over, it has suddenly become considerably smaller. Even the clockwork precision of *Home Alone*'s much-admired home-defense sequence is not without its foibles. Joe Pesci's bruised criminal Harry Lime is tarred and feathered at an early stage in his burglary of Kevin McCallister's home, and yet as the housebreaking continues he appears to be conspicuously less feather-laden as time goes by. Similarly, when Kevin is soaking the steps leading up to the house's front door, they quickly freeze, making it perilous for the burglars to enter and suggesting that the exterior temperature is sub-zero. Yet nearer the conclusion, when Kevin is racing away from the house, the ground is clearly free from ice and he is able to break into a sprint without any danger of skidding or falling.

Hughes was a director who prided himself on his ability to observe and comment perceptively on the human condition, and the occasional errors that were to crop up in his films only heightened the fact that—just like his characters—even the most exacting perfectionists cannot claim to be without fault. While none of the mishaps affecting a Hughes film were ever likely to seriously impede audience enjoyment, their very presence nonetheless underscores the fact that even this renowned stickler for fine detail managed to get things wrong occasionally.

26

You Don't Spell It, Son, You Eat It

Restaurants and Dining in John Hughes Films

Eating and dining out is a recurring motif in several John Hughes movies. Given the importance placed by Hughes on family life, the act of sharing a meal—whether at home or beyond the domestic environ-ment—could often be a significant one. Sometimes, dining functioned as a way of delineating a character's particular motivations or intentions, or occasionally as a means of advancing a film's plot. At other points, food itself was the focus of the audience's attention, either as a cultural reference or a subtle in-joke. At times where cafés, diners, and restaurants proved to be consequential venues for Hughes's characters, there was often specific relevance for these eating places within respective nar-ratives, while the choice of food was often meaningfully selected in its own right.

Pull up a Chair: The Family Meal in John Hughes's Cinema

Eating together could be a pleasurable experience for families within John Hughes's movies, but it could just as easily lead to disastrously awk-ward interplay between clashing personalities which unintentionally draws out long-standing conflicts or other differences. Rarely was this seen so starkly as in *Sixteen Candles* (1984), when the Baker family and their soon-to-be in-laws, the Ryszczyks, get together for a family meal prior to the marriage between Rudy (John Kapelos) and Ginny (Blanche Baker). The sequence, set at a local club in town, seems deliberately calculated to focus not on interpersonal tension so much as a comedy of errors between two well-meaning families who are struggling to find common ground and overcome differences. The likable but arguably over-personable Ryszczyks and the self-consciously discomfited Bakers, led by patriarch Jim (Paul Dooley), play out this incongruous bonding exercise in interesting ways. Mr. Ryszczyk baffles Jim with an account of his tenuously defined business practices, which include everything from trucking to video game arcades to laundry services and cigarette machines, leading Jim to suspect that the family's commercial activities are not entirely above board. Then Mrs. Ryszczyk steers the conversation into dangerous territory by warning Rudy that his days of unrestricted dating will be over once the marriage is finalized, leading her son to respond in a way which immediately makes everyone present question the prospects of his long-term fidelity. The humorous scene with the capricious Ryszczyks is played in deliberate contrast to the much more formally conducted family dinner that is arranged by the grandparents of Samantha Baker (Molly Ringwald), prior to her school dance, as she is baffled by the ability of exchange student Long Duk Dong (Gedde Watanabe) to so effortlessly charm her elderly relatives with his amiable conversation. Samantha is peeved by Long Duk's prowess in winning over her family with such charismatic force of personality, not least as she feels that his obvious desire to help around the household is showing her own demeanor in a bad light. However, the scene is played out with great tongue-in-cheek wit and droll subtlety, in skillful juxtaposition to more dramatic family meals which took place in later Hughes-produced movies. This included the often-tense emotional discourse which takes place between Keith Nelson (Eric Stoltz) and his goodhearted but overbearing father Cliff (John Ashton) in *Some Kind of Wonderful* (Howard Deutch, 1987), whose stubborn temperaments and strong characters clash over the direction of Keith's future during a seemingly harmless domestic dinner. For Cliff and his wife, Carol (Jane Elliot), the family sharing mealtimes represent its

Chevy Chase (1943–   ), television and film comedian.

cohesion and mutual support; for the headstrong Keith, it is symbolic of the stifling expectations of social conformity and domestic conventions. Similarly, in *Home Alone* (Chris Columbus, 1990), a family meal presents young Kevin McCallister with the exact opposite of a welcoming environment; on the eve of his relatives' departure for a holiday in France, an accidental mishap leads to his being castigated by everyone present. The fact that all of his immediate kin are gathered together to eat makes the censure he receives seem all the more intense, precisely because he feels bereft of allies, and this aggrieved sense of injustice fuels his subsequent sense of independence when he discovers that he has been left to fend for himself while his family has departed for foreign climes.

Overseas dining prove to be no less of a strain for Clark Griswold and his family during their whirlwind tour of continental Europe during

National Lampoon's European Vacation (Amy Heckerling, 1985). While their brief dalliances with British and German cuisines leave much to be desired, the apex of their brush with European food arrives during a visit to a French restaurant. Obviously exulting in the anticipation of ordering a meal from a Parisian bistro, given France's worldwide reputation for gastronomic excellence, Clark soon encounters the obstacle of his lack of linguistic agility. Unable to read the menu or understand the staggeringly insulting rhetoric of the waiter (Philippe Sturbelle), he ends up with no real idea of the actual content of the meal he has ordered, leading to a tremendously acerbic sequence during which—behind the scenes of the restaurant—we see an obviously bored chef inelegantly dashing an unappetizing microwaveable meal onto a plate, thus revealing their attempt at "sophisticated" French dining to be represented by something that could have been purchased from any American supermarket's frozen food section.

The luckless Griswold clan fare little better dining at home. During the events of *National Lampoon's Christmas Vacation* (Jeremiah S. Chechik, 1989), there is a deliberate attempt by Hughes to subvert his own fairy tale–like Thanksgiving conclusion of *Planes, Trains and Automobiles* (1987) by instead presenting the turkey dinner from hell. Served up in the family's beautifully decorated dining room, surrounded by relatives both cherished and barely tolerated, Clark carves into a succulent, immaculately presented turkey—only for it to collapse into a desiccated husk. It transpires that Cousin Catherine (Miriam Flynn), keen to get involved in the Griswolds' festivities, had grossly overcooked the unfortunate fowl, leading to its current shriveled state. Desperate to avoid hurting her feelings, everyone then forces themselves to chew excruciatingly through the parched vestiges of the turkey, the inedible nature of their meal being painfully obvious. Indeed, it says everything about the meal that when a visiting cat manages to electrocute itself after chewing through the power cord of the electric lights on the Griswolds' Christmas tree, Clark almost seems to consider the unfortunate feline's tragic situation to be a welcome distraction from enduring any further dehydrated remnants of the Christmas dinner.

Making a Meal of It: John Hughes, Dining, and Popular Culture

The choice of food selected by Hughes's characters could often say quite a bit about their lives and personal outlook, as could the venue in which they consumed it. Sometimes their meals lend an insightful glimpse into how they think and behave, while on other occasions it gave Hughes an opportunity to toy with the audience's expectations. In the extended broadcast cut of *Sixteen Candles*, for instance, Samantha's visit to the cafeteria of Shermer High School reveals that the eclectic menu there (though only briefly glimpsed) features such peculiar culinary fare as meatball salad, senior burger and fries, chipped [sic] pork on bun, jumbo fish-dog, cornaroni, gelatin balls, cream of lunch soup, brisket of meat with sauce, and canned brownies in light syrup; drinks include iced tea, warm milk, and "grape beverage." The intriguingly named "vitamin cobbler" is enigmatically listed on the menu as being free of charge. If much of this gastronomic lineup seemed to verge on the inedible, Hughes provides the perfect punch line when—at the conclusion of the scene—Samantha spots the object of her affections, Jake Ryan (Michael Schoeffling), and hastily abandons her lunch altogether, believing she will seem less attractive to him if he should see her consuming anything at all (much less any of the questionable selections on the school's menu).

Lunch choices also give an important insight into the lives of the various members of *The Breakfast Club* (1985). During a midday sequence, the students open up their packed lunches to reveal a very diverse range of diets. The chic Claire Standish (Molly Ringwald) opts for a sophisticated box of sushi, while bookish Brian Johnson (Anthony Michael Hall) instead unveils a rather less urbane lineup of soup, apple juice, and a peanut butter and jelly sandwich. Thus, the refinement of Claire's lunch (rice, seaweed, and fish) reveals the worldly refinement that is afforded her by the affluence of her family background, though that same material prosperity inadvertently isolates her from the others, while Brian's somewhat artless selection of comfort food instead suggests that he is being mollycoddled by his own parents, remaining in thrall to their own desires for his future rather than allowing his own independence of identity to break through. The unconventional Allison Reynolds (Ally

Sheedy) chooses a curious sandwich filled with Pixy Stix (a sweet-and-sour powdered candy) and Cap'n Crunch cereal; this sickly sweet, deeply unpalatable culinary nightmare is perfectly in keeping with her kooky persona. But arguably the starkest contrast among the group's lunches lay between the muscular Andrew Clark (Emilio Estevez)—who reveals an array of snacks consisting of three sandwiches, chocolate cookies, a bag of chips, a banana, an apple, and some milk—and rebellious John Bender (Judd Nelson), who brings nothing to eat at all. While Andrew's veritable feast can be explained by the fact that, as a wrestler and athlete, he requires considerable sustenance as part of his personal training program, it may also indicate some aspect of his father's overbearing influence over every aspect of his life—including his dietary choices. By contrast, Bender's apparent nonchalance over his total lack of food does little to distract from the fact that his own family cares so little for his well-being that not only have they neglected to ensure that he has anything to eat, there is apparently no provision at his home for him to prepare a lunch for himself.

In *Ferris Bueller's Day Off* (1986), the crafty protagonist and his friends manage to sneak into the opulent, upscale Chez Quis restaurant in downtown Chicago for lunch. Ferris only manages to secure lunch for the trio thanks to an impromptu scheme which sees him impersonating Abe Froman—"the sausage king of Chicago"—after spotting the businessman's name in the reservations book. This leads to a battle of wits between Ferris and the restaurant's snooty maître d' (Jonathan Schmock), which is aided by the fortunate outcome of the real Froman never actually turning up for the table he has booked (presumably due to an unexpected development at work) and ultimately allowing Ferris to take his place without his cover story being compromised. Deleted material from the film would have featured an extended sequence at Chez Quis, explaining Ferris's later enigmatic line that the trio had eaten pancreas during their visit, but certainly there is no denying, even in the extant cut, that Ferris and his friends obviously dine in high style—thanks, in no small part, to the contrition of the thoroughly outmaneuvered maître d'. The name of the classy restaurant was a deliberate pun on Hughes's part; "Chez Quis" was purposely chosen to sound like "Shakey's," a reference to Shakey's Pizza—the first franchise pizza chain in the U.S., which was founded in

1954 and is still in operation today. (The closest translation of the expression into English is actually "Chez Qui," which, in French, means "the House of Whom.")

Although the exterior of the Chez Quis restaurant was actually a redressed private home in Chicago's West Schiller Street, in keeping with the movie's Chicago-based action, its interiors were instead filmed at the lavish L'Orangerie restaurant in West Hollywood, Los Angeles. L'Orangerie was among the foremost eating places in the Los Angeles until its closure in December 2006; the building was later extensively remodeled. Because of the visual sumptuousness of its elaborate interior, L'Orangerie also appeared in several other prominent movies of the 1980s, among them *The Blues Brothers* (John Landis, 1980), *St. Elmo's Fire* (Joel Schumacher, 1985), and *Brewster's Millions* (Walter Hill, 1985).

Another One Bites the Crust: Food Facts in John Hughes Movies

One unusual aspect of food and drink in Hughes's cinema is how often cola features as a part of the narrative—both as a cultural reference and as an issue of continuity. During a scene in the cafeteria of Shermer High School during *Sixteen Candles*, Samantha Baker selects a can of Diet Coke which she places on her food tray, and yet when she enters the main eating area a few moments later the can has inexplicably changed to regular Coke. Intriguingly, a similar phenomenon was mirrored a few years later in *Pretty in Pink* (Howard Deutch, 1986), when Andie Walsh (Molly Ringwald) enters her room during a study session with her friend "Duckie" Dale (Jon Cryer) holding a can which is printed with the Pepsi-Cola logo on one side, and the Coca-Cola insignia on the other. In *The Breakfast Club*, the characters can be seen drinking from Coca-Cola cans which bear the emblem of the 1984 Los Angeles Olympics, a throwback to the time of the movie's production, when that year's Olympic Games were still being widely publicized.

Hughes was no stranger to the power of branding, and his awareness of marketing issues—which had been built up through an early career in advertising—was often evident by the choices made in several of his films. For instance, in *The Breakfast Club* we see that Andrew has stored his lunch in a Happy Foods paper bag, which drew attention to a real-life chain of grocery stores operated (and indeed continue to do business) in the Chicago area. Similarly, in *The Great Outdoors* (Howard Deutch, 1988), Hughes underscored the Wisconsin location of his action by introducing bottles of Point Beer, a popular alcoholic beverage, which is brewed in the state by Stevens Point Brewery, and helped to provide additional authenticity to the setting. Similarly, in *Home Alone* Kevin orders take-out pizza from a business named Little Nero's, the imperial Roman name being an obvious spoof of the famous Little Caesars company. Founded in Michigan in 1959, Little Caesars rapidly grew to become the third-largest pizza chain in the entire U.S., after Pizza Hut and Domino's.

Finally, one of the most noteworthy feasts in any Hughes screenplay is alluded to in *Home Alone 2: Lost in New York* (Chris Columbus, 1992), when young Kevin—reveling in the high-quality room service that is made possible by his father's credit card and the glamorous city hotel where he is staying—ends up overindulging on sweet treats during his unexpected vacation in the Big Apple. It is only when the audience is given a glance of his supersized hotel bill that we realize the full extent of Kevin's determination to dine like a king: according to the itemized list, we can see that he has consumed two chocolate cakes, six chocolate mousses, six custard flans, eight strawberry tarts, a pastry cart, thirty-six chocolate-covered strawberries, and strawberry, vanilla, and chocolate ice cream sprinkled with M&Ms, chocolate sprinkles, nuts, cherries, marshmallows, whipped cream, bananas, and a range of syrup flavors, such as caramel, strawberry, and chocolate. While being lost in one of the biggest cities on the planet would seem daunting to any adolescent, Kevin nonetheless seems unwavering in his desire to make the most of his time there, and nothing sums up the essence of his wide-eyed enthusiasm quite like his impossibly ostentatious menu—surely the stuff of any youngster's dreams.

27

The Place Is Like a Museum

Eighties Pop Culture and Set Design in John Hughes Films

The homes and workplaces of John Hughes's many protagonists often present the viewer with a veritable time capsule of 1980s popular culture—the posters on the bedroom walls of his teen characters, the considered snapshots of classroom life, and the thought-provoking flashes of a culture in a state of rapid transition. Set design and prop choice was a crucially important factor in Hughes's films, with scrupulous effort expended on providing the most exacting of details, and in many instances he employed carefully composed surroundings in order to explore characters' personalities and to reflect the vibrancy and complexity of American society at the point of each respective movie's production.

Rooms with a View: Hughes's Composition of Teenage Living Spaces

In a John Hughes movie, living space is used to communicate a great deal about his characters and their individual personalities, and never was this truer than in the case of his teenaged protagonists. When carefully constructing the bedroom of Samantha Baker in *Sixteen Candles* (1984), Hughes collaborated with actress Molly Ringwald, who actually brought various belongings from her own home to apply an additional layer of authenticity to Samantha's personal living zone. The result was a fully functioning illustration of a young woman experiencing her mid-teens in the eighties; a quick glance at the shelving in Samantha's room reveals the obligatory music system (complete with tape deck and record turntable), cosmetics, a quirky selection of dolls and plush toys, an eclectic variety of books, and even a pair of ice skates. Perhaps most noticeable of all is the way in which Hughes illustrates—seemingly in a casual manner, and yet very effectively in practice—so much of Samantha's character through her taste in popular culture. On the walls of her home we can see posters for British new wave bands Culture Club and Squeeze, rockabilly group Stray Cats, and Sammy Hagar—vocalist, musician and eventual lead singer of Van Halen. Thus, with no additional exposition, the viewer is immediately able to glean some aspect of Samantha's diverse tastes in music, piecing together a workable idea of what makes her tick even before the movie's events encourage us to empathize with her.

Hughes expanded upon this strategy in interesting ways during *Weird Science* (1985). Given the technological interests of protagonists Gary (Anthony Michael Hall) and Wyatt (Ilan Mitchell-Smith), it was important to highlight something of their scientific prowess in the scenes taking place in Wyatt's room, and yet we are left in no doubt that for all their proficiency with mathematics and physics we are still dealing with teenagers with all the sophisticated and varied creative tastes that implies. Thus all of the computer paraphernalia in the room is reflected in Wyatt's prominent poster which features *The Wave of the Future*, a lithograph created by design company Grafik for an advertising campaign operated by VM Software Inc. in 1981. While the image's connotations to the world of computing are clear enough, its basis in historical art—specifically *The Great Wave Off Kanagawa*, a famous woodblock print which was arguably the most famous work to be created by Japanese artist Katsushika Hokusai (1760–1849)—suggests a greater cultural awareness than is necessarily obvious from the poster's marketing origins. But if this may indicate artistic preferences which are relatively uncommon for the general age group of the main characters, it exists alongside more conventional teenage fare, such as posters for Californian heavy metal group Y&T (specifically, their sixth studio album *In Rock We Trust* from 1984), and rock band Talking Heads. The

Matthew Broderick (1962–   ), stage and screen actor as well as a vocalist, he is noted for his success in musical theater.

latter was to provide an interesting continuity discrepancy, as the mysterious arrival of Kelly LeBrock's Lisa is to result in the poster being torn, only for it to later appear undamaged and then—shortly afterwards—it can be seen to be ripped once again.

Perhaps the acme of Hughes's attempts to create the perfect teenage bedroom was that of the urban sophisticate Ferris Bueller in *Ferris Bueller's Day Off* (1986). Containing a vast array of pop culture memorabilia and other eccentric items, Hughes presented a setting which may have appeared to be superficially chaotic, but in reality was a meticulously constructed manifestation of his lead character's wide-ranging interests and ebullient personality. Although we see his classy (for the time) home computer system and eye-wateringly expensive synthesizer, along with a similarly big-ticket music system (complete with graphic equalizer), being used in various sequences—thus articulating the creative and tech-savvy aspects of Ferris's character—Hughes is just as proficient in showcasing the smaller details of the room's composition. Whereas seemingly innocuous items, such as a baseball glove and sports trophy, later prove to have greater significance as part of Ferris's jury-rigged inventions used to hoodwink his parents, the room is peppered with pleasingly off-the-wall affectations such as a mounted stag's head wearing a life preserver and plastic pig's snout; an industrial *EXIT* sign above the door; twin flags of the United States and the United Kingdom; various toys and miniature statuettes; and a photo of Elvis Presley taken during his 1956 performance on CBS's *The Ed Sullivan Show*. His range of wall art is no less extensive; among the more prominent posters are those which feature British band Cabaret Voltaire's album *Micro-Phonies* (1984); synthpop group Blancmange's albums *Mange Tout* (1984) and single "The Day Before You Came" (1984); rock band The Damned's album *Phantasmagoria* (1984); singer-songwriter Bryan Ferry's single "Slave to Love" (1985), and—perhaps most significantly of all—Scottish rock group Simple Minds' song "Don't You Forget About Me" (1985), which had so memorably accompanied Hughes's earlier *The Breakfast Club* (1985). Yet just as eclectic is the fact that, nestling among prints of music stars such as The Clash, The Who's Pete Townshend, and Buddy Holly and the Crickets, is the somewhat offbeat choice of a large poster showing a portrait of French monarch Francis I (1494–1547) of the House of Valois, a key figure in the French Renaissance who remains well known in history for his enthusiasm towards—and patronage of—a wide variety of artistic disciplines during his lifetime. By emphasizing the fact that Ferris's room is chock-full of unconventional and inspired belongings, very effectively delineating the wily teen's own highly individual persona, Hughes also succeeds in skillfully contrasting the character's attention-grabbing living space with that of his hypochondriacal best friend, Cameron (whose own bedroom more closely resembles a hospital isolation area, given that it is packed to the brim with medicines, cold cures, and various other health-related paraphernalia) and arch-nemesis Ed Rooney (where his soulless, fastidiously tidy office is so utterly devoid of charm that its most idiosyncratic feature appears to be a half-eaten packet of antacid tablets lying next to the desk nameplate—a hint, perhaps, that Rooney's constant exasperation towards his student body has already led him to develop a peptic ulcer).

There is Here and Here is There: Hughes and Set Construction

Just as important as the dressing of Hughes's movie sets were the stories which lay behind their construction. Hughes went to considerable lengths to ensure that the interior scenes of his films were credible representations of real-life living areas, but generating this element of verisimilitude often required some out-of-the-box thinking.

Perhaps most famously, during the production of *The Breakfast Club*—which was filmed in the then-closed Maine North High School—Hughes intended to set the action in the building's library, only to find that the location was too cramped and confined for the purposes of shooting all of the required scenes which would take place there. Thus, the library depicted in the movie was actually built from scratch in the school's capacious gymnasium. This allowed Hughes and his cast far greater scope, and ensured that the filming area could be composed exactly to his specifications rather than making do with the facilities which already existed on location. Maine North High School first opened in 1970, but closed in 1981 due to a falling population of students in the area that it served (in Maine township, northwest of Chicago). After its closure it would serve as a training facility for the Chicago Blitz, a team in the United States Football League of 1983–1985, and, later, as a mortuary college before eventually becoming a district headquarters building for the Illinois State Police Department. Because Hughes could see the potential of the former school's utilitarian corridors and rows of abandoned lockers, he would return there for the filming of interior scenes during *Ferris Bueller's Day Off*—albeit that the exterior of the fictitious "Ocean Park High School" in that later movie would actually be located at Glenbrook North High School in Northbrook. However, when Ed Rooney (Jeffrey Jones) and Sloane Peterson (Mia Sara) emerge from what appears to be the school's main entrance, they were actually leaving the doorway to the Center for Performing Arts, located elsewhere on the school campus.

Hughes was no stranger to constructing elaborate sets in gymnasiums, having used the same technique in *Sixteen Candles* and later movies such as *Uncle Buck* (1989). He was also adept at juxtaposing locations in different geographical areas to good effect; for instance, in *Pretty in Pink* (Howard Deutch, 1986), the interiors of the fictional "Meadowbrook High School" were filmed at Burroughs Junior High School in Los Angeles's Hancock Park while its exterior was shot at the rather more imposing John Marshall High School in Silver Lake, Los Angeles—one of the three schools used as the setting for Rydell High School in *Grease* (Randal Kleiser, 1978), and which would subsequently be used as the setting for *Buffy the Vampire Slayer* (Fran Rubel Kuzui, 1992). On other occasions, Hughes employed the most unlikely locations to double as the setting for a particular scene. For instance, the fictitious "Shermer Police Station" in *Ferris Bueller's Day Off*—located in the Chicago suburbs—was actually the headquarters of Hills Brothers Coffee, based in Los Angeles. (The commanding building would later be occupied by the Southwestern Bag Company.) Interior scenes were shot in the building's upstairs office area, redressed to appear as though it was a functioning police station. The effect was compelling enough that the same location was used to double for police premises in other productions in later years, most notably in *Beverly Hills Cop II* (Tony Scott, 1987). Surprisingly, a contrary feat of sleight-of-hand was achieved some time later in *Home Alone* (Chris Columbus, 1990), where scenes set at the local police station actually took place in the repurposed office of a high school.

Hughes's fastidious attention to detail reached something of a highpoint with the production of *Planes, Trains and Automobiles* (1987). The inviting home of Steve Martin's Neal Page was filmed in a capacious redbrick Colonial-style home built in 1916 and based in Kenilworth, Illinois. Hughes spent considerable time and effort in dressing every part of the house's interior that is shown throughout the movie—including the hallway, kitchen, bedrooms, and living room. This process was said to have taken considerable time to complete, but in spite of the expense involved, Hughes's determination to transform the home into a warm and appealing Thanksgiving-themed paradise seemed justified given the fact that it was to form the tantalizing endpoint of Neal's quest to defy overwhelming odds and make it back to his family. He knew that the house had to look the part, and, in the end, his efforts paid off handsomely. Arguably more involved was the sequence set at the fictional Marathon Car Rental company, where—in one of the movie's most memorable sequences—Neal suffers a profanity-laden meltdown in the face of the firm's inflexible bureaucracy. Due to the implied ineptitude of the organization that is depicted for comic effect, it would have been unreasonable to expect a real business to consent to the use of their premises to film the sequence, and, thus, Hughes ordered the construction of a facsimile business to appear in the film instead. This would ultimately involve corporate emblems and staff uniforms that had been invented solely for this purpose, all situated within a set that would resemble the kind of rent-a-car facility that might be available in proximity to any city airport while simultaneously not reflecting visual similarity to any real-life company.

An Object Lesson: Prop Design and Placement in Hughes Movies

The choice of effective movie props is an often-overlooked part of film production, and yet Hughes was to place just as much importance on making the right selection as he did with fashions and music. This was true not only of features he directed, but for those he wrote or produced. It is difficult to imagine John Candy's kindhearted but nerve-grating Del Griffith without his outsized, sticker-festooned traveling trunk in *Planes, Trains and Automobiles* (all the more poignant when we later discover how little it actually contains), or *Weird Science*'s Wyatt and Gary conducting their experiments into creating life from lifelessness unless they were equipped with bras on their heads, and an unfortunate Barbie doll hooked up to their computer system.

Sometimes even the most innocuous props take on significance in a Hughes movie. When Ferris Bueller makes a fruitless and somewhat cacophonic attempt at playing a clarinet in his bedroom, it is all the more pleasing to consider the fact that Matthew Broderick discovered the instrument on the set and decided to give it a whirl—in spite of the fact that neither he, nor by extension Ferris, had ever been trained to play it. Likewise, when Chevy Chase first donned his Chicago Bears baseball cap as Clark Griswold in *National Lampoon's Vacation* (Harold Ramis, 1983), it is unlikely that he would have imagined that the character would end up wearing the same piece of sports apparel in later entries of the series. When the audience sees a record turntable rotating with a pizza on top of it, rather than a vinyl album, in *Sixteen Candles*, it is unlikely that the shot would have lodged itself quite so convincingly in the annals of pop culture if Hughes had not chosen the stalwart Denon DP-62L as his musical equipment of choice. Nor would the McCallister house of *Home Alone* have seemed quite as festive if its interior had not been so visibly decorated in Christmas-themed colors of green and red, including many of the characters' clothing items and several props within numerous scenes, all of which helped to underscore its late-December setting. On other occasions, props were used to communicate subtle in-jokes, such as in *The Breakfast Club* where we discover that Shermer High School's guidance counselor has a desk sporting a name plate which reads *R. Hashimoto*—a tip of the hat to production supervisor Richard Hashimoto—and a campaign poster for the prom queen features the name *Michelle Manning*, the movie's co-producer.

Some movies to feature a Hughes screenplay include timely items, to comic effect. In *National Lampoon's Christmas Vacation* (Jeremiah S. Chechik, 1989), for example, Clark Griswold is keen to ingratiate himself with his permanently irritable boss Frank Shirley (Brian Doyle-Murray) by presenting him with a Christmas gift. Upon arriving at Shirley's office, however, Clark is dismissively told to leave his wrapped present alongside all of the others that have already been imparted by his fellow employees. Moving to a table nearby, Clark is somewhat crestfallen to discover that everyone else has bought Shirley exactly the same gift—rows of identically shaped wrapped presents are already there, jockeying with his own in a fruitless battle for significance. The humor of the sequence is generated by the fact that a late-eighties audience would be all too aware from the profile and dimensions of the gifts what lay underneath the wrapping: a desk organizer, arranged at a right-angle to accommodate pens on one side and supplies, such as paperclips and staples, on the other. Thus, the gift choice not only gives some indication of the mindset of the office's workforce, clearly unwilling to take any risks by purchasing a present that may be displeasing to the grouchy senior executive, but also Shirley's own lack of imagination, suggesting that none of his colleagues know him well enough to purchase anything other than the safest and most generic of festive offerings.

28

You Can't Tell a Book by its Cover

The Literary Allusions and Cinematic Tributes of John Hughes

John Hughes was a keen student of classic cinema, literature, and art. Many of his films are packed with tributes to famous movies and well-received books of bygone years, while others feature prominent visits to museums and galleries, showcasing works of art which are meaningful to the characters in one way or other. This offered a sophisticated commentary on areas of intersection between art and popular culture, highlighting his deep respect for creativity in all its forms. But whether he was presenting audiences with recognizable homages to the movies, literature, music, and artwork of years past, or toying playfully with the boundaries between different modes of creative expression, Hughes was never afraid to draw on his formidable knowledge of cultural phenomena to infuse his screenplays and productions with a comprehensive variety of artistic references.

Behind the Camera: John Hughes's Allusions to Classic and Modern Cinema

Whether acting as writer or director, Hughes was never afraid to introduce the occasional reference to cinema past and present—often by subtle means, though at times there was no mistaking his respectful nods to the filmmaking greats of years gone by. Among the most noteworthy is his inclusion of a TV broadcast of the classic Universal Pictures horror movie *Frankenstein* (James Whale, 1931) within *Weird Science* (1985), along with a rather more understated sound sample from the later sequel *Bride of Frankenstein* (James Whale, 1935), in which Colin Clive's character, Dr. Henry Frankenstein, and Ernest Thesiger's Dr. Pretorius, are shown in the process of animating the monster's bride (Elsa Lanchester) just as Wyatt (Ilan Mitchell-Smith) and Gary (Anthony Michael Hall) involve themselves in the creation of Kelly LeBrock's Lisa. Thus, Hughes indicates the shared parthenogenetic ground between the theme of Mary Shelley's 1818 novel, where a mutilated corpse is resurrected, and his own teenaged characters' efforts—more clearly grounded in the modern day—to bring about a living, conscious being solely via technological means (albeit with some unexplained, unnatural assistance into the bargain).

There are similarly numerous references to classic cinema throughout *Home Alone* (Chris Columbus, 1990). While killing time in Paris waiting for their flight home, the McCallister family wind up watching a French broadcast of Yuletide staple *It's a Wonderful Life* (Frank Capra, 1946)—a fact that would prove to be strangely appropriate, given that the *Washington Times* critic Hal Hinson was later to describe *Home Alone* as a cinematic collision between the emotional sentimentality of Frank Capra and the cartoon mayhem of animator Chuck Jones. A broadcast of *It's a Wonderful Life* would briefly appear again in *Home Alone*'s sequel, *Home Alone 2: Lost in New York* (Chris Columbus, 1992), but less well remembered is the classic Christmas movie's appearance in *National Lampoon's Christmas Vacation* (Jeremiah S. Chechik, 1989), where it is being aired alongside the Griswolds putting up their household Christmas tree. In an intriguing twist of fate, the grandson of *It's a Wonderful Life*'s famed director, Frank Capra III, worked as an assistant director on *National Lampoon's Christmas Vacation*.

Other cinematic allusions in *Home Alone* include a clever homage to the advertising poster for Fritz Lang's crime thriller *M* (1931), which featured the palm of Peter Lorre's character Hans Beckert bearing a branded letter "M." In *Home Alone*, Joe Pesci's burglar Harry Lime unsuspectingly grabs an electrically heated doorknob, which is engraved with the initial letter of the McCallister family. Once the burn has cooled, Harry discovers that the flesh of his hand has become imprinted with the aforementioned letter, in a manner identical to that of the Lang movie's poster motif. Similarly, Macaulay Culkin's Kevin McCallister brandishes a Daisy Red Ryder air rifle, which is an low-key tribute to the prized BB gun so greatly desired by Peter Billingsley's Ralphie Parker in the modern Yuletide classic *A Christmas Story* (Bob Clark, 1983), while Kevin's beloved gangster movie *Angels with Filthy Souls* (and its *Home Alone 2* equivalent, *Angels with Even Filthier Souls*) was a tribute to influential *film noir* crime-drama *Angels with Dirty Faces* (Michael Curtiz, 1938). Amusingly, though Hughes makes clear the fact that Roberts Blossom's seemingly terrifying Old Man Marley is not a mass-murderer but actually a kind and caring elderly gentleman, Blossom had received some degree of notoriety due to his starring role in *Deranged: The Confessions of a Necrophile* (Alan Ormsby and Jeff Gillen, 1974), in which he had portrayed a serial killer named Ezra Cobb. By comparison, Mr. Marley's counterpart in *Home Alone 2*—Brenda Fricker's destitute "Pigeon Lady," who befriends Kevin—seems to be rather more innocently based on Jane Darwell's aged "Bird Woman" in the Walt Disney Company's adaptation of *Mary Poppins* (Robert Stevenson, 1964).

Hughes peppered many of his movies with shrewd references to well-known cinematic features, many of them fairly contemporary. In *Planes, Trains and Automobiles* (1987), for instance, as Neal (Steve Martin) and Del (John Candy) lament the wreckage of their rental car, a road sign can be seen nearby which states that Chicago is 106 miles away. This mirrors the famous line from *The Blues Brothers* (John Landis, 1980)—a film which had also featured John Candy—that stated the characters were exactly 106 miles to Chicago. *The Blues Brothers* had also starred Dan Aykroyd as Elwood Blues, and *The Great Outdoors* (Howard Deutch, 1988)—in which Aykroyd portrays nominal antagonist Roman Craig—features a song entitled "Dragboat," performed by none other than The Elwood Blues Revue. Another musical reference can be found in *Sixteen Candles* during a brief dining scene in which Rudy Ryszczyk's (John Kapelos) family explains to soon-to-be father-in-law Jim Baker (Paul Dooley) about their somewhat nebulous business practices. Accompanying the sequence is Nino Rota's "Love Theme" from *The Godfather* (Francis Ford Coppola, 1972), reflecting the Bakers' suspicions about the Ryszczyks' seemingly shady commercial dealings.

Other allusions were considerably more cunning. In *National Lampoon's European Vacation* (Amy Heckerling, 1985), Eric Idle's incredibly apologetic English "Bike Rider" is struck by a car driven by tourist Clark Griswold (Chevy Chase), but politely dismisses his serious injuries as being merely a flesh wound. This was an off-the-cuff reference to *Monty Python and the Holy Grail* (Terry Gilliam and Terry Jones, 1975), wherein Idle (and the rest of the cast) played a number of parts, as John Cleese's Black Knight stubbornly claimed that he too had suffered only "a flesh wound" even as he was brutally dismembered by swordplay. The often-unpredictable Griswold patriarch would again evoke his capacity for causing injury in *National Lampoon's Christmas Vacation*, in which he trims an oversized Christmas tree while dressed in a Jason Voorhees–style hockey mask—a clear visual reference to *Friday the 13th* (Sean S. Cunningham, 1980)—while swinging around a chainsaw in the manner of Leatherface, the fearsome adversary of *The Texas Chain Saw Massacre* (Tobe Hooper, 1974). Rather more innocently, *Pretty in Pink* (Howard Deutch, 1986) has Iona (Annie Potts)—manager of record store Trax—answering the phone with the brusque inquiry "Whaddya want?"; this mirrored the frankness of Potts's memorably straight-talking secretary Janine Melnitz, who had used the exact same greeting in *Ghostbusters* (Ivan Reitman, 1984).

When the cunning Ferris Bueller (Matthew Broderick) uses his hacking skills during *Ferris Bueller's Day Off* (1986) to break into the network of his high school and reduce the number of absences he has clocked up over the current term, the scene reflects a similar incident in *WarGames* (John Badham, 1983) where Broderick's tech prodigy David Lightman successfully manages to increase his grades by infiltrating his school's database. Keeping with the science-fiction theme, Vernon Wells—who portrayed Lord General, the leader of a gang of mutant bikers in *Weird Science*—was very clearly reenacting his earlier role as the post-apocalyptic henchman Wez in *Mad Max 2: The Road Warrior* (George Miller, 1981), from his studded-leather costume to his lethal proficiency with motorbikes. In *Planes, Trains and Automobiles*, Hughes re-used an insert of a Boeing 707 in flight through a storm to chart Del and Neal's abortive journey to Chicago; the shot had originally been used for Trans American Flight 209 in Paramount's surreal comedy *Airplane!* (Jim Abrahams,

David Zucker, and Jerry Zucker, 1980), and appropriately foreshadowed the many comic incidents. Also in *Planes, Trains and Automobiles*, the opening sequence in New York City sees Steve Martin's Neal Page racing against Kevin Bacon's "Taxi Racer" in an attempt to reach a yellow cab, paralleling a similar chase in the stock market–themed drama *Quicksilver* (Thomas Michael Donnelly, 1986), wherein Bacon's character Jack Casey finds himself involved in an urban bike pursuit.

Hughes's most unusual cinematic crossovers take place in *Planes, Trains and Automobiles* and the later *She's Having a Baby* (1988). Dialogue from *She's Having a Baby* can be heard on a television broadcast, featuring an argument between Kristy Briggs (Elizabeth McGovern) and her husband, Jake (Kevin Bacon), suggesting that the film is being aired by a TV channel even though it hadn't at that point premiered in theaters. Bacon, who had a cameo in *Planes, Trains and Automobiles*, would star in *She's Having a Baby*. Candy—one of the two leads in the previous feature—makes a short appearance in the end credits of the later movie.

Films featuring a Hughes screenplay occasionally offered up an in-joke to other movies in his filmography, or referenced the work of production crew members. For instance, when Josie McClellan (Jennifer Connelly) is browsing through an array of audio cassettes while accidentally trapped in a department store during the events of *Career Opportunities* (Bryan Gordon, 1991), the camera momentarily lingers on the tape release of the original soundtrack album for *The Breakfast Club* (1985). Likewise, during a scene in record store Trax in *Pretty in Pink*, the soundtrack cover for the fantasy-adventure movie *Ladyhawke* (Richard Donner, 1985) can be seen; that film had starred Ferris Bueller actor Matthew Broderick, and had been produced by Lauren Shuler, who was also the producer of *Pretty in Pink*. While Clark Griswold tries in vain to read a copy of *People* magazine while relaxing in *National Lampoon's Christmas Vacation*, his hands covered in sap from his freshly trimmed Christmas tree, the cover design of the publication shows none other than the film's director, Jeremiah S. Chechik. *Ferris Bueller's Day Off* features an affable detective named Steven Lim (Robert Kim), who reassures Katie Bueller (Cindy Pickett) after her daughter, Jeanie (Jennifer Grey), has been taken to Shermer Police Station; this was a nod to the movie's first assistant director, albeit that his name was actually spelled Stephen Lim. *Ferris Bueller's Day Off* would itself become a reference in a later Hughes film; in the events of *Curly Sue* (1991), the offices of Kelly Lynch's lawyer Grey Ellison are based in the Bueller Building, an upscale Chicago high-rise.

By the Book: The Literary Allusions of John Hughes Movies

Though his literary references were less plentiful than his allusions to other cinematic works, Hughes's keen interest in the written word was also reflected in his screenplays. Just as the original *National Lampoon's Vacation* (Harold Ramis, 1983) had been inspired by a short prose work he had penned—"Vacation '58," which appeared in a 1979 issue of *National Lampoon* magazine—so too was the later *National Lampoon's Christmas Vacation* loosely based on another of his early stories: "Christmas '59," which was first published by the magazine a year later, in 1980. When Clark Griswold is seen trapped in his attic, rummaging through old home movie reels as he attempts to kill some time, he discovers a dusty film can labeled "Xmas '59."

Hughes's literary allusions ranged from the classic to the modern. For instance, in *Home Alone* the name of Roberts Blossom's Old Man Marley is a fairly obvious reference to Jacob Marley, the deceased money-lender who was once partner to the miserly Ebenezer Scrooge in Charles Dickens's often-adapted novella *A Christmas Carol* (1843). Like Dickens's Marley, Hughes's character demonstrates a major transformation in attitude as the story unfolds: in his case, changing from an ominously frightening figure to a supportive, avuncular individual who unexpectedly saves the day. In the same movie, the name of Joe Pesci's antagonist Harry Lime is a tribute to the enigmatic central figure of Graham Greene's novella *The Third Man* (1959), which was written by Greene as preparation for his screenplay for Carol Reed's famed 1949 *film noir* of the same name. (In the Reed movie, Lime was portrayed with sphinxlike inscrutability by Orson Welles—quite a contrast when juxtaposed with Pesci's dimwitted, bumbling burglar character.)

On occasion, Hughes's literary references could tend more towards the spiritual than the fictional. When Dean of Students Ed Rooney tries to

National Lampoon's European Vacation. Director: Amy Heckerling. Release date: July 26, 1985.

offer comfort to the seemingly grieving Sloane Peterson in *Ferris Bueller's Day Off*, he awkwardly recites a brief extract from an anthem drawn from the "Burial of the Dead" section of *The Book of Common Prayer*, which has been published and used by the Anglican Church since 1549. The particular anthem that Rooney recites is drawn from the Old Testament book of Job 14:1–2, and Hughes uses the sequence to provide humor in two ways. First, the contrite dean of students (wrongly believing he has insulted Sloane's father) is uneasily trying to pour oil on troubled waters by using consoling religious imagery to offer solace to his student, but his efforts turn out to be amusingly inept. And second, because Rooney is characterized as a spiteful and vindictive character who is the very opposite of humble piety, his attempts at religiosity cannot help but appear hypocritical at best and utterly self-serving at worst.

Interestingly, not all of the literary sources called upon by Hughes had any bearing in real publications. In *Planes, Trains and Automobiles*, John Candy's Del Griffith can be seen reading a pulpy paperback entitled *The Canadian Mounted*. This was a comical evocation of Candy's nationality; though he often played American characters, he was actually Canadian by birth, hailing from Newmarket, Ontario. Hughes continued the joke the following year in *The Great Outdoors*; during dinner, while Candy's character, Chet Ripley, orders the colossal "Old 96er" steak, his wife, Connie (Stephanie Faracy), instead asks for the "Royal Canadian Mounted Beef Barley Soup," recalling the gag from the earlier movie.

Painting on a Wide Canvas: The Artistic Allusions of John Hughes

As someone with a keen interest in visual art, it was no surprise that Hughes also included numerous tips of the hat to a wide variety of artwork throughout his movies. On occasion, this even extended to the marketing of films; *National Lampoon's Vacation*, for instance, have poster artwork by Peruvian fantasy artist Boris Vallejo, with both the original feature and its sequel *National Lampoon's European Vacation* aping the marketing imagery for the famous poster created by artist Renato Casaro for *Conan the Barbarian* (John Milius, 1982)—complete with Chevy

A Sunday Afternoon on the Island of La Grande Jatte (*Un dimanche après-midi à l'Île de la Grande Jatte*), painted by Georges Seurat in 1884.

Chase's hapless Clark Griswold striking a heroic central pose in place of Arnold Schwarzenegger's musclebound Cimmerian warrior.

In a number of instances, characters' interest in (or ownership of) artwork is used by Hughes to reveal something about their personality. During *Ferris Bueller's Day Off*, Cameron Frye becomes fixated on Georges Seurat's pointillist masterpiece *A Sunday Afternoon on the Island of La Grande Jatte* (1884) while visiting the Art Institute of Chicago. Though the sizeable canvas painting depicts a large number of people situated in a park near the River Seine in Paris, Cameron becomes especially preoccupied with the image of a small, happy child standing next to its mother. The more Cameron attempts to focus on the small details of the child's face, because of the pointillist technique (where small colored dots are carefully arranged in patterns to form a larger image) he finds himself increasingly unable to do so. The scene is used by Hughes to rather poignantly emphasize Cameron's troubled formative years, the tenderness of the relationship between the mother and child in the painting being starkly juxtaposed with the distant and discontented familial connection that exists between the anxious teen and his own parents.

Likewise, during *Sixteen Candles* Hughes places an intriguing artifact on the wall of Jake Ryan's (Michael Schoeffling) bedroom. Whereas the living spaces of most other Hughesian teens tend to be plastered with posters of rock bands and other music groups, Jake instead has a print above his bed which shows the *Vasa*, a Swedish warship which was sunk in August 1628. Later salvaged in 1961 outside Stockholm Harbor with its hull still largely intact, the ship has since gone on display and has become a hugely popular tourist attraction. The presence of this historical shipwreck marked Jake as a somewhat deeper and more contemplative individual than many of his contemporaries, suggesting a level of cultural understanding not shared by his asinine girlfriend Caroline Mulford (Haviland Morris) and laying the groundwork for a more fulfilling relationship with Molly Ringwald's smart, sensitive Samantha Baker.

Perhaps most conspicuous of all allusions to visual art is *Home Alone*, which features—both in promotional posters, as well as in the film itself—the famous scene in which Macaulay Culkin's Kevin McCallister silently shrieks with his hands clapped to either side of his face: a gesture which closely imitated Edvard Munch's famous 1893 painting *The Scream*. While that work has become forever associated with existential dread and internal angst, and has been endlessly referenced and parodied in popular culture, its influence on *Home Alone* was instead to be one which presented a rather more innocent depiction of childhood panic and youthful exuberance. Later replicated in the film's 1992 sequel, this distinctive tableau has been recreated by Culkin on various occasions in the years since, and is now synonymous with the *Home Alone* franchise.

A Finger on the Pulse: Music and Pop Culture Allusions in John Hughes's Cinema

Such was Hughes's fascination with popular culture that many homages to recognizable figures and well-known cultural phenomena are present in his work. This was particularly evident in the *National Lampoon's Vacation* series. Whereas Walley World—the ultimate goal of the Griswolds' unfortunate journey across America—is a sprawling California-based theme park that was very obviously modeled after Disneyland, the comparison is made all the more blatant by including Roy Walley (Eddie Bracken), whose general appearance mirrors that of both Walt Disney and his nephew Roy Edward Disney. A similar tactic was used in *National Lampoon's European Vacation* with the introduction of smarmy, over-familiar TV host Kent Winkdale (John Astin), the presenter of game show *Pig in a Poke*, whose appearance and demeanor seemed intended to be a satire of ingratiating TV entertainers of the seventies and eighties. His name was suggestive of Wink Martindale, disc jockey and game show host, who became best known for presenting TV quizzes *Gambit* (1972–1976) and *Tic Tac Dough* (1978–1985), though others have pointed to Richard Dawson—a panelist on *Match Game* (1973–1978) and the host of *Family Feud* (1976–1985)—as another possible inspiration.

Hughes's knowledge of light entertainment was also evident in the use of *The Breakfast Club*, now an expression forever associated with high school detention. However, the distinctive moniker likely has its origins in *Don McNeill's Breakfast Club*, a long-running radio show broadcast from Chicago between June 1933 and December 1968 (as well as briefly airing on television in the early fifties). The Breakfast Club was also the name of a New York City–based synthpop group, active between 1979 and 1990, which initially featured Madonna as its drummer and (later) on lead vocals. However, it is likely that the Don McNeill radio show was the more credible influence of the two; for all the eclectic range of music on the movie's soundtrack, the work of The Breakfast Club does not feature, and even when Allison Reynolds (Ally Sheedy) is perusing the cover of an LP during lunch it turns out to be Prince's fifth studio album *1999* (1982). Other notable cultural references to appear in Hughes's eighties screenplays include Gary and Wyatt of *Weird Science* being faced with the appearance of a Pershing II atomic warhead after it is reproduced from the cover illustration of the January 31, 1983, issue of *Time* magazine. Ocean Park High School's sympathetic nurse, Florence Sparrow (Virginia Capers), who offers condolences to the seemingly grief-stricken Sloane in *Ferris Bueller's Day Off*, is quite unambiguously named after historical nursing pioneer Florence Nightingale, while the railroad worker friend mentioned by John Candy's Del Griffith in *Planes, Trains and*

Automobiles—Burt Dingman—is a sly reference to Robert O. Dingman Jr., the president of the New York and Lake Erie (NYLE) Railroad.

Given Hughes's love of music, it is no surprise that his movies and screenplays contain many tributes to songs and recording artists. Among them is the fact that the central characters of *Some Kind of Wonderful* (Howard Deutch, 1988) feature names which correlate with band members of the Rolling Stones: Eric Stoltz's Keith is an allusion to Keith Richards, Mary Stuart Masterson's Watts homages Charlie Watts, and Amanda Jones—as played by Lea Thompson—refers to "Miss Amanda Jones," the eleventh track of the band's studio album *Between the Buttons* (1967). *The Breakfast Club* opens with a quotation from David Bowie, drawn from "Changes"—a song which appeared on his 1971 album *Hunky Dory*, and was later released as a single in January 1972. *Weird Science* features Van Halen's 1982 cover of Roy Orbison's "(Oh) Pretty Woman," which is reflected in a sequence when Wyatt and Gary scan a photographer of the band's frontman David Lee Roth into their computer as one of the stylistic influences which later affect the creation of Kelly LeBrock's Lisa. On other occasions, Hughes would toy with the audience's cultural assumptions about particular music for comic effect. For instance, John Candy's Buck Russell playfully irritates his niece, Tia (Jean Louisa Kelly), by deliberately mistaking her beloved eighties rap music for rock band The Grass Roots, who charted most regularly between the late 1960s and mid-1970s. The humor is generated not only from Tia's lack of recognition of a band which had appealed widely to an earlier generation, but also from Buck's premeditatedly fallacious misidentification of two vastly dissimilar musical styles.

Sometimes a particular song could become closely associated with a Hughes film, such as Bert Kaempfert's "Danke Schoen" (1962) which crops up not once but four times throughout *Ferris Bueller's Day Off*. Whether hummed or sung, "Danke Schoen" can be heard when Ferris takes a shower, when Ed Rooney waits around after ringing the doorbell of the Bueller residence, as Jeanie heads down the stairs of the local police station, and—most notably of all—when Ferris mimes along to Wayne Newton's 1963 recording of the song during the Von Steuben Day Parade in Chicago. But, on other occasions, Hughes could use music as a means of foreshadowing events within a movie's plot. During *Pretty in Pink*, Jon Cryer's Phil "Duckie" Dale is switching between stations on Andie's (Molly Ringwald) car radio, only to hear "If You Leave" (1986) by Orchestral Manoeuvres in the Dark. Duckie promptly points out that he can't stand the song, and yet it is the same track which later sets the mood for the conclusion, when—at the school prom—Andie decides to pursue a romance with wealthy Blane McDonnagh (Andrew McCarthy) at the cost of a relationship with Duckie himself. Thus, his distaste for the synthpop composition lays the groundwork for the disappointment which would later befall him.

He Loves Them Yeah, Yeah, Yeah: John Hughes and The Beatles

Though he had admiration for many different music groups, Hughes was especially fond of The Beatles, and several of his films contain references to that most singular of British bands. Though the allusions were often quite restrained in nature, there was no shortage of ingenious evocations of The Beatles and its members. Sometimes the homage was fairly direct, such as Anthony Michael Hall's "Farmer" Ted singing "Birthday" (from the 1968 album *The Beatles*) to Samantha Baker in a doomed attempt to impress her during *Sixteen Candles*, or an incidence of "You Never Know" on the soundtrack of *Curly Sue* (1991), performed by former Beatle Ringo Starr and written by Steve Dorff and John Bettis. In *Pretty in Pink*, Andie hands a copy of *In His Own Write* (1964)—John Lennon's surrealistic book of poetry and short fiction—to Blane when he visits the Trax record store, whereas in *The Breakfast Club* the character of irritable Assistant Principal Richard Vernon (Paul Gleason) shares his name with the British actor who portrayed Johnson (a train commuter) in *A Hard Day's Night* (Richard Lester, 1964), a musical-comedy which starred The Beatles and was released when Beatlemania was at its cultural peak. The Beatles connection also surfaces later in the movie when Vernon asks John Kapelos's Carl—the school janitor—what he had dreamed of being when he was still a youth, and his colleague replies that he'd always hoped to become John Lennon.

While *Ferris Bueller's Day Off* contains one of Hughes's most instantly familiar Beatles tributes in the form of Matthew Broderick miming along to the group's 1963 cover of The Top Notes' "Twist and Shout" (which is on The Beatles' 1963 debut studio album *Please Please Me*), there were other, less conspicuous references to the Fab Four scattered throughout the film. Ferris briefly quotes from John Lennon's song "God," which appeared on Lennon's 1970 debut solo studio album, *John Lennon/Plastic Ono Band*. There is an even subtler allusion in the Detroit Red Wings logo worn on the ice hockey jersey worn by Cameron (Alan Ruck), which matched the team decal that ornamented Paul McCartney's Epiphone Texan acoustic guitar from 1976 onwards. During a performance with his band Wings, McCartney was gifted the sticker by Mike Kudzia—an employee of Detroit's Olympia Stadium—on the first night of a weekend performance, and it has been associated with the instrument ever since.

29

You Couldn't Ignore Me If You Tried

The Box-Office Performance of John Hughes's Cinema

While John Hughes is famous for his ability to generate sizeable profits from movies filmed on modest budgets, it is interesting to note that some of his most enduring successes were not always commercial smash hits at the time of their initial release. Similarly, not all of his less critically regarded motion pictures would prove to be financial flops. Some surprising contradictions were to lie behind the box-office performance of many of Hughes's movies, sometimes explaining their eventual waning from public interest, but—conversely—often underpinning their continued ability to appeal to viewers many years after their debuts.

The box-office figures and other statistical data for this chapter have been sourced from The Numbers (http://www.the-numbers.com), Box Office Mojo (http://www.boxofficemojo.com), and the Internet Movie Database (http://www.imdb.com).

Lights, Camera, Accountant: The Commercial Performance of John Hughes as Director

Due to John Hughes's lengthy and successful career as a screenwriter and producer, it is a regularly unobserved fact that he was to take up directorial responsibilities for movies on only eight separate occasions. However, those features were to include some of his best-known contributions to cinema, and their profitability—along with their critical success—was to cement his reputation as one of the most prominent cultural figures of the 1980s.

Hughes's directorial debut, *Sixteen Candles* (1984), immediately brought him to the attention of the studios; with an estimated budget of $6.5 million, the movie was to make back $4,461,520 in the opening weekend alone, eventually grossing $23,686,027 domestically. The performance of *Sixteen Candles* was arguably bolstered by the fact that its release did not coincide with any particularly high-profile competition. Also debuting in theaters across the United States on May 4, 1984, were the comedies *The Buddy System* (Glenn Jordan, 1984) and *Rent Control* (Gian Luigi Polidoro, 1984); the historical-drama *Memed My Hawk* (Peter Ustinov, 1984); the wartime-thriller *Purple Hearts* (Sidney J. Furie, 1984), and the dramas *Breakin'* (Joel Silberg, 1984), *Alphabet City* (Amos Poe, 1984), and *Wildrose* (John Hanson, 1984). Arguably the most prominent challenger came in the form of lavish maritime-epic *The Bounty* (Roger Donaldson, 1984), recounting the fateful voyage of Captain William Bligh and featuring the weighty star billing of Anthony Hopkins and Mel Gibson.

Hughes's second movie as director was to be one of the most instantly identifiable of his entire career, and would prove to be even more profitable than his inaugural feature. *The Breakfast Club* (1985) was produced on an estimated budget of $1 million, and would go on to make its money back quite comfortably in the opening weekend, when it grossed $5,107,599. It would eventually reach a domestic total of $45,875,171, with a further $5,650,000 raised in foreign ticket sales—a total revenue of $51,525,171. This was clearly a huge success for Hughes given the movie's negligible budget, and was a victory for his prioritization of dialogue and characterization over special effects and spectacle. As had been the case with its predecessor, *The Breakfast Club* met with fairly light commercial opposition at the time of its release on February 15, 1985. Among the other features being screened for the first time on that date were the dramas *Fast Forward* (Sidney Poitier, 1985), *The Bay Boy* (Daniel Petrie, 1985), and *Vision Quest* (Harold Becker, 1985), the international-drama *Beyond the*

Walls (Uri Barbash, 1985), the comedies *Turk 182!* (Bob Clark, 1985) and *Lost in America* (Albert Brooks, 1985), and the thrillers *The Mean Season* (Phillip Borsos, 1985) and *Into the Night* (John Landis, 1985).

By the time *Weird Science* (1985) appeared in theaters later that year, Hughes's star was well and truly in ascendance, as was reflected in the funding for his new production. With an estimated budget in the region of $7,500,000, the film enjoyed solid opening weekend profits of $4,895,421, before going on to a domestic gross of $23,834,048 and foreign takings of $15,100,000. With a cumulative box-office total of $38,934,048, *Weird Science* could be considered a success, and if the extent of its profitability seemed qualified in relation to that of *The Breakfast Club*, it was only due to the fact that its budget (in line with the high-tech trimmings of its sci-fi premise) was substantially increased over the scant production values of its immediate predecessor. *Weird Science* also benefited from a release date which featured little competition in the line of a comedy/sci-fy; also to be launched, on August 2, 1985, were the satirical historical-drama *Insignificance* (Nicolas Roeg, 1985), the horror-comedy *Fright Night* (Tom Holland, 1985), the thought-provoking French-thriller *Peril* (Michel Deville, 1985), the off-kilter *Phenomena* (Dario Argento, 1985), and the family-oriented *Sesame Street Presents Follow That Bird* (Ken Kwapis, 1985).

Next was to come one of Hughes's defining teen movies: the inimitable *Ferris Bueller's Day Off* (1986). Another extremely successful contribution to the genre, from an estimated budget of $5.8 million, the film was to make that back on its opening weekend, with a box-office take of $6,275,647. Eventually making a total domestic gross of $70,136,369, the feature was a huge hit for Hughes and would, of course, go on to become one of his best-loved movies of the 1980s—a fact borne out by its continued relevance to popular culture. Going into general release on June 11, 1986, *Ferris Bueller's Day Off* faced little in the way of commercial opposition in cinemas; the only other film to debut in American theaters on the same day was *The Eyes of the Birds* (Gabriel Auer, 1983), making its U.S. debut after its original run in France, three years earlier.

A sidestep from teen movies to mainstream comedy then followed, in the form of *Planes, Trains and Automobiles* (1987). Another feature which has stood the test of time, the film was not to reach quite the same heights of profitability at the time of its release. With a budget estimated to be in the region of $30 million, the opening weekend was to see $7,009,482 being raised, eventually leading to an overall domestic gross of $49,530,280. While still profitable, *Planes, Trains and Automobiles* could not claim to be quite as successful as Hughes's earlier directorial efforts. However, favorable critical reception has led to it being re-released numerous times on home-entertainment formats. In keeping with the film's Thanksgiving setting, *Planes, Trains and Automobiles* debuted in theaters on November 25, 1987, and faced stiff competition from *Three Men and a Baby* (Leonard Nimoy, 1987), a popular and very profitable American remake of Coline Serreau's *Trois Hommes et un Couffin* (1985), which would enjoy a long run in theaters.

Hughes was to focus on mainstream drama for his next film, *She's Having a Baby* (1988), where his usual insightful comedy was tempered by family-oriented contemplation. While the budget for the film is not known and, indeed, is not even to be found in an estimated form, it earned $3,827,520 in its opening weekend, leading to an eventual total domestic gross of $16,031,707. This was markedly below the level of profit enjoyed by Hughes's other movies thus far, and the comparative lack of commercial impact made by *She's Having a Baby* has led to it becoming one of his lesser-known directorial efforts. While the more introspective drama of the movie may have seemed incompatible with the expectations of those anticipating a straightforwardly comedic experience, its underwhelming box-office performance may also have been explained in part by the varied lineup released on the same date. Also debuting on February 5, 1988: the drama *The Unbearable Lightness of Being* (Philip Kaufman, 1988), the crime-drama *Cop* (James B. Harris, 1988), the horror film *The Serpent and the Rainbow* (Wes Craven, 1988), and the sci-fi/action movie *Cherry 2000* (Steve De Jarnatt, 1988). The same date would also see American premieres for three movies which had previously been released in foreign markets—the British crime-comedy *The Supergrass* (Peter Richardson, 1985), the Polish drama *The Promised Land* (Andrzej Wajda, 1975), and the Italian mystery-thriller *Julia and Julia* (Peter Del Monte, 1987).

A commercial return to form would be made by Hughes the following year, thanks to the popular *Uncle Buck* (1989). His decision to revisit perceptively observed suburban comedy soon paid dividends, for with a budget estimated at $15 million, the movie would go on to earn $8,794,501 in its opening weekend, eventually leading to a domestic gross of $66,758,538 and takings from foreign markets reaching $12,500,000. With an overall worldwide gross of $79,258,538, *Uncle Buck* was to see Hughes returning to the kind of profitability that had been experienced by many of his earlier movies, and the film's popularity among audiences has led to it becoming one of his most enduring non-teen comedies in subsequent years. Its impressive opening weekend performance may well have been aided by the fact that it faced little in the way of commercial challenge; the only other movie to be launched on August 16, 1989, was the comedy *Rude Awakening* (David Greenwalt and Aaron Russo, 1989). However, in a summer that was noted for its exceptionally strong cinematic lineup, *Uncle Buck* did very well against such formidable competition as Steven Spielberg's *Indiana Jones and the Last Crusade*, Robert Zemeckis's *Back to the Future: Part II*, and, most especially, Tim Burton's *Batman*.

Hughes's directorial swan song came two years later in the form of family-comedy *Curly Sue* (1991). Striking a decidedly kid-friendly tone which would inform many of his screenplays throughout the 1990s, it was a marked departure from the earlier features he had helmed, though it would struggle to capture either the tone or popularity of his other family-oriented films. With a hefty estimated budget of $25 million, the movie had a tepid opening weekend, grossing $4,974,958; its total domestic gross came to a discouraging $33,691,313. Though the film had proven successful enough to make back its budgetary costs, the disappointing profit margin marked a frustratingly lukewarm end to a directorial career that had otherwise proven to be critically efficacious and commercially gainful. *Curly Sue* faced reasonably light competition at its time of release; also debuting in the U.S. on October 25, 1991, was horror-anthology *Two Evil Eyes* (Dario Argento and George Romero, 1991), action-thriller *The Hitman* (Aaron Norris, 1991), and whimsical comedy *The Butcher's Wife* (Terry Hughes, 1991). While the box-office performance of *Curly Sue* may not have been the career conclusion that Hughes would ideally have sought, his time behind the camera was only one part of a multifaceted contribution to cinema.

Top of the Flops: The Commercial Failures of John Hughes

Though Hughes enjoyed considerable public acclaim for his directorial career, it was as a producer and screenwriter that he established even greater longevity. But while he has become widely recognized for his success at the box-office, his filmography was also not to be without the occasional lapse in financial performance.

The early years of his screenwriting career were to produce a few significant duds before his rise to prominence within popular culture, with *National Lampoon's Class Reunion* (Michael Miller, 1982) achieving a total domestic gross of $10,054,150—a far cry from its predecessor, the hugely profitable *National Lampoon's Animal House* (John Landis, 1978)—and the later *Nate and Hayes* (Ferdinand Fairfax, 1983) proving to be a far greater disappointment, delivering a domestic gross of only $1,963,756 from an estimated budget of approximately $5 million. Occurring at an early point in his career, and in relation to lesser-known entries in his filmography, the underperformance of these movies did nothing to tarnish his reputation given that they were surrounded by other, much more lucrative features and prior to the success of his emergence as a noteworthy director.

While Hughes's screenwriting throughout the eighties would reach far greater heights as the years progressed, he was to hit upon another wave of less-than-successful commercial results from the early nineties onwards. *Career Opportunities* (Bryan Gordon, 1991), which was considered derivative and lackluster by many critics, grossed only $11,336,986 at the domestic box-office—a figure far below the kind of revenue expected by a Hughes feature at this stage in his career—whereas *Dutch* (Peter Faiman, 1991) has come to be regarded as one of his most visible commercial failures, drawing a comparatively paltry domestic gross of $4,603,929, which could only be considered a financial blow given the movie's estimated budget of $17 million. The critically panned *Baby's Day Out* (Patrick Read Johnson, 1994) would face a similar fate; with a hefty budget estimated to be in the region of $48 million, the movie was to amass a domestic box-office revenue of $16,827,402 along with foreign takings of $10,700,000, leading to a loss-making total gross of only $27,527,402, and putting paid to the notion of any potential sequels.

Hughes's attempt at small-scale independent film production, *Reach the Rock* (William Ryan, 1998) was something of a special case; with a limited release—meaning that the film screened in only three theaters nationwide—the movie was to gross only $4,960 domestically. However, an unprofitable outcome also awaited the final film to which he would contribute as a screenwriter. *Just Visiting* (Jean-Marie Poiré, 2001) was produced on an estimated budget of $35 million, and went on to raise only $4,781,539 at the domestic box office, along with foreign ticket sales of $11,395,193—a cumulative total of just $16,176,732, and a particularly unfortunate example of unprofitability at this late stage in his career.

Just the Ticket: John Hughes's Box-Office Triumphs

While Hughes's features had occasionally met with poor financial results, he remains far better known for the resounding successes. Nowhere was this better illustrated than with the first three films in the *Home Alone* series. The meteoric monetary achievement of the original *Home Alone* (Chris Columbus, 1990) retains a reputation not only as the pinnacle of Hughes's commercial viability in a writer/producer role, but as one of the most profitable movies of the 1990s. Produced on an estimated budget of $15 million, the film had made back $17,081,997 by the end of its opening weekend alone. It enjoyed a long run in theaters, eventually grossing $285,761,243 in the domestic market and a further $190,923,432 in foreign territories: a remarkable combined worldwide gross of $476,684,675. At the conclusion of its theatrical run, *Home Alone* had been responsible for more than 67.7 million ticket sales in the United States, becoming the third highest-grossing movie of all time at that point.

Given the huge financial success of the movie, a sequel was all but inevitable, and *Home Alone 2: Lost in New York* (Chris Columbus, 1992) was to meet with similarly positive commercial results when released two years later. With a larger budget estimated at around $18 million, the sequel more than comfortably made its money back in the opening weekend alone; box-office proceeds came to $31,126,882. *Home Alone 2* would

Home Alone 3. Director: Raja Gosnell. Release date: December 12, 1997.

eventually gross $173,585,516 domestically, with a further $185,409,334 in foreign-ticket revenue, leading to an overall total of $358,994,850. While not quite reaching the heady heights of its predecessor, there was no doubting the achievement in recreating such a robust box-office return in the wake of such a lucrative original. This led some years later to the production of *Home Alone 3* (Raja Gosnell, 1997), which marked a down-turn in the financial fortunes of the series. With an increased budget estimated to be in the region of $32 million (almost twice that of the first sequel), the film met with a disappointing opening weekend that raised $5,085,482, and its domestic box-office takings were similarly a pale shadow of the first two movies in the series, coming to $30,882,515. While the foreign gross was $48,200,000, leading to an overall figure of $79,082,515 by the time its theatrical run was over, there was little doubt that audience appetite for the series' once-innovative home-defense sce-nario had been on the wane since the early nineties, meaning that later sequels would be in the form of made-for-television movies.

Hughes met with earlier success thanks to the financial performance of another film series, namely the *National Lampoon's Vacation* cycle. The original movie, *National Lampoon's Vacation* (Harold Ramis, 1983), was one of the most profitable features in Hughes's seminal years as a screenwriter; from the film's estimated production budget of $15 million, it was to raise a solid $8,333,358 in the opening weekend and would go on to amass a total domestic gross of $61,399,552. This trend continued in the sequel, *National Lampoon's European Vacation* (Amy Heckerling, 1985), for which Hughes was credited as co-screenwriter. Though generally less well regarded by critics, there was no ignoring its commercial performance; with an increased budget estimated at $17 million, the film enjoyed healthy opening-weekend takings of $12,329,627, eventually leading to a domestic total of $49,364,621. The final *Vacation* movie of the 1980s, and also the last entry in the series which would feature any involvement from Hughes, *National Lampoon's Christmas Vacation* was similarly a success in theaters. With a budget in the region of $27 million—far in excess of the first two films in the cycle—the Griswold family's Yuletide misadventures secured a substantial $11,750,203 in its opening weekend, leading to a substantial domestic gross of $71,319,526.

Many of Hughes's other eighties movies also performed convincingly in theaters. For example, *Mr. Mom* (Stan Dragoti, 1983)—one of Hughes's earliest screenplays to be developed into a feature film—had an underwhelming opening weekend, drawing in only $947,197, and yet it would eventually attract a total domestic gross of $64,783,827. The teen movies which he produced and wrote in the mid-eighties also fared well, albeit not to the same extent enjoyed by those he had directed himself. *Pretty in Pink* (Howard Deutch, 1986) was to make $6,065,870 in its opening weekend, making back two-thirds of its estimated $9 million budget, and went on to attract an overall $40,471,663 domestically. The following year's *Some Kind of Wonderful* (Howard Deutch, 1987) made less of an impact, earning $3,486,701 in its opening weekend and eventually achieving a total domestic gross of $18,553,948—less than half of *Pretty in Pink*'s commercial takings. Hughes's later family comedy *The Great Outdoors* (Howard Deutch, 1988) was to fare more compellingly; with an ample budget estimated at $24 million, it experienced a tepid opening weekend, with $6,121,115 in takings before continuing to domestic box-office earnings of $41,455,230. Along with modest foreign returns of $2 million, the movie would eventually go on to a gainful overall gross of $43,455,230.

Though often treated less favorably by the critical community than his prolific 1980s output, Hughes's family movies throughout the nineties were to be among the most resoundingly profitable of his entire career. *Beethoven* (Brian Levant, 1992) turned a production budget estimated at $18 million into domestic takings of $57,114,049 and foreign income of $90,100,000, leading to a highly successful overall gross of $147,214,049 worldwide. Comic-strip adaptation *Dennis the Menace* (Nick Castle, 1993) was produced on a weightier budget in the region of $35 million, but went on to a domestic gross of $51,270,765 and foreign ticket sales of $66 million, cumulating in a total of $117,270,765 at the box office. Perhaps because of its seasonal setting, which was more explicitly situated than had been the case with his other Christmas-themed movies, his mid-nineties remake of *Miracle on 34th Street* (Les Mayfield, 1994) was a more qualified success; after a distinctly lukewarm opening weekend that raised $2,753,208, the film was to earn $17,320,136 domestically and $28,944,248 from foreign markets, ultimately grossing $46,264,384 in total.

Hughes's two creative collaborations with Walt Disney Productions were also to yield considerable profitability. The live-action remake of *101 Dalmatians* (Stephen Herek, 1996) was made on a sizeable budget estimated at $75 million, and experienced a highly lucrative opening weekend that earned $33,504,025. The movie would eventually end its run with a domestic gross of $136,189,294 and foreign takings of $184,500,000, leading to a remarkable combined total of $320,689,294. The following year's *Flubber* (Les Mayfield, 1997) was also to meet with no small amount of success. With one of the largest production budgets of any movie of Hughes's career—an amount estimated to be in the region of $80 million—the film benefited from a rewarding opening weekend tally of $26,725,207. Though *Flubber* was to comfortably make its money back with its domestic gross of $92,977,226, its substantial foreign revenue of $85 million was to lead to a total amount of $177,977,226 by the end of the movie's run in theaters.

While not every film to feature a Hughes screenplay guaranteed profitability, it seems fair to say that his victories greatly outnumbered his failures. Yet it is intriguing to consider that while the eighties movies for which he has become best known were financially successful in the main, it was in the latter phase of his career—when he was almost entirely preoccupied with child-friendly family features—that his creative output was to be at its most profitable. Though Hughes's versatility and artistic dexterity were well documented by many critics, it seemed almost ironic that his most commercially gainful movies were among his least regarded.

30

One Day I'll Look Back on It and Laugh

The Legacy of John Hughes

John Hughes casts a long shadow over filmmaking even now, with his teen movies and eighties comedies in particular being regarded as the definitive benchmark for their genre. But what aspects of his creative approach led to this enduring appeal, such that his popularity and influence still shows no sign of fading? Many different qualities of John Hughes's cinematic career have contributed to his lasting success among fans and critics, and these varied attributes of his work have helped to ensure that his cultural relevance remains pertinent. Yet Hughes's lasting influence may be in the extent to which later filmmakers—and popular culture in general—have been inspired by his body of work, even many years after his death.

The Man Behind the Curtain: Public Perception of John Hughes

For all of his critical and commercial success, Hughes's withdrawal from the glare of the Hollywood spotlight was to establish him as something of a man of mystery. As his public appearances lessened following the conclusion of his directorial career, his reclusiveness—particularly from the turn of the millennium—became the stuff of pop culture legend. His conspicuous elusiveness was to be the focus of the documentary film *Don't You Forget About Me* (Matt Austin, 2009), a feature which not

Don't You Forget About Me. Director: Matt Austin. Release date: November 3, 2009.

only illuminated the significance of Hughes's self-motivated departure from the public eye, but the scope of his contribution to modern cinema. Though no one could have realized it at the time, because the film was released in the same year as Hughes's death it would inadvertently help to spark a new wave of interest in his already-popular movies.

Largely due to the fact that his output had been so squarely focused on popular genres such as the teen movie and romantic comedy, Hughes's work had remained largely under-analyzed in the annals of academic discourse. While the considerable profitability of many movies produced by Hughes has meant that his filmography has never been entirely ignored, scholarly discussion of the themes of his various features was essentially neglected until the years following his death. In recent times, however, the more refined nuances of his work—both as a director and screenwriter—have come under the microscope of critical discussion, with a deserved re-evaluation now underway regarding the social and cultural concerns underlying Hughes's range of cinematic narratives.

In spite of his string of box-office smash hits, Hughes was almost entirely overlooked at awards ceremonies during his lifetime. While an entire section of the 82nd Academy Awards in 2010 was given over to a posthumous tribute to Hughes, his work at the height of his career was ignored by AMPAS and the Golden Globes. Indeed, his most high-profile honor was the Producer of the Year Award at the 1991 ShoWest Convention (one of a series of worldwide annual events once operated by the Film Group unit of Nielsen Business Media). However, the extent of his industry recognition forms only one part of a much more complex story. For while Hughes's movies may have been shunned by awards organizations and often treated with skepticism by critics and film scholars, their popularity with fans has never diminished. With his mid-eighties to early-nineties output generally proving (with a few exceptions) to have an immediate impact with moviegoers at the time of their first appearance in theaters, his most enduring features have continued to prove successful on home-entertainment formats—and now Internet video streaming services—with an unprecedented ability to attract new viewers among successive generations.

Part of the reason for Hughes's success lies in his central determination to, first and foremost, tell a good story well. Though someone who staunchly held to his political beliefs, the ideological content of Hughes's cinema was almost always oblique in nature, ensuring that it did not risk alienating members of the audience who had competing views. That being said, Hughes was not about to enfeeble his personal opinions for the sake of commercial expediency; the points he made may well have been subtle in nature, but they were never obscured entirely. At a time of profound ideological discord, he knew that offering a worldview which was appealing and encouraged the public to relate specific fictionalized situations to their own lives was a far more effective way of communicating particular themes than taking a more direct approach. Even his knockabout eighties comedies concealed surprising satirical bite beneath their boisterous façades.

Today, as was the case during his lifetime, Hughes remains an enigmatic figure. Someone who clearly preferred to let his work do the talking, Hughes has become largely defined by the solitary nature of his later years, suggesting a complex and deeply perfectionistic man who gradually became less comfortable with the high-pressure world of moviemaking. The general impression is one of an individual who preferred to keep his family life separate from his public persona, and whose ongoing reinvention—from teen-movie innovator to creator of mainstream comedies, to (eventually) a producer of family features—was sparked as much by a willingness to try new things as it was by an economic impetus to capitalize on the box-office success of different genres which best reflected audience tastes over a turbulent and sharply changeable period of film history. Though various actors over the years have spoken of their artistic disagreements with Hughes, especially during the zenith of his fame in the eighties, just as many have painted a picture of a genuine visionary who cared deeply about his work and fought hard to maintain the highest level of professional integrity in order to present the best possible creative product to his audiences. Yet while the complex and intensely private Hughes has bequeathed a rather inscrutable status as a figure of some ambiguity, his prolific output has nonetheless guaranteed him a degree of cinematic longevity, ensuring that as long as 1980s movies are being discussed, the name of John Hughes will never be ignored.

More Unites Us Than Divides Us: The Themes and Fictional Worlds of John Hughes

One of the most remarkable things about Hughes's films is their ability to retain universal appeal. His use of relatable environments, suburban locales, and domestic situations have all combined to create memorable features which continue to resonate not only in the United States, but in many other countries across the globe. This is particularly striking when—by the standards of the modern world—the scope of Hughes's movies may be considered somewhat restricted in the eyes of more recent audiences due to the films' lack of representation of characters from ethnic minority backgrounds or those with LGBTQ sexual identities. Though not as obvious at the time of production as it is in today's more enlightened times, Hughes's central characters—especially in his teen movies—were invariably Caucasian, heterosexual, and often had their eyes fixed firmly on the conspicuous affluence of a white-collar future. Yet while such an approach would prove problematic in our current times simply because its dearth of balanced representation would ignore all but the narrowest interpretation of contemporary American society, when considered as period pieces Hughes's movies have largely escaped censure due to his focus on individualism, self-determination, meaningful cooperation, and other universal drives which are relevant to everyone regardless of gender, sexuality, or race. While social mobility is usually perceived to be an advantageous incentive, Hughes places far greater emphasis on independence, creativity, and non-conformity as true agents of empowerment in a culture where quick thinking and inventiveness were increasingly essential factors in standing apart from the crowd.

Hughes explores individual motivation and personal determination with a laudable degree of nuance, applauding ambition while censuring greed and opportunism. Thus, while Andie Walsh of *Pretty in Pink* (Howard Deutch, 1986) is not oblivious to the material advantages of a relationship with the affluent Blane McDonnagh, her attraction to him is driven by genuine affection rather than acquisitiveness or cynicism, and she is always shown to be talented and highly creative, emphasizing that—however her romantic ambitions played out—she was more than capable of being highly successful in her own right. Conversely, Keith Nelson of *Some Kind of Wonderful* (Howard Deutch, 1986) rejects not only the prosperous trappings of the lives enjoyed by Amanda Jones's upscale acquaintances, but is also highly skeptical of the conventional path to prosperity via educational attainment; by instead choosing a relationship with Watts, he reaffirms the need for true fidelity and a sincere meeting of minds over any attempt to use romance as a means for social advancement. Hughes's exploration of the corrosiveness of greed arguably reached its apex in the covetous yuppie Roman Craig in *The Great Outdoors* (Howard Deutch, 1988), wherein this nominal antagonist knows the price of everything and yet the value of nothing; the maladroitness of Roman's financial dealings have led his family into a downward spiral from which he lacks the ability to free them, and yet he remains so oblivious that his entire worldview continues to be centered on reducing every resource and situation to base economic worth rather than acknowledging that the things that really matter in life—such as the people who eventually come to his aid—are beyond price.

The value of the family unit is almost certainly the predominant theme throughout Hughes's work, and yet while he regularly drew attention to its virtues he was similarly aware of the difficulties of maintaining good relationships with immediate relatives. In the *National Lampoon's Vacation* cycle—and especially throughout the events of *National Lampoon's Christmas Vacation* (Jeremiah S. Chechik, 1989)—Hughes regularly depicts the quarrels and disputes which break out among the unconventional extended Griswold family before we invariably witness them coming together. In other movies, such as *Curly Sue* (1991), disparate characters who are unrelated by blood ties nevertheless find themselves forging a simulacrum of the nuclear family unit which proves to be just as nurturing and adaptable as a more conventional relational bond. Yet while Hughes regularly espoused the significance of family, he did not consider it to be beyond reproach. *The Breakfast Club* (1985) relentlessly depicts the dangers of neglectful or overbearing parenting, exploring the ill-effects on the lives of the film's troubled protagonists, while Tom and Katie Bueller of *Ferris Bueller's Day Off* (1986) are supportive and well-meaning but also prove to be gullible and so preoccupied with their professional lives that they are easily (and repeatedly) duped by their charismatic son. Jim and Brenda Baker of *Sixteen Candles* (1984) manage to completely forget their daughter Samantha's milestone sixteenth birthday due to their anxieties over wedding arrangements, causing them guilt and unease as they struggle to rectify their oversight, while *Some Kind of Wonderful*'s Cliff Nelson is so determined to encourage his son Keith into escaping the same blue-collar existence he has lived through that he ends up alienating him altogether. However, more often than not family is the key motivating factor in a Hughes narrative, whether a reunion of the family unit forms the central aim—as in *Planes, Trains and Automobiles* (1987) or *Home Alone* (Chris Columbus, 1990)—or where it stimulates a capacity to change and grow as a result of dawning responsibility or mutual supportiveness, in films such as *She's Having a Baby* (1988) or *Uncle Buck* (1989).

Hughes's take on the human condition was multidimensional and rarely offered straightforward moral solutions. *The Breakfast Club* made the point that adulthood had the capacity to leave individuals jaded and disillusioned if they felt their youthful ambitions had been unrealized, laid bare in the pessimism of the autocratic, burned-out Richard Vernon. In *Career Opportunities* (Bryan Gordon, 1991), the results of heavy-handed or abusive parenting are clearly shown to have far-reaching and directly detrimental effects. But while growing older is an inevitable part of life, growing up tends to be a much more elective choice. The freewheeling Buck Russell in *Uncle Buck* enjoys a life that is free from serious professional or emotional responsibility, but—as he later realizes—this eventually makes him realize that he has become listless and isolated from those around him. Ferris Bueller likewise prizes his individuality above all else, but—while the morally ambiguous outcomes of his actions are obscured by his charm and wit—at the end of *Ferris Bueller's Day Off* the audience becomes aware that he is actually all too aware that his easygoing lifestyle is finite and that his carefree existence is likely to be challenged by the encroachment of adulthood. Thus, while Hughes holds up autonomy and individuality as virtues to be commended and cherished, he also stipulates that responsibility and duty are just as key to a happy and fulfilling life. The way in which his characters choose to accept and deal with this accountability can vary widely, however.

Hughes also had a predisposition towards being extremely dubious of authority figures, with particular suspicion being cast upon the public school system. While Richard Vernon of *The Breakfast Club* veritably drips with contempt towards the misfit students in his charge, desiring that they conform at all costs, Anita Hoargarth of *Uncle Buck* is shown to be even more singularly obsessed with submission to conventionality, to the extent that she disdains creative thought and artistic expression and expects her students to be little more than mindlessly obedient automata. Though played more for laughs than dramatic effect, Ed Rooney of *Ferris Bueller's Day Off* is preoccupied with instilling order and discipline because it justifies his existence as his school's dean of students; his vendetta against Ferris is not impelled solely by his disdain for rule-breaking, but as a means of saving face when his authority is challenged by a quick-thinking and endlessly creative adversary. In all of these cases, Hughes pitches an antagonist who seeks to suppress critical thought and individual behavior against characters who see the value in personal freedom and intellectual autonomy. By projecting machinations of attempted behavioral control onto these representatives of the state, Hughes issues a subtle warning to remain vigilant throughout life towards the collusions of those who would seek to influence and regulate the way in which people think, communicate, and envision the world. While ambition and innovation can offer ways of getting ahead in the world, he shows, autocratic attempts at restricting freedom of thought and action are restrictive and never truly serve the goals of the individual.

Above all else, John Hughes was a patriotic American. He believed that in a world of uncertainty and fast-moving cultural change, holding true to his country's central values of personal liberty, equality, and self-government could help to advance traditional principles of fair play and ethical justice for all. To some, these optimistic themes may have seemed an awkward fit alongside many of the darkly comic situations presented in Hughes's movies, and indeed some critics have even pointed towards a highly understated vein of nihilism lurking beneath the skin of even his more upbeat features. This was particularly true of those who have drawn attention to his deliberately out-of-touch adult characters' invariable sense of ineffectualness and anxiety, comparing them to the savvier teen characters who—it is sometimes hinted—might one day succeed their elders in the same march towards apathetic cluelessness as they grow older. However, the fact remains that Hughes knew even his most multifaceted characters could operate in morally gray areas while still aiming to uphold overarching standards which were greater than themselves. Ferris Bueller may have been scheming, manipulative, and self-serving, but he was also a supportive friend, devoted partner, and someone who seemed to care sincerely for the local community that he was repeatedly hoodwinking. Neal Page considers his nominal friendship with Del Griffith to be riven with divisions based on class difference and personal disparities, but when he discovers the truth about Del's circumstances his actions in welcoming him into his own family unit are motivated just as much by moral responsibility as they are by the fraternal bond which has grown between them during their nightmarish journey. And Buck Russell, who believed that his life could be one long string of insouciant activities financed by legally dubious opportunities, discovers that embracing personal accountability and financial dependability is the path back into the arms of his family and, by extension, greater mainstream social acceptability.

Hughes may have identified major challenges facing the society of his time, but he did not attempt to present easy answers. While it is true that he extols the virtues of family, community, and American values, he does not pretend that the road ahead is a smooth one: only that by remaining true to the guiding principles which had made his country great, people still had a chance to improve their lives while retaining a moral center which could favor the individual as well as the collective, working towards a future which is prosperous but also agreeable and satisfying. At the height of the "greed is good" culture of the 1980s, he showed that when tempered by moral responsibility the free market had the potential to empower not just the individual but also to encourage greater affluence for the country at large; that if personal dignity and self-worth are respected, society operates better and more efficiently than when people and communities are left behind by the relentless march of free enterprise. Thus, when Roman Craig faces ruin as a result of his sharply declining financial fortunes in *The Great Outdoors*, he is offered a safety net by a supportive family unit who—though his competitive personality grates on them—can see that sustaining him in a time of crisis, rather than casting him adrift, is the right thing to do. As Jack Butler of *Mr. Mom* (Stan Dragoti, 1983) is unceremoniously made redundant from his career in engineering, his situation would have been all the worse if he had not been married to a skilled and talented advertising professional who is able to provide for their family while he struggles to find a new role for himself. And while Buck Russell's family resents the fact that he relies on illicit schemes to keep himself afloat while they work hard to sustain themselves by honest means, by eventually embracing a conventional job he is able to redeem himself and be re-incorporated into the family unit—a development which is to the benefit of all. This may have seemed like a relatively restrained mode of social commentary at a period which witnessed the barbed satire of John Landis's *Coming to America* (1988), and the indignant morality play of Walter Hills's *Brewster's Millions* (1985). But Hughes always seemed to be most concerned with presenting ways of encouraging people to improve their outlook and enhance their lives, rather than inspiring them to save the world single-handedly. If his audience felt moved to enjoy their lives and help to improve those of others around them, in a manner which was to the betterment of all, then they had been compelled by the fundamental motivation that has helped to make the best of Hughes's films as life-affirming today as they were at the time of their original release.

The Sun Never Sets on Shermer: The Lasting Influence of John Hughes's Cinema

While Hughes's screenplays for his family features of the 1990s may have been hugely lucrative at the box office, and the comedies that he scripted throughout the eighties met with general critical approval, it is for his teen movie cycle that he will always be most keenly remembered. Hughes's thoughtful approach and considered depth of characterization, which was evident throughout all six of his teen movies, would come to influence the style and approach of many later films, including Cameron Crowe's *Say Anything . . .* (1989), Whit Stillman's *Metropolitan* (1990), Kevin Smith's *Mallrats* (1995), and, arguably, even elements of Richard Linklater's *Dazed and Confused* (1993). His characters, and many of the standout sequences from his films, have been saluted and parodied in music videos, TV commercials, video games, and, of course, later movies by other directors, while tributes to his work have appeared in everything from situation comedies to animated series. His seismic contribution to the teen movie genre, from presenting flawed but believable protagonists to the unerringly authentic ring of his dialogue, has been just as celebrated as his painstaking choice of music, unforgettable one-liners, and keen eye for fashion and artwork, both contemporary and classical.

Hughes left an indelible impact not just on youth cinema, but on the 1980s movie industry in general. It is difficult to find an account of the decade's movies that does not feature at least one of his many films, with *The Breakfast Club*, *Pretty in Pink*, and *Ferris Bueller's Day Off* all listed prominently as gold standards of the genre. While his mainstream comedies such as *Planes, Trains and Automobiles*, *Uncle Buck*, and the various entries in the *National Lampoon's Vacation* series have continued to win over new viewers in the years since, his status as a cultural icon seems fated to be forever grounded in his work between 1984 and 1990; though the proven profitability of his family-oriented movies throughout the nineties cannot be denied, his status as a leading figure of pop culture had begun a gradual decline from the early part of the decade onwards—a process which would only accelerate with his eventual retreat from the public eye.

Today, for all his prolific body of work, Hughes will always be synonymous with the 1980s and his exceptional ability to capture the zeitgeist of the period. While his record with the critics may have been patchy even at the height of his fame, there is no negating the ability of his movies to continue to achieve immediate recognition among audiences of all ages—including those who had not been born during the pinnacle of Hughes's creativity. For so many people, the sight of a 1961 Ferrari 250 GT California will always suggest a magic ticket allowing a departure from everyday responsibility, the sound of Oingo Boingo's "Weird Science" will forever evoke the possibility of Kelly LeBrock being created from the keystroke of a Memotech MTX512, and John Bender triumphantly punching the air at the end of *The Breakfast Club* will eternally act as a signifier for every teenager who has ever defiantly declared his or her sense of independence. And this, perhaps, is John Hughes's greatest and most persistent legacy: that his movies have comfortably survived the era and the culture that created them, meaning that while they naturally conjure up considerable nostalgia for their 1980s setting, they have also managed to transcend their era of production to achieve a kind of immortality in popular culture that is in no danger of diminishing in the foreseeable future.

Image Credits

Introduction: Image of John Hughes is Copyright © Paul Natkin, all rights reserved, and is reproduced by kind permission of the photographer.

Chapter 1: Image of Lake Forest by Slo-mo is licensed under the Creative Commons Attribution-Share Alike 3.0 Unported license. [https://creativecommons.org/licenses/by-sa/3.0/]

Chapter 3: Image of Ferrari 250 GT California by Torroid is licensed under the Creative Commons Attribution 2.0 Generic license. [https://creativecommons.org/licenses/by/2.0/]

Chapter 3: Image of Wagon Queen Family Truckster by Adam Lautenbach is licensed under the Creative Commons Attribution 2.0 Generic license. [https://creativecommons.org/licenses/by/2.0/]

Chapter 3: Image of Chrysler LeBaron Town & Country Station Wagon by Dave_7 is licensed under the Creative Commons Attribution 2.0 Generic license. [https://creativecommons.org/licenses/by/2.0/]

Chapter 5: Image of IBM PCjr by Rik Myslewski. Public domain image.

Chapter 5: Image of E-mu Emulator II by John R. Southern is licensed under the Creative Commons Attribution-Share Alike 2.0 Generic license. [https://creativecommons.org/licenses/by-sa/2.0/]

Chapter 5: Image of Memotech MTX500 by Bilby is licensed under the Creative Commons Attribution 3.0 Unported license. [https://creativecommons.org/licenses/by/3.0/]

Chapter 6: Image of Great Sand Dunes National Park by Tpsdave at Pixabay. Public domain image.

Chapter 6: Image of Yosemite National Park by Tpsdave at Pixabay. Public domain image.

Chapter 7: Image of Gedde Watanabe by Rob DiCaterino is licensed under the Creative Commons Attribution 2.0 Generic license. [https://creativecommons.org/licenses/by/2.0/]

Chapter 8: Image of Wrigley Field by SecretName101 is licensed under the Creative Commons Attribution-Share Alike 4.0 International license. [https://creativecommons.org/licenses/by-sa/4.0/]

Select Bibliography

Austin, Joe, and Michael Nevin Willard, eds. *Generations of Youth: Youth Cultures and History in Twentieth-Century America*. New York: New York University Press, 1998.

Base, Ron, and David Haslam. *The Movies of the Eighties*. London: Portland, 1990.

Batchelor, Bob, and Scott Stoddart. *The 1980s*. Westport: Greenwood, 2006.

Bernstein, Jonathan. *Pretty in Pink: The Golden Age of Teenage Movies*. New York: St. Martin's Griffin, 1997.

Bleach, Anthony C. "Postfeminist Cliques? Class, Postfeminism, and the Molly Ringwald–John Hughes Films." *Cinema Journal* 49. Number 3. (Spring 2010): 24–44.

Clarke, Jaime, ed. *Don't You Forget About Me: Contemporary Writers on the Films of John Hughes*. New York: Simon Spotlight Entertainment, 2007.

Evans, Richard. *Remember the 80s*. London: Portico, 2008.

Falk, Gerhard, and Ursula A. Falk. *Youth Culture and the Generation Gap*. New York: Algora Publishing, 2005.

Freeman, Hadley. *Life Moves Pretty Fast*. London: 4th Estate, 2015.

Gora, Susannah. *You Couldn't Ignore Me If You Tried: The Brat Pack, John Hughes, and Their Impact on a Generation*. New York: Three Rivers Press, 2010.

Honeycutt, Kirk. *John Hughes: A Life in Film*. New York: Race Point Publishing, 2015.

Jordan, Chris. *Movies and the Reagan Presidency: Success and Ethics*. Westport: Greenwood, 2003.

Karp, Josh. *A Futile and Stupid Gesture: How Doug Kenney and National Lampoon Changed Comedy Forever*. Chicago: Chicago Review Press, 2006.

Kaveney, Roz. *Teen Dreams: Reading Teen Film from* Heathers *to* Veronica Mars. London: I. B. Tauris, 2006.

Lewis, Jon. *The Road to Romance & Ruin: Teen Films and Youth Culture*. London: Routledge, 1992.

Mallan, Kerry, and Sharyn Pearce. *Youth Cultures: Texts, Images, and Identities*. Westport: Greenwood, 2003.

Mansour, David. *From Abba to Zoom: A Pop Culture Encyclopedia of the Late 20th Century*. Riverside: Andrews McMeel, 2005.

Mitchell, Jeremy, and Richard Maidment, eds. *The United States in the Twentieth Century: Culture*. London: Hodder and Stoughton, 1994.

Müller, Jürgen, ed. *Movies of the 80s*. Köln: Taschen, 2002.

Palmer, William J. *The Films of the Eighties: A Social History*. Carbondale: Southern Illinois University Press, 1993.

Prince, Stephen. *A New Pot of Gold: Hollywood Under the Electronic Rainbow, 1980–1989*. Berkeley: University of California Press, 2002.

Prince, Stephen, ed. *American Cinema of the 1980s: Themes and Variations*. Chapel Hill: Rutgers University Press, 2007.

Quart, Alissa. *Branded: The Buying and Selling of Teenagers*. Jackson: Basic Books, 2004.

Rettenmund, Matthew. *Totally Awesome 80s*. New York: St. Martin's Press, 1996.

Ryan, Michael, and Douglas Kellner. *Camera Politica: The Politics and Ideology of Contemporary Hollywood*. Indianapolis: Indiana University Press, 1988.

Schultze, Quentin J., Roy M. Anker, James D. Bratt, William D. Romanowski, John W. Worst, and Lambert Zuidervaart. *Dancing in the Dark: Youth, Popular Culture, and the Electronic Media*. Grand Rapids: William B. Eerdmans, 1990.

Shary, Timothy. *Generation Multiplex: The Image of Youth in Contemporary American Cinema*. Austin: University of Texas Press, 2002.

Shary, Timothy. *Teen Movies: American Youth on Screen*. London: Wallflower Press, 2005.

Simmons, Matty. *If You Don't Buy This Book We'll Kill This Dog: Life, Laughs, Love and Death at the National Lampoon*. Fort Lee: Barricade Books, 1995.

Simpson, Paul, ed. *The Rough Guide to Cult Movies*. London: Haymarket Customer, 2001.

Tropiano, Stephen. *Rebels and Chicks: A History of the Hollywood Teen Movie*. New York: Back Stage Books, 2006.

Index

THE FAQ SERIES

AC/DC FAQ
by Susan Masino
Backbeat Books
9781480394506...$24.99

Armageddon Films FAQ
by Dale Sherman
Applause Books
9781617131196.........$24.99

The Band FAQ
by Peter Aaron
Backbeat Books
9781617136139 ....$19.99

Baseball FAQ
by Tom DeMichael
Backbeat Books
9781617136061........$24.99

The Beach Boys FAQ
by Jon Stebbins
Backbeat Books
9780879309879..$22.99

The Beat Generation FAQ
by Rich Weidman
Backbeat Books
9781617136016 ....$19.99

Beer FAQ
by Jeff Cioletti
Backbeat Books
9781617136115 ....$24.99

Black Sabbath FAQ
by Martin Popoff
Backbeat Books
9780879309572..$19.99

Bob Dylan FAQ
by Bruce Pollock
Backbeat Books
9781617136078 ......$19.99

Britcoms FAQ
by Dave Thompson
Applause Books
9781495018992 ....$19.99

Bruce Springsteen FAQ
by John D. Luerssen
Backbeat Books
9781617130939.......$22.99

Buffy the Vampire Slayer FAQ
by David Bushman and Arthur Smith
Applause Books
9781495064722.....$19.99

Cabaret FAQ
by June Sawyers
Applause Books
9781495051449......$19.99

A Chorus Line FAQ
by Tom Rowan
Applause Books
9781480367548 ...$19.99

The Clash FAQ
by Gary J. Jucha
Backbeat Books
9781480364509 ..$19.99

Doctor Who Faq
by Dave Thompson
Applause Books
9781557838544....$22.99

The Doors FAQ
by Rich Weidman
Backbeat Books
9781617130175........$24.99

Dracula FAQ
by Bruce Scivally
Backbeat Books
9781617136009 .....$19.99

The Eagles FAQ
by Andrew Vaughan
Backbeat Books
9781480385412.....$24.99

Elvis Films FAQ
by Paul Simpson
Applause Books
9781557838582.....$24.99

Elvis Music FAQ
by Mike Eder
Backbeat Books
9781617130496......$22.99

Eric Clapton FAQ
by David Bowling
Backbeat Books
9781617134548 ......$22.99

Fab Four FAQ
by Stuart Shea and Robert Rodriguez
Hal Leonard Books
9781423421382.......$19.99

Fab Four FAQ 2.0
by Robert Rodriguez
Backbeat Books
9780879309688...$19.99

Film Noir FAQ
by David J. Hogan
Applause Books
9781557838551......$22.99

Football FAQ
by Dave Thompson
Backbeat Books
9781495007484 ...$24.99

Frank Zappa FAQ
by John Corcelli
Backbeat Books
9781617136030.......$19.99

Godzilla FAQ
by Brian Solomon
Applause Books
9781495045684 $19.99

The Grateful Dead FAQ
by Tony Sclafani
Backbeat Books
9781617130861.........$24.99

Guns N' Roses FAQ
by Rich Weidman
Backbeat Books
9781495025884 ..$19.99

Haunted America FAQ
by Dave Thompson
Backbeat Books
9781480392625.....$19.99

Horror Films FAQ
by John Kenneth Muir
Applause Books
9781557839503 ....$22.99

Jack the Ripper FAQ
by Dave Thompson
Applause Books
9781495063084....$19.99

James Bond FAQ
by Tom DeMichael
Backbeat Books
9781557838568.....$22.99

Jimi Hendrix FAQ
by Gary J. Jucha
Backbeat Books
9781617130953.......$22.99

Johnny Cash FAQ
by C. Eric Banister
Backbeat Books
9781480385405.. $24.99

KISS FAQ
by Dale Sherman
Backbeat Books
9781617130915.........$24.99

Led Zeppelin FAQ
by George Case
Backbeat Books
9781617130250 ......$22.99

Lucille Ball FAQ
by James Sheridan and Barry Monush
Applause Books
9781617740824.......$19.99

MASH FAQ
by Dale Sherman
Applause Books
9781480355897.....$19.99

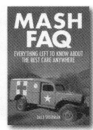
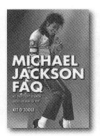

HAL•LEONARD®
PERFORMING ARTS
PUBLISHING GROUP

Prices, contents, and availability subject to change without notice.

FAQ.halleonardbooks.com